The Clean Run Book of Agility Games

For Lee Ann
Have great fun! It is all but a game!
Bud Houston

2nd edition

by Bud Houston

The Clean Run Book of Agility Games, 2nd Edition

For information contact:

Clean Run Productions, LLC
35 N. Chicopee St.
Chicopee, MA 01020
Phone: 413-532-1389 or 800-311-6503
Fax: 413-532-1389
Website: www.cleanrun.com

Book design and typesetting by Robin Nuttall, www.ddgraphix.com

Cover design by Robin Nuttall

Cover Photo by Alissa Behn, www.pet-personalities.com

Editing by Nini Bloch and Marcille Ripperton

Printing by Hadley Printing Company, Inc.

First printing September 2003

ISBN 1-892694-09-3

dedication

This book is dedicated to my wife Marsha, who can no longer bear to edit my work... to agility fans everywhere who enjoy the game of agility for the fun of it and for the simple love of dogs... and to my loving pack of wild dogs (Bogie, Birdie, Par, Tack, Ringer, Banner, Wizard, and Dash), without whom there's not much reason to play the game.

table of contents

Introduction

Games

Appendix

introduction

It is with great pride that I present to you the second edition of *The Clean Run Book of Agility Games*. In the original version, I collaborated with Stuart Mah; in this version, he declined participation in view of his busy schedule.

I find myself in the unique position of being a historian and perhaps the only historian of agility games. With delight, I've documented more than 125 agility games and many specific variations played around the world.

The purpose of this book is to provide agility enthusiasts with an easy-to-use and clearly written reference to nearly any agility game they might want to try. The types of games I've included range from the hard-bitten games of competition to silly games for fun and recreation to games that teach valuable handler skills.

The ultimate goal is having fun with your dog.

Why is it unsafe for a dog to leap off a dogwalk at a height of 16" or so and yet perfectly acceptable for a dog to fall more than 26" on the landing side of a jump? Why is it unsafe (a fly-off!) for a 3-pound dog to jump the final 2" at the end of a teeter in his impatience for the plank to settle on the ground? What profound individual explained the technical definition of a refusal? True refusals are quite rare. Artificial definitions allow the agility judge to make calls without thinking and without exercising judgment. In the Australian National Kennel Club (ANKC), a dog may circle the table and will not be called for a refusal if the circling continues to bend the dog closer to the table. Is this any more or less rational than the International definition? Certainly not; it's just amusing.

You should keep in mind the irrational nature of rules as you play any agility game. Bend the rules to your will if you must. Make the game your own variation. You can't be any more or less rational than the person who originally defined performance in agility.

It is the rules that make the game a contest. In our hearts, we love the contest, we love the struggle, and we love the opportunity to rank ourselves. We especially love the win. These are human conditions, which are possibly not shared with any enthusiasm by the dog.

Every now and again, I hear an old-timer lamenting the loss of the "old days when agility was fun." While I understand that lament, I have to disagree with the sentiment. We are all responsible for our own sense of fun. None of the hubbub of title-chasing, national championships, World Cup aspirations, double-Q-ing, super-Q-ing, Top Ten lists, or other egoistic measures of validation should affect us one whit. Agility is a private thing. Agility is a game we play in the park on the weekends with our dogs.

A fairly recent development on the agility scene is "league play" (see page 104). An agility league is organized somewhat like a bowling league, except that the participants don't bowl; they play agility. League play has been responsible for an explosion of new games and the more rigorous definition of (irrational) sets of rules. An agility league is the perfect tonic for the person who truly aspires to have fun with his dog and doesn't get caught up in the hype that the "standard" run is the defining game of dog agility.

League play is not yet a widespread variation of agility. Think about it from the perspective of those who'd necessarily be champions of the idea. It's inexpensive and recreational. It takes a pretty special person to champion a game that promotes neither profit nor ambition.

I'm pleased finally to put this work to print. I'm committed on each reprinting of the book to update the content to reflect new games and new variations. I hope this book will prove to be the ultimate reference to dog agility games.

Bud Houston; Ostrander, Ohio.

notes on this edition

No attempt has been made to summarize the scoring systems and rules of every agility organization in the English-speaking world, much less every agility organization in the world. This is an American version and subscribes to the rules of the American agility organizations.

For a more comprehensive discussion of rules and activities, you can contact the organization directly.

American Kennel Club (AKC)
5580 Centerview Drive, Suite 200
Raleigh, NC 27606-3390
Email: agility@akc.org
www.akc.org
Offers Standard and Jumpers With Weaves

Canine Performance Events (CPE)
P.O. Box 805
South Lyon, MI 48178
Email: k9cpe@hotmail.com
www.k9cpe.com
Offers Standard, Colors, Wildcard, Snooker, Jackpot, Full House, Jumpers

Just For Fun Agility (JFF)
8738 Slocum Road
Ostrander, OH 43061
Email: info@dogwoodagility.com
www.dogwoodagility.com
Offers a host of games listed on the web site; new games added frequently

North American Dog Agility Council (NADAC)
11522 South Hwy 3
Cataldo, ID 83810
Email: info@nadac.com
www.nadac.com
Offers Standard (Regular), Jumpers, Gamblers, Tunnelers, Touch N Go, and Weavers

Teacup Dogs Agility Association (TDAA)
P.O. Box 69
Ostrander, OH 43061
Email: info@dogwoodagility.com
www.dogagility.org
Offers a host of games listed on the web site; new games added frequently

United Kennel Club (UKC)
100 East Kilgore Rd.
Kalamazoo, MI 49002-5584
(269) 343-9020 or fax (269) 343-7037
www.ukcdogs.com/
Offers Standard agility only

United States Dog Agility Association (USDAA)
P.O. Box 850995
Richardson, TX 75085-0955
(972) 487-2200 or fax (972) 272-4404
E-mail: info@usdaa.com
www.usdaa.com
Offers Standard, Jumpers, Gamblers, Snooker, and Relay

Australian Shepherd Club of America (ASCA)
P.O. Box 3790
Bryan, TX 77805-3790
(800) 892-ASCA
lola@asca.org
www.asca.org
Offers Standard (Regular), Jumpers, Gamblers, Tunnelers, Touch N Go, and Weavers

The American Mixed Breed Obedience Registry (AMBOR)
179 Niblick Rd., #113
Paso Robles, CA 93446
805-226-9275
Ambor@Amborusa.org
www.amborusa.org
AMBOR registered dogs compete in a number of agility venues, including ASCA, NADAC, and USDAA

Agility Association of Canada (AAC)
RR#2
Lucan, Ontario, Canada
N0N 2J0
(519) 657-7636
www.aac.ca
Offers Standard, Jumpers, Gamblers, Snooker, and Relay

documenting the games

Most games in this book could be played under the rules set of any of the agility organizations—except under trial conditions, in which the sanctioning organization would surely insist on using its own rules. Every game documented makes some recommendation for which rules basis should be applied to the game. This shouldn't keep the sponsor of the game in an informal setting from applying whichever organization's rules he wants.

This book documents each game according to the following format:

- **Briefing**—Contains the rules of play and an overview of the game, as the game might be explained to a class of exhibitors.
- **Scoring**—Explains the rules basis for the game: how it is scored, how faults are assessed, and how a winner is determined. Exhibitors also might receive much of this information in a briefing.
- **Course Design**—Describes the principles for designing courses for the game. It is a guide for judges and instructors faced with the task of designing such a game for fun, for practice, or for competition, according to available space and equipment inventories.

  Every game is presented with one or more sample courses as an aid to the course designer and to the exhibitor so that they may better understand how the game is played and what such a game might look like when set on the ground. All games are illustrated on a grid. Each square on a grid represents 10' x 10'.
- **Strategies**—Discusses strategies and provides hints for developing a winning strategy for the game.
- **Qualifying and Titles**—Describes various titling programs that may exist for a specific game.
- **Variations**—Lists and describes variations of a game which differ in some manner from the basic rules for that game.

Please note that as of this printing, the charts and tables in this book were correct, but are subject to change. Please check with the appropriate agility organization for their accuracy.

future volumes

It is the intention of this book's editor to update this reference periodically to properly reflect current agility games. Therefore, we would like to know about:

- Any new games you have discovered in the dog agility community.
- Existing games for which there are rules refinements.
- Experiences you have with the games in this book. We would like to have new course diagrams that are appropriately marked with the judge's name and the date and location of the event.
- Corrections for errors in this volume.

Please provide us with the name of the game and indicate whether it is a new game, a variation of a game described in this book, a new sample of a game in this book, or a correction to information in this book. For guidelines on creating a new game or variation of an existing game, see page 177.

Mail your contributions to:

Bud Houston
8738 Slocum Road
Ostrander, OH 43061
info@dogwoodagility.com

cautionary note

Any sort of competition, whether it be a simple training game at practice or a USDAA Steeplechase final, can make the handlers' and their dogs' adrenaline flow. The resulting excitement and exposure to new game formats, equipment, props, and/or handler emotional states can make a dog's behavior less predictable. Dogs may have to contend with soccer balls on course, their handlers dressing up in baggy clothing, baton exchanges at close quarters with strange dogs, screaming and laughing competitors, and cheering crowds. For dogs with little experience in such settings, or for dogs that stress easily, take your time in acclimating them. Make sure they have fun in a safe environment. Watch for signs of aggression. Use common sense.

For instance, Basketball requires that the handler try to toss a tennis ball through a tire. Since many dogs will go for the tennis ball, be careful when playing this game with jumps and other obstacles that the dog doesn't injure himself on the equipment by crashing into things. It's possible, too, that excitement about an unaccustomed toy on course will bring out aggressive traits in some dogs.

contributors

Anderson, Leslie
Anderson, Sharon
Anderson, Webb
Atkinson, Barbara
Bayne, Kathryn
Beam, Mary
Berger, Mary Ellen
Boone, Sheri
Brown, Jonathan
Brown, Lorraine
Brownschilde, Lisa
Bryant, Sherry
Carr, Anna
Ceranko, Al
Cheek, Marq
Cheek, Rebecca
Choate, Tara
Cockerham, Carrie
Creel, Nancy
Culley, Terry
Dean, Becky
Dege, Dan
Del Page, Lora
Dombourian, Donna
Dominey, Deb
Dominey, Simon
Duke, Katie
Egyed, Cynthia
Eickholdt, Linda
Erin Friedeman
Evans, Elizabeth
Everline, Terri
Fairweather, Helix
Fender, Brenna
Flanigan, Amy
Franks, Tracie
Friedeman, Erin
Fuge, Heidi
Gadsby, Martin
Garrett, Susan
Gloor, Karen
Gyes, Nancy
Hanson, David
Harvey, Francis
Harvey, Melinda
Helmke, Kathy
Houston, Bud
Houston, Marsha
Jones, Sally
Juliano, Pam
Kirkwood, Natalie
Koukkari, Will
Laubach, Tim
Lavin, Mary Jo
Lewis, Stephen
MacKenzie, Jean
Mah, Stuart
Maillioux, Karen
Manchester, Laura
McArthur, Betty
McCleskey, Adra
McGunigle, Brian
Mecklenburg, Linda
Mersereau, Mary
Miele, Chris
Miller, Kay
Morse, Susan
Nelson, Sharon
Nichols, Lyndal
Northrop, Linda
Osborn, Tiffany
Ostrowski, John
Redl, Shirley Ann
Rhodes, Arlene
Rhodes, John
Richey, Deb
Ring, Ken
Robinson, Rob
Rukis, Ilze
Scheich, Tammie
Schmit, Lisa
Schultz, Lori
Schwartz, Claire
Seibert, Fran
Simmons-Moake, Gordon
Skogan, Matt
Slanker, Becky
Sminkey, Mary Jo
Smith, Anne
Sobey, Joyce
Stall, Tricia
Sterling, Bill
Steward, Marilyn
Stone, Tammi
Tanner, Rae
Tatsch, Kenneth
Thomas, Denise
Thomas, Eleanor M.
Thompson, Hazel
Thompson, J.C.
Thompson, Sharon
Thuot, M.J.
Tovino, Sue
Valencia, Bob
Van Deusen, Wayne
Varney, Cheryl
Vroman, Michelle
Wheeler, Ray
White-Cotterman, Heather
Wilkins, Jean
Woz, Darlene
Zerbian, Lee
Zelinger, Joan

agility

Nearly 20 years ago, the game of dog agility was introduced to the United States. The sport has grown steadily since then and is played today by more than 10,000 enthusiasts. People of all ages, sizes, and degrees of fitness play the game. By all indications, agility will continue to be one of the fastest-growing sports in the U.S. because it is instant fun for both handler and dog. The handler gets to play and bond with the canine members of his family. For the dogs, agility provides an outlet to perform honest work and contribute to the pack.

Many variations of agility are played. The most common form of the game is the Standard (or NADAC Regular) course. In the Standard course, the judge lays out a pattern of obstacles, designates the order in which they must be performed, and sets a minimum course time for performing them. It's significant that none of the exhibitors have ever seen the course that the judge lays out on a given day. Courses are never the same.

Briefing

The dog is required to perform each obstacle on the course at the handler's direction in the sequence and within the time period designated by the judge. The handler may use voice commands and signals, but may not touch the dog or any obstacle. The competition is between dogs at a given jump height and skill level and the clock.

Before running the course, the exhibitors are allowed to walk it without their dogs to decide their handling strategies. After the course walk-through, the competition begins.

Scoring

Agility is scored faults then time. The winner is the dog with the fewest faults. If two dogs have the same number of faults, then time breaks the tie.

Faults are assessed for exceeding the standard course time as well as for a number of performance errors. The following table summarizes performance faults for agility in the various organizations, based on rules at the time of this printing.

Standard Agility Faults Chart

	AKC	NADAC	USDAA Starters*	USDAA Advanced	USDAA Masters	JFF	TDAA	CPE
Displaced bar	E	5	5	5	5	5	5	5
Missed contact	E	10	5	5	5	5	5	15
Refusal	5	N/F	N/F	5†	5	N/F	5†	N/F
Off-course	5	10	5	20	E	5	5	5
Missed weave pole that's fixed	5	N/F	N/F	5	5	N/F	5	5
On and off table	2	N/A	5	5	5	5	5	N/F
Failure to perform	E	20	20	E	E	20	20	15
Touching dog or obstacle	E	N/F to E	5 to E	5 to E	5 to E	N/F to E	5 to E	5
Collar on dog	N/F	E	E	E	E	N/F	N/F	E
Banking‡	N/A	N/A	5	5	5	N/F	5	5

E = Elimination
R = Faulted as a refusal
N/F = Not faulted
N/A = Not applicable

* *These faults apply to both USDAA Starters and Novice classes*
† *Only faulted on contact obstacles*
‡ *Banking refers only to wall jumps or the wishing well. Touching the aperture of the tire is not faulted. Banking is not faulted on a standard bar jump so long as the bar stays up.*

Course Design

The design of agility courses varies greatly, depending on the design criteria specified by the sanctioning organization and the level of competition. AKC judge Lori Schultz designed the courses shown here for three levels of Standard agility and presented at the Columbus All Breed AKC trial on April 7, 2002.

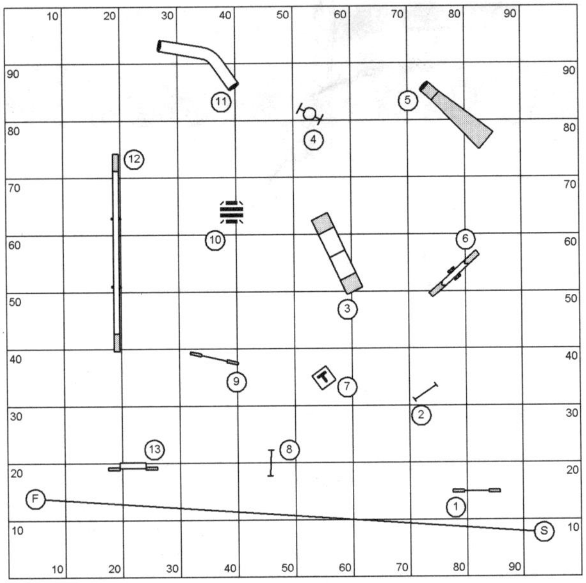

For Novice Standard, Lori Schulz designed a course with a simple, easy flow and wide, open spaces between the obstacles, consistent with AKC course design philosophy.

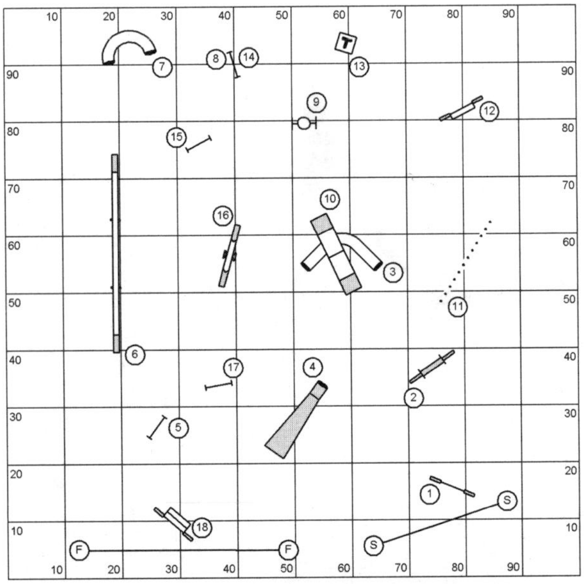

Lori Schulz designed this Open Standard course with a few more obstacles and more complex challenges.

Qualifying and Titles

Standard agility is used as a core titling game in all North American agility organizations. For more information on a particular agility organization and its programs, see page 8, or consult the appropriate web site.

Variations

- **Anything But a Collie**—Also called ABC, this British variation is standard agility for any dogs but collies. For the purposes of entry in this class, a collie is defined as a smooth or rough collie, a working sheep dog, or a border collie cross. Collies must compete in a separate class.
- **Black and Whites**—This British variation is standard agility for black and white border collies only (or black and white dogs with any hint of BC in them).
- **Junior Handlers**—Also called JH, this is standard agility for younger handlers. The age limit is usually under 19 years. AKC, NADAC, and USDAA all have titling programs expressly for Junior Handlers. It's worthwhile to note that the titling is for the handler, not for the dog. Junior Handlers can either train their own dogs or handle a dog trained by someone else. There is no distinction made for the level of qualification dogs have achieved under an adult handler.
- **Veterans**—In some agility venues, canine partners of advanced age compete in their own class. The minimum age is usually set at seven years. Jump heights are reduced, the A-frame lowered, and spread jumps prohibited. Both USDAA and NADAC have titling programs expressly for veteran dogs. This variation of agility is known as Golden Oldies in the U.K.
- **Time plus faults**—For titling purposes in standard agility classes, all the sanctioning organizations in the U.S. base their scoring on a faults-then-time basis. However, agility can also be scored on a time-plus-faults basis. When course faults are added to time, the dog with the lowest score wins. In a match or game setting, time plus faults is often the scoring system of choice.
- **Open entry**—Dogs can compete in a class regardless of titles earned. This is called open entry. For instance, in an open entry USDAA class (like Steeplechase), dogs that normally compete in Starters, Novice, Advanced, or Masters are all eligible to enter and compete against one another.

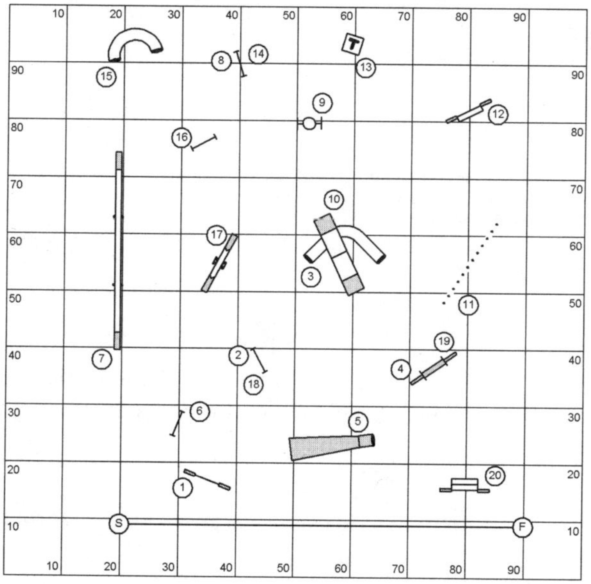

Lori Schulz's Excellent Standard course contains 20 obstacles and considerably more technical challenges.

agility with a twist

This game probably should have been called "twisted agility." It features, among other things, a wooden scaffold used to tie three pipe tunnels together into a large pretzel. It also puts the wings of jumps to work as a weaving sequence. The invention of Darlene Woz, Agility With a Twist is a game both of strategy and agility.

Briefing

The goal of this game is to collect exactly 21 points—no more and no less.

Obstacles may be taken more than once and in any order, but never back-to-back. One paw commits the dog to doing an obstacle. Once committed, the dog must complete an obstacle successfully before going on to another.

The dog can begin anywhere along the designated start line and will have 35 seconds to score points. The timekeeper will blow a whistle at the end of this period.

The handler can direct the dog to the clock-stopper (a table or pause box) at any time during the 35 seconds. If the handler goes to the clock-stopper to end time before the whistle blows, each second under 35 will be added to the points the dog accumulated on course. Time adjustments are in whole seconds only. For example, if the dog earns 20 points on course and stops the clock at 33.1, two points would be added to the dog's score (drop the fraction of a second and subtract 33 from 35). The dog's final score is 22 points.

If, on the other hand, the handler waits for the whistle to go to the clock-stopper and end time, each second over 35 will be subtracted from the points the dog earned on course. For example, if the dog earns 20 points on course and stops the clock at 40.2seconds, 5 points would be subtracted from the dog's score. The dog's final score is 15.

Scoring

The team closest to 21 points, without going over, is the winner. Any ties for first place will lead to a runoff on a predetermined course design. Fastest time wins.

Faults are judged under USDAA Starters/Novice rules. If a dog faults an obstacle, however, there is no penalty beyond having to retry the obstacle until successfully completed.

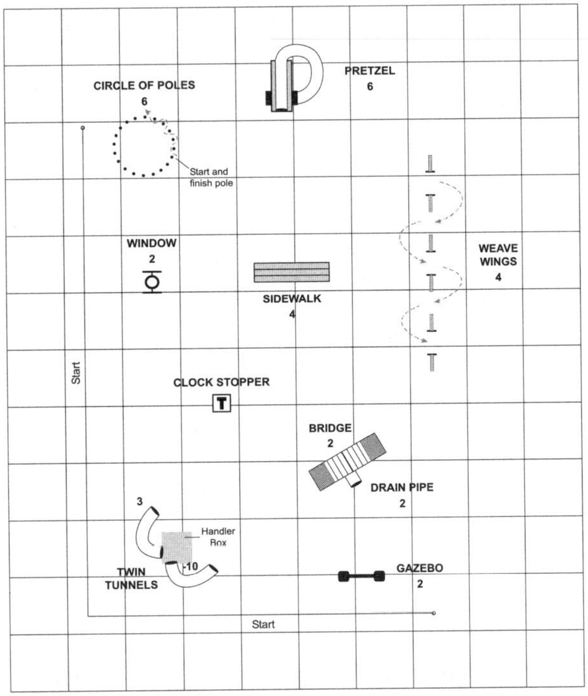

This is the original Agility With a Twist course designed by Darlene Woz.

Course Design

Agility with a Twist is usually designed using the materials at hand.

- Dogwalk planks are placed side by side on the ground to form the Sidewalk. The dog is required to walk the length of the sidewalk.
- The Bridge is the A-frame set at a height of 4'.
- 20 stick-in-the-ground weave poles are arranged in a circle to make the Circle of Poles. The dog must enter between two poles designated as the start and weave counterclockwise around the circle of poles. The handler may work outside or inside the circle.
- The barrel of the collapsed tunnel is used to make the Drain Pipe.
- Six jump wings are arranged end to end, about 4' apart, to form the Weave Wings. The dog is required to weave in and out through the spaces between the wings.
- The Window might be a wishing well jump or a tire.
- The Gazebo might be set up by securing together pieces of lattice from the ring enclosure.
- The Pretzel is 30' of pipe tunnel fixed upon a scaffold and requires a three-dimensional performance

  Note: Plans for building the scaffold for the Tunnel Pretzel are included on page 179.
- The Twin Tunnels represent a distance challenge and a discrimination trap. The handler is not allowed to step into the handler exclusion box. Performance of one tunnel is rewarded with 3 points. Performance of the second tunnel is penalized by a loss of 10 points.

Strategies

The honest approach to this game would be to calculate how many obstacles the dog can do in 35 seconds and then make adjustments for the point values of the obstacles and the over/under time implications. Then, go out and give it your best run.

The crafty approach might be to leverage the over/under points to arrive at the desired 21 points without worrying about performing a long sequence of obstacles.

agility y

Agility Y is a game for beginners and is designed to ensure a positive and successful experience. It's a great introduction to competition, and an early test of the dog's training and readiness for real competition. In the USDAA, the game Agility Y is sometimes known as Pre-Starters or Beginners.

Briefing

The dog is required to perform each obstacle on the course at the handler's direction in the sequence designated by the judge.

A safety rule will be observed on contact obstacles. If the dog commits to a contact obstacle with all four-paws and then bails off the obstacle, the judge will direct the handler to skip the obstacle and continue on course. A failure-to-perform fault will be assessed. If the handler directs his dog back onto the obstacle, the dog and handler will be dismissed.

At the handler's option, the dog may perform on leash. If so, it is the responsibility of the handler to manage the leash in a safe manner. For instance, the handler must lift the leash over jump standards, keep the leash slack and out of the way on contact obstacles, and release the leash as the dog goes through tunnels. A dog will be excused if the handler uses the leash in an unsafe manner.

Jumps and the table will be set one height lower than the dog's regulation jump height. Contact obstacles will also be set at a reduced height. The recommended height for the A-frame is 4'6", and the recommended height for the dogwalk is 2'6".

Scoring

Agility Y is scored time plus faults. The dog with the lowest score wins. Traditionally faults are judged under USDAA Starters/Novice rules.

A 5-point fault is assessed per occurrence if the handler uses the leash to jerk or pull the dog in any way.

Course Design

Only 10 to 13 obstacles should be used on the course. The course design should not be completely trivial. An element of the sequence should challenge the handler to analyze the implications of a handling position and decide what handling might be needed to entice the dog to perform the sequence successfully.

Prohibited obstacles include the seesaw, weave poles, and spread hurdles. The tire is optional. The height settings for contact obstacles should be indicated on the course diagram for the benefit of course-builders.

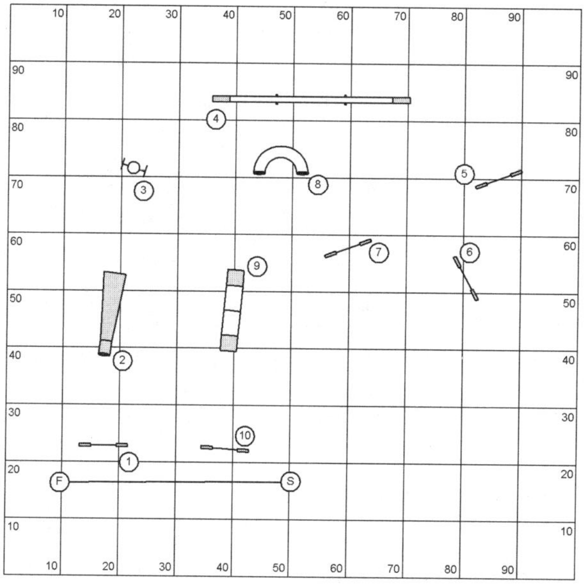

This typical example of an Agility Y or Pre-Starters course has no crossing patterns and requires only one change of sides.

Variations

- **Agility Y games**—Any agility game (such as Jumpers or Snooker) can be designed for Agility Y. However, the course designer must keep in mind that dogs and handlers at this level are usually not ready for challenging handling sequences.

april's fool

The invention of Joyce Sobey of Richmond, Virginia, April's Fool is suitable for a club outing or casual competition.

Briefing

The April's Fool course is essentially a standard run with a twist. Handlers direct their dogs through the course in the order and direction specified by the judge's numbering of the course. Before each dog and handler team run, however, they will be required to turn their backs to the course. A runner will mark two obstacles on the course with an "APRIL'S FOOL" sign. Marked obstacles must be *skipped* during the run.

After the course is marked, the dog and handler team must immediately run the course.

A dog taking an obstacle marked April's Fool will incur an off-course penalty (5 faults).

When the next handler/dog team is up to run, another person is selected to re-mark the course, omitting two obstacles. So, the course is basically different each run and offers a good chance to work on call-offs.

It turned out to be lots of fun, and people were much better at call-offs than they thought they would be.

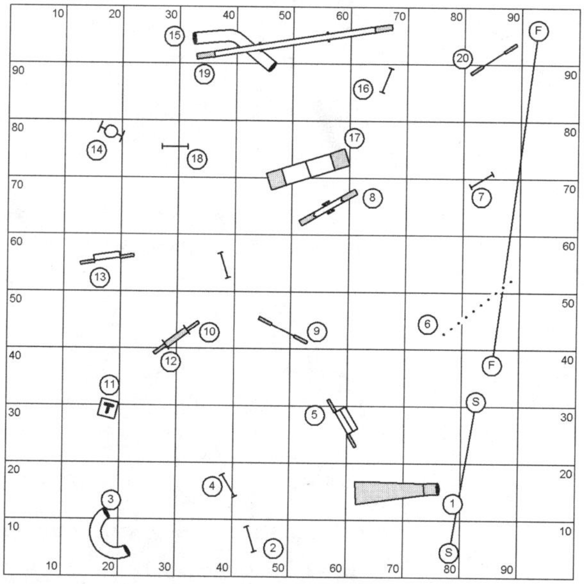

This is the original April's Fool Course designed by Joyce Sobey and played in a JFF league in Richmond, Virginia.

Scoring

April's Fool is scored time plus faults. The dog with the lowest score wins.

JFF rules for obstacle performance are used to determine course faults.

- Dropped bars, off-course, missed contacts—5 faults
- Failure to perform—20 faults
- Refusals—not faulted
- Missed weave poles—not faulted, but the performance must be corrected, or the dog earns a failure to perform.

Course Design

April's Fool is adaptable from any course in which a sequence is specified. It could be a standard course, for example, or a jumpers course.

barrel racing

The Barrel Racing game can take several forms, each borrowed with some variation from the rodeo crowd. It is guaranteed to showcase the directional and distance-working capabilities of the dog-and-handler team. This game uses a nonstandard agility obstacle: a barrel, set on end, with a hard top. The form of the game shown here is the invention of Lyndal Nichols of Queensland, Australia, where it is played as a serious game of competition. Lyndal's version is based upon a set of rules originally defined by Kim Duff in the U.S.

Briefing

As with the equine version, three barrels are placed in a triangular formation, which the dogs must gallop around in a set pattern indicated by the judge. The dogs are run off lead, and the handler may guide the dog around the barrels in any fashion that encourages it to run accurately and quickly, but he may not touch the dog, touch the barrel, or enlist outside help from the spectators.

There are two courses, one which turns right around the first barrel and then left around the second and third. The other course does the opposite, left around the first barrel and right around the second and third. The dogs must run through the start and finish poles to record a time. There is no fault for running the wrong course, but the handler must correct the dog's path to record a time.

The handler may carry a toy or ball to promote speed and enthusiasm and can throw it across the finish line to ensure a fast run home.

Scoring

Barrel racing is scored time plus faults. The lowest score wins.

There are two height divisions:

- Mini: up to and including 16" in height at the withers.
- Unrestricted: no restriction in height.

Time faults are caused by:

- Handler deliberately touching the dog—3-second penalty

- Handler touching the barrel—3-second penalty
- Dog or handler knocking the barrel over—5-second penalty

Course Design

Australians run barrel racing on the equine course reduced by two-thirds, but the game is open to other alterations. Spacing of the barrels is often an important consideration.

Strategies

Barrel Racing is a game that does not require the handler to be particularly fit. A dog can be taught to scoot around the barrels at some distance from the handler, leaving the handler to run the least distance, perhaps even standing in the middle of the formation, using commands and hand signals to guide the dog.

In the American variation, notice from the sample courses that the handler's position is dictated by downstream handling, probably more so than in standard agility. Since the dog turns most naturally in the direction of the handler, the handler must be constantly aware of where he needs to be to best promote the successful performance of the dog in this fast-paced game. In training, it's necessary for the dog and handler to develop a vocabulary for direction of movement. In general, the handler cannot micromanage the dog's movements as in standard agility. This is a fast event, requiring broad sweeping motions by dog and handler alike, and just a few, well-timed commands to communicate direction and action to the dog.

Like anything else, the communication is likely to be awkward at first as the handler struggles to provide the right command with good timing, and the dog tries to learn and understand what the handler is asking him to do.

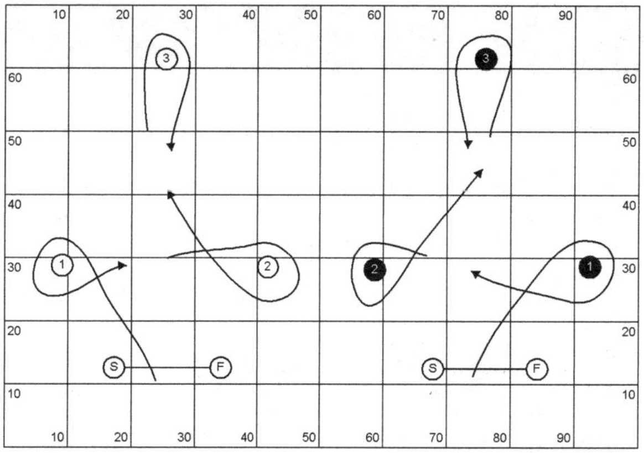

These are the two legitimate courses recognized in Australia. The barrels are set up in an area with a minimum spacing of 48 to 63 yards between them. This is the equine course reduced by approximately two-thirds. One course turns right, left, left around the barrels; the other turns left, right, right around the barrels.

There is no reason why an enthusiastic dog should not run as fast if not faster around a Barrel Racing course than a horse. The dog can get in close around the barrel and does not have to balance a rider. However, the best time so far around the course set up as in the diagram is 9.43 seconds. This is definitely a time to smash, since it is only half the time a horse takes on a course three times as long. A worthy aim is to get dogs tearing around the reduced course in six seconds!

Variations

American variation—The course may be set up in several patterns, as shown in the sample course at right. The dog is required to negotiate each barrel in the course in the sequence and in the direction indicated by the judge. The judge may specify that all barrels be taken in a common direction or may change the direction of performance several times in the course.

The handler may run with his dog but is not required to.

Barrels may be placed a minimum of 20' apart. No maximum distance is specified, which allows some interesting transitional routes for both dog and handler. However, placing a barrel in the dog's path between two barrels in sequence is not allowed.

Competition courses should involve six or more barrels. Barrels may be used more than once in the course, but the course designer cannot specify back-to-back performance.

The American variation of Barrel Racing is scored time plus faults. The lowest score wins. Faults are assessed for the following infractions:

- Refusal (turning back or jumping on the barrel)—5-faults
- Off-course (wrong barrrel or barrel in the wrong direction)—5 faults
- Failure to perform—elimination

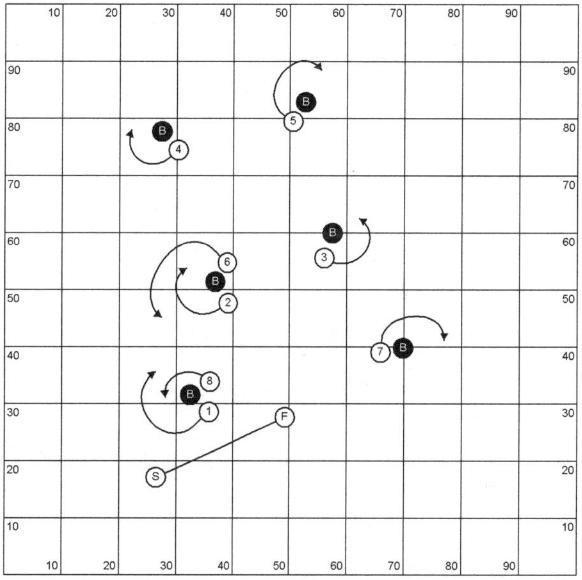

The American variation allows multiple barrels and variable patterns of placement. The judge will stipulate in which direction the dog must move around each of the barrels and clearly indicate these on a course map or in the briefing to exhibitors.

baseball

Like the great American pastime, Baseball is a delightful just-for-the-fun-of-it game for a summer afternoon in a park with a band of agility enthusiasts and their dogs. This game is also a useful training exercise for modest distance work. Baseball is the invention of Terry Culley of Bosque, New Mexico.

Briefing

The dog is required to perform the obstacles in sequence at the handler's direction and in the order designated by the judge.

Bonuses are awarded for each base the dog gets to while the handler stays on the pitcher's mound. A home run (25 bonus seconds) may be scored if the handler leaves the dog in a stay at the start line, stands inside the area designated as the pitcher's mound (roughly the center of the course), and remains on the pitcher's mound throughout the dog's performance. If the handler leaves the pitcher's mound before the dog completes the course, the dog will be faulted, and no subsequent bonus will be earned.

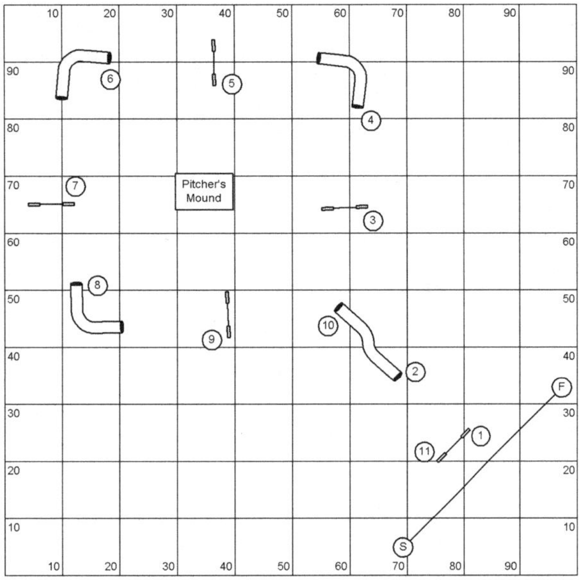

This is a relatively simple Baseball course, demonstrating the basic design elements.

The game can be played in two ways: for individual scores, or the field can be divided into an equal number of dogs and handlers on each side for a cumulative score.

Scoring

Baseball is scored time plus faults, minus bonus. The team with the lowest score wins.

The schedule of faults will be:

- Dropped bars—5 faults
- Off-course—5 faults
- Stepping off the pitcher's mound—5 faults
- Failure to perform—20 faults
- Refusals—not faulted

The schedule of bonuses will be:

- 1st base—5 seconds
- 2nd base (overall 2nd base would be worth 10 seconds)—5 seconds
- 3rd base (overall 3rd base would be worth 15 seconds)—5 seconds
- Home run (overall the home run would be worth 25 seconds)—10 seconds

Course Design

The course is diamond-shaped and flows around the pitcher's mound. Notice that the path from the start and finish line (home plate) to the pitcher's mound is a re-used sequence. It points toward the pitcher's mound at the beginning of the course and straight away from the pitcher's mound towards "home plate" at the end of the course.

If tunnels are not available, jumps may be substituted; and the tire may be used at home base. Use of contacts and weave poles is not recommended.

Qualifying and Titles

TDAA

Baseball is eligible as a qualifying game under TDAA rules. When using this game as a TDAA qualifier, a baseline for the standard course time should be established by the judge that reflects the yards per second in the Standard classes for the respective level of the dog. When the handler steps outside the box, earning a 5-point penalty, the dog's ability to earn a qualifying score is significantly affected, but not totally eliminated.

JFF

Baseball is eligible as a qualifying game under JFF rules. When using this game as a JFF qualifier, the game should be scored faults then time. No standard course time should be established. Qualifying criteria should reflect the skill level of the dog and handler team:

- Games I—15 or fewer faults
- Games II—5 faults
- Games III—zero faults

Variations

The Egyed variation—In this variation, invented by Cynthia Egyed for a club outing, the table serves as the pitcher's mound. Handlers must stand on the table. If a dog takes the table with the handler, the handler will be required to run the course without his dog.

basketball

Basketball is the invention of John and Arlene Rhodes. The game was originally played on May 25, 2002 after the first agility match put on by Zippity Do Dogs Sports Club in Grand Junction, Colorado, and has been modified slightly here to simplify the rules and to speed up play.

Briefing

Basketball is a two-part game. The first part is the point-accumulation period. The second part is the basketball period in which point scores can be multiplied.

Please note: two jumps are marked SD for "Sudden Death." If the dog takes either of these jumps at any time, sudden death occurs, and the dog must run to the table to stop time. The dog retains any previously earned score but cannot earn any more points.

To start, a ring steward loads a tennis ball on the table.

Point accumulation—The team will have 50 seconds to accumulate points. Time starts after a ring steward has "loaded" the table and when the dog crosses the start line. Points are earned for each obstacle the dog successfully performs. Although the dog can take jumps any number of times, he can take other scoring obstacles no more than twice.

During point accumulation, if the dog removes the ball or causes it to fall off the table, the handler must replace it before continuing. Point accumulation ends on the 50-second whistle.

The basketball game—If the tennis ball is left on the table at the end of the opening period, the team will have 15 seconds to shoot a basket. A basket is made when the shooter tosses the tennis ball though the tire. A basket doubles the team's score, provided that both the dog and the handler are behind the line when the shot is made (the dog can be on the table). If the handler can then entice the dog to go through the tire to give chase to the ball, the dog's score is tripled.

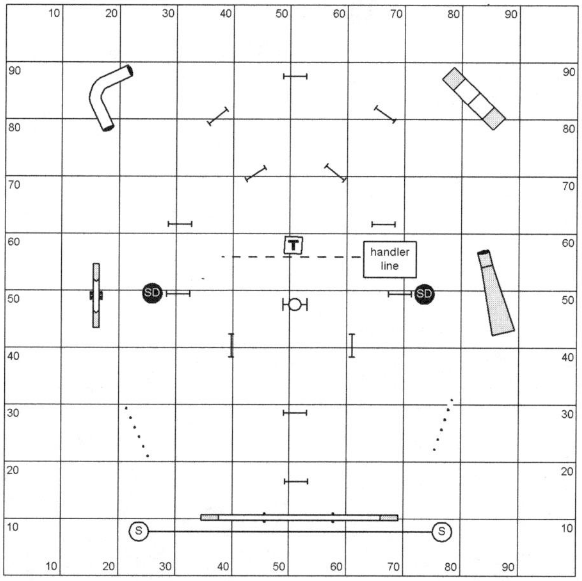

In this sample course, the judge stipulated that the collapsed tunnel and teeter may only be taken one time each. Note both are performed in the same direction (toward the starting line).

If the ball rolled off the table during play or was carried off by the dog, and the handler doesn't replace it before the start of the basketball game, then the handler's shot is forfeited, and the dog must go to the table to stop time.

Scoring

Basketball is scored points then time. Time is a tiebreaker only. Scoring is:

- Jumps—1 point
- Tunnels—3 points
- Contacts and weave poles—5 points
- Tire (in the point-accumulation round)— minus 3 points

The basketball round only multiplies the score; it cannot add any points.

Course Design

Rearranging the obstacles will vary the game. The arrangement of the tire and table are a required element of the game. The doubling line is set at 7' from the basket.

Strategies

The best strategy appears to be for the handler (or dog) to pick the best line of obstacles for point accumulation and then do the line back-to-back.

beat the clock

Beat the Clock has long been a favorite warm-up game in the USDAA. It is a simple, open-entry game in which novice dogs and handlers can compete with more advanced teams. By cutting down on the distance that the handler must run on course, Beat the Clock can help teach the dog to work at a distance from the handler.

Briefing

The objective is for the team to perform the clock of obstacles before the time runs out. Typically, the standard course time is 60 seconds.

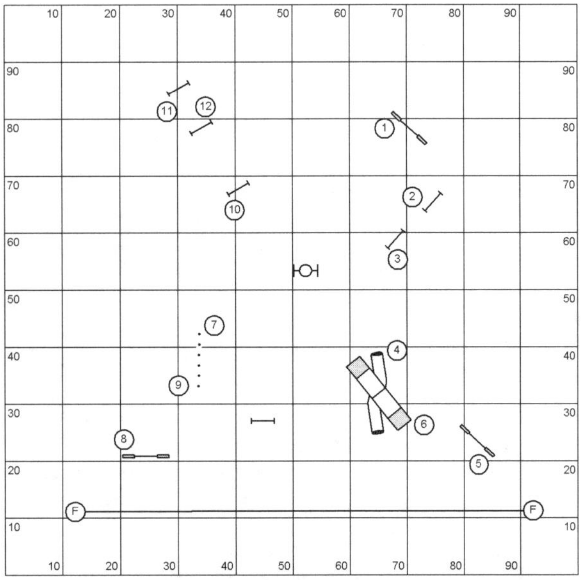

This typical example of a Beat the Clock course was designed by Bud Houston and originally played in the agility league at Dogwood Training Center in Ostrander, Ohio.

The dog and handler begin in the center of the clock where the dog must perform an obstacle that begins course time and then perform a quarter of the obstacles on the course (first #1 through #3; then #4 through #6, and so forth). The handler must direct the dog to the obstacle at the center of the clock face prior to beginning each quarter of the obstacles on the clock. After completing the final sequence of obstacles, #10 through #12, the dog must be directed to the finish line or to a table, at which time the clock is stopped. After completing #12 while on the way to the table or finish line to stop time, the dog will not be faulted for taking additional obstacles.

If a dog faults an obstacle in a designated sequence, the judge will call "fault." The handler must direct the dog back to the obstacle at the center of the clock face and reattempt the same sequence. Any points previously won in that group are lost. The dog may not continue on to the next sequence until he successfully finishes the faulted one.

Faults are assessed for dropping bars, missing contacts, and taking an obstacle out of order (or from the wrong group). Refusals may be faulted at the discretion of the judge and course designer.

Scoring

Beat the Clock is scored points then time with the highest score winning. The team earns the clock value of each obstacle successfully performed. If two or more dogs have the same number of points, time breaks the tie.

A total of 78 points is possible.

Course Design

A Beat the Clock course consists of twelve obstacles, numbered from #1 to #12. The layout is roughly circular with the #12 obstacle positioned at 12 o'clock and the other obstacles arranged in a clock-like fashion.

Strategies

The handler should find the sweetest path for his dog and push for as much speed as possible without sacrificing the reliability of the dog's performance.

The different variations of Beat the Clock offer greater opportunity for strategy and daring. In the Cuckoo variation, the handler should carefully measure the length of his dog's course. From this measurement, the handler should get a pretty good idea whether it's possible to complete the cuckoo and earn the cuckoo bonus points within the allotted time. During the run, if there is a bobble that takes any amount of time to correct, the handler might think hard about abandoning any attempt at the cuckoo.

In the Dealer's Choice variation, the handler should carefully analyze each three-part sequence to find the most efficient line for the dog. Indeed, the tire should always be considered a fourth obstacle to close the three-part sequences. The handler should consider what approach to the tire completing each sequence would give his dog.

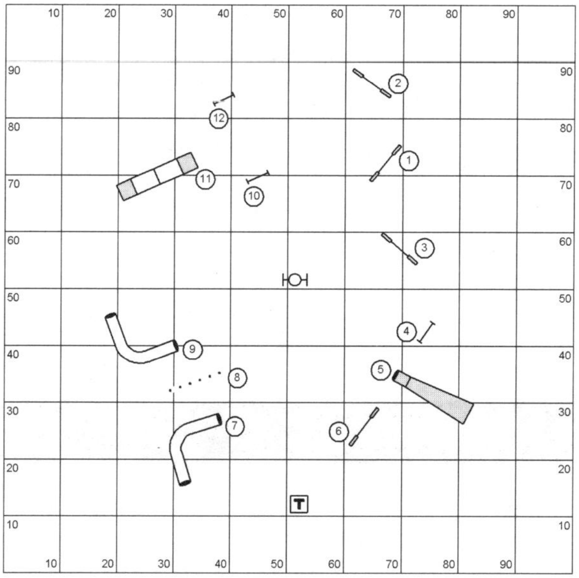

In the Dealer's Choice variation of Beat the Clock, the obstacles in each group may be numbered, but these numbers do not indicate the order and direction in which the obstacles must be taken. This is left to the handler— or the dog—to determine.

Qualifying and Titles

In the TDAA and JFF, qualification should be set on the basis of points and time; the points the dog can earn should be doable and appropriate to the level of play. For example:

- Games I—For a score of 9 or better
- Games II—For a score of 12 or better, in 60 seconds or fewer
- Games III—For a score of 12 or better, in 50 seconds or fewer

In the Cuckoo variation, this might be changed to require the Master handler to go for the Cuckoo to win the higher games qualifier.

- Games I—For a score of 9 or better.
- Games II—For a score of 12, in 60 seconds or fewer.
- Games III—For a score of 24, in 50 seconds or fewer.

Variations

- **Combination obstacles**—In this variation, combination obstacles (a series of obstacles that count as a single point value) might be used much as they are used in USDAA-style Snooker. This option is especially useful when nesting courses for novice and advanced levels. The more advanced competitors would have to do the combination obstacles while the Novice level competitors would use only a single obstacle from any combination. Combination obstacles can be used with any standard or variant Beat the Clock game. In the Dealer's Choice variation, the judge may specify that the combination obstacle has to be taken in a certain order or direction.
- **Cuckoo**—Credited to Gordon Simmons-Moake, this variation of Beat the Clock adds a 13th obstacle to the clock. If a dog and handler have completed the first 12 obstacles and believe they have enough time left, they may attempt to perform the cuckoo. If the team completes the cuckoo

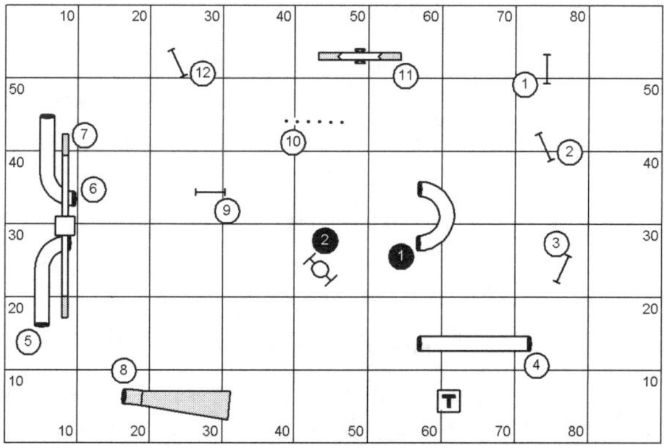

In this Strategic Teams course, different dogs start each quadrant by performing the tunnel-tire combo at the center of the clock face. One or more dogs can perform the quadrants. However, each dog on the team must perform obstacles in one or more of the quadrants. The table stops time.

within the original 60 seconds, then the team's score is doubled. If the team attempts the cuckoo but does not perform it correctly within course time, then all points are forfeited.

When using the Cuckoo variation, it is important to specify whether the dog must be directed to the obstacle at the center of the clock's face before (or after) attempting the cuckoo obstacle.

- **Dealer's Choice**—This variation of Beat the Clock allows the handler to choose the order and direction of obstacles to be performed in the segments of the clock and may allow the handler to choose the order of the segments themselves.
- **Strategic Teams**—Invented and inspired by Wayne Van Deusen for JFF league play, this variation of Beat the Clock is played by a relay team with a more aggressive time limit than when one dog is playing and may be combined with the Cuckoo variation. Each dog is required to perform at least one obstacle in each of the "quadrants" of the clock. Also, no dog is allowed to do consecutive performances of the intro obstacles at the center of the clock face.

In strategic pairs or teams, if a dog faults an obstacle, that obstacle has to be performed by a different dog. If the obstacle faulted is a jump, the handler whose dog dropped the bar must reset it before the team can continue.

biathlon

The invention of Stuart Mah, this game was the runner-up in the 1995 Clean Run *magazine games contest. Biathlon is a combination of Pairs Pursuit, Boxed Pairs Relay, and the Olympic Biathlon event.*

Briefing

A side consists of two dog-and-handler teams: a shooting team and a penalty team. Both teams on the side begin in a start box, which is designated by the judge.

The shooting team begins a sequence designated by the judge in which two areas are marked as shooting stations. Both dog and handler of the shooting team must remain in the box as the handler tries to knock over a target with one of three tennis balls (ammo) supplied at the shooting station.

If the handler successfully knocks down the target, the team continues on the shooting course. When the first team completes the course, the teams swap places: The penalty team becomes the shooting team that must complete the shooting course in the same manner as the first team, and the shooting team becomes the penalty team.

If the shooting team incurs a penalty, the dog on the penalty team runs the assigned penalty course. The shooting team must remain in place until the penalty team has completed its course. A penalty is assessed:

- Any time the dog on the shooting team faults an obstacle
- Any time the shooter's dog leaves the shooting station before the ammo has been exhausted

If the dog running the penalty course incurs obstacle performance faults, those faults are added to the side's course time. Any obstacle omitted in the penalty course will incur a failure to perform (20 faults).

If the dog on the penalty team leaves the start box or the penalty course to pick up loose ammo, there is no penalty except the time it takes to get the dog back under control.

If the shooter fails to knock down a target in three tries, the penalty team must run the assigned penalty course.

During the course run, ammo that is dropped by the shooter will be considered unusable and must be left on the field.

There is no penalty if a shooter's dog picks up and carries ammo on the course. However, this ammunition is considered unusable by the shooter.

Handlers who are not on course may hold onto their dogs.

Scoring

Biathlon is scored time plus faults. The side with the lowest score wins.

Traditionally, USDAA Advanced rules are used for judging faults.

Course Design

The shooting course should be designed using 9 to 12 obstacles and should be suitable to the level of the dogs. Use mainly jumps and tunnels and, occasionally, weave poles or a contact obstacle.

The penalty course ideally should consist of no more than two or three obstacles, other than contacts.

The target is placed 10' to 15' away from the shooting station. Some possible targets are: a tire with a net on the end to catch the ball, or soft dog toys set on a table or other suitable surface. In addition, if hitting the target will be difficult to judge, it is advisable to use jump stewards as target judges. They can signal with a flag if the target is hit.

Variations

- **Hurry Up and Wait**—In this variation of Biathlon, a typical two-dog Relay course is run. In each leg of the relay is a shooting station, equipped with six balls and a target. The handler on course must pause at the shooting station and attempt to hit the target. The shooter can proceed on course only after hitting the target or exhausting all his ammunition.
- **Single shooting station**—The Biathlon shooting course can be reduced to one shooting station.
- **Alternative penalty course**—There may be two different penalty courses set: one course for the dogs and one course for the handlers that is more handler-friendly.

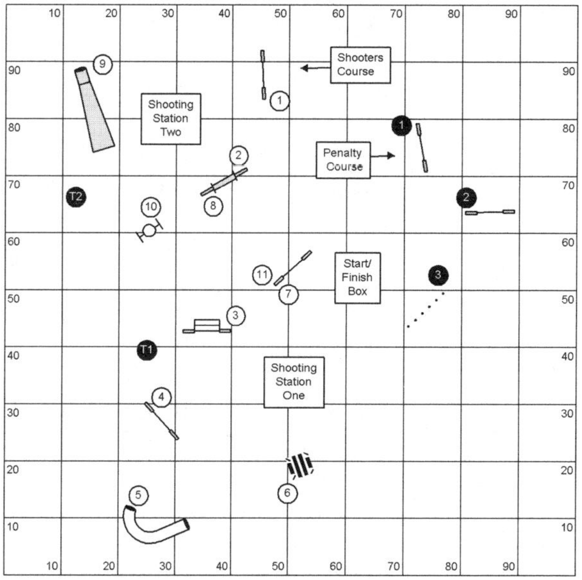

The shooters course, shown in white numbers, uses 9 to 12 obstacles. The penalty course, shown in black numbers, uses 2 or 3 obstacles. The targets are labeled "T1" and "T2." This course was designed by Stuart Mah.

black hole

Black Hole is the invention of Ilze Rukis, who was looking for a different spin on the usual agility game. Some games reward repetitions of certain obstacles. Others give higher points for some obstacles over others. She determined to create something where the focus is to avoid taking a particular obstacle. What could be better than the ever-inviting tunnel opening that so many dogs just love to dive into? The game is intended to help to develop the dog's discrimination and the handler's control skill. It's particularly handy now that NADAC has Tunnelers classes.

Briefing

Black Hole starts and ends at the table. The handler will direct the dog on the numbered course, accumulating points for each obstacle performed successfully. The dog can continue to earn points unless it goes into a pipe tunnel (the black hole). Scoring stops once the dog goes off-course into a tunnel. The handler must direct his dog to the table to stop time.

Scoring

Black Hole is scored points plus bonus, then time. Time is a tiebreaker only. The schedule of points will be:

- Jumps—1 point
- Tire or 6 weave poles—3 points
- Contact obstacles and 12 weave poles—5 points

Faulted obstacles will earn no points. Refusals are not faulted. A wrong course (except into a tunnel) is not faulted. Errors in weaving are not faulted. However, the handler must correct the dog's error or earn failure to perform.

The dog earns a bonus of 10 points for doing this course in 50 seconds or less. The bonus is added to the dog's score.

Course Design

The Black Hole course should be designed to suggest a logical path to the dog that presents on-course tunnels as inviting opportunities. These teasing options should be presented with some frequency.

Strategies

The chief reasons that a dog goes off course into a pipe tunnel are that the handler has logically presented the tunnel to the dog or that the handler worries so over the potential for an off-course at the tunnel that his body gives inadvertent "focus" to the tunnel. Where you have a tunnel-sucking dog, you usually have a tunnel-sucking handler.

The handler might "trust the force" of his own movement while moving confidently and reliably in the direction of the true course without giving the tunnels much attention. On the other hand, the handler could also seek to create a path for the dog that does not present the pipe tunnels to the dog.

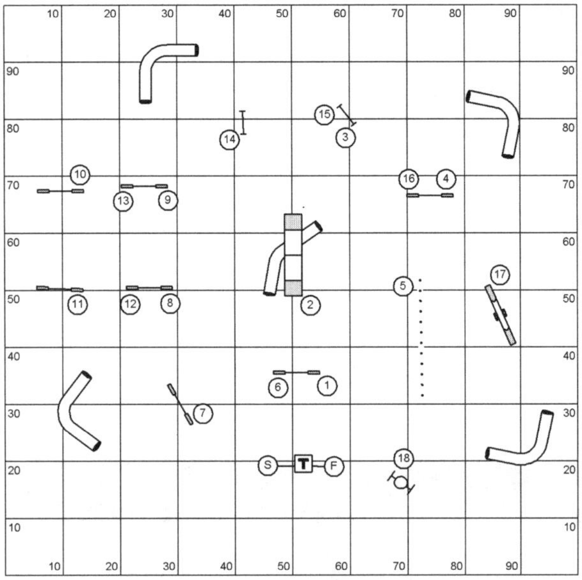

In this example of a Black Hole course, the benchmark time for earning the bonus points is based on an arbitrary yards-per-second calculation. This course is about 160 yards long. The 50-second benchmark would be based on something better than 3 yards per second.
In a more technical course, the standard course time might be set at .5 yards per second less than in this more open and flowing course.

Qualifying and Titles

JFF

JFF and league play qualification should be set with the expectation that the Games III (Masters) dog will earn all available points and lose none. Games II might require a clean course but not the time bonus. Games I should be set at some doable level that demonstrates that the dog is working and biddable.

- Games I—For a score of 20 or better
- Games II—For a score of 32
- Games III—For a score of 42

Note that the Games III qualifying reflects the 10-point bonus for blazing the course in 50 seconds or less but leaves little room for faults incurred on the course.

TDAA

Black Hole can also be a titling game for the TDAA, though the course would have to be tighter than the one shown in the sample course design. The TDAA uses a transitional distance averaging about 7' or 8' between obstacles and tunnels with 16" apertures and shorter overall length.

The benchmark for a bonus should be based on the yards-per-second calculation for the respective level.

blackjack

Blackjack is the invention of Jonathan Brown, former President of the Agility Association of Canada (AAC). While Blackjack now is no longer a titling game for Canine Performance Events (CPE), JFF and TDAA still offer it as a titling game. The Vegas variation of Blackjack is possibly more exciting and challenging than the original version.

Briefing

The purpose of this game is to accumulate 21 points in the fastest time. Accumulating more than 21 points disqualifies the team.

At least one corner, one side, and one jump must be completed successfully. Corners are typically made from tunnels placed in the corners of the course; sides are always contact obstacles and weave poles, which are placed along the sides of the course. The jumps are arranged in a random fashion in the middle.

The judge will choose the first obstacle, but the order of subsequent obstacles will be the handler's choice. The handler must attempt the first obstacle or points that are double the value of the opening obstacle are deducted from the dog's score.

No contact obstacles may be taken back to back. At least one obstacle must be taken between contact obstacle attempts, whether successful or not. Four-paws are required for commitment to any obstacle. No obstacle may be successfully performed more than twice for points.

Dogs shall accumulate points within a time period established by the judge, usually 60 seconds. If 21 points are accumulated under the time limit set by the judge, the dog and handler go to the table to stop time.

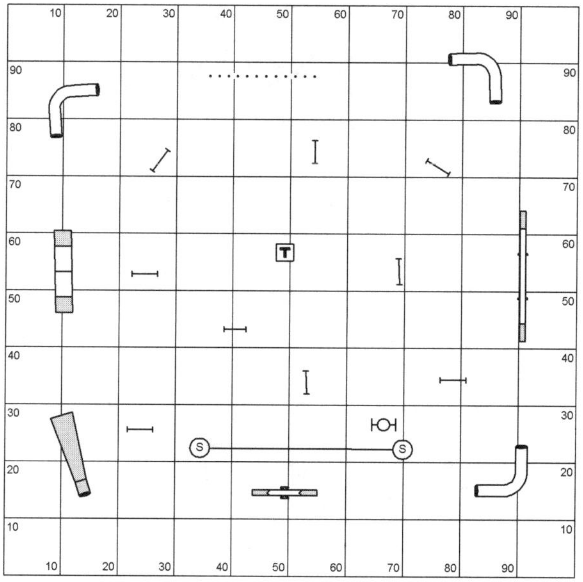

In a typical JFF Blackjack course, the corners are worth 2 points and the sides are worth 3 to 4 points.

Scoring

Blackjack is scored points then time. The highest point value under 21 wins. A team scoring more than 21 points is eliminated. If two or more dogs have the same number of points, then time breaks the tie.

Points are awarded as follows:

- Jumps—1 point
- Tunnels, tire, window—2 points
- Contact obstacles—3 points
- Weave poles—4 points

Course Design

A typical Blackjack course includes the table used to stop the clock (near the center of the course), surrounded by six to eight single-bar, non-winged jumps. The contact obstacles and weave poles are arranged on the outer perimeter of the course. The four corners include a collapsed tunnel, and three pipe tunnels

Strategies

It is important in Blackjack to make a good estimate of the quickest way for a given dog to earn the necessary 21 points. Aside from the required obstacles to be performed and the prohibition against back-to-back performance of contact obstacles, the handler must take into account the specific strengths and weaknesses of his dog.

The handler also must be able to add up the point values of the obstacles to arrive at exactly 21 points. If something goes wrong on course, the handler will have to change the plan, but still do the arithmetic on the fly to get 21 points.

In the Vegas variation, the handler's ability to keep the math straight will be somewhat more difficult. If the handler attempts a gamble, but fails because of an off-course or a refusal, the dog will earn the simple value for the obstacles completed, but not the gamble bonus. According to the rules, the handler is eliminated for going to the table with more than 21 points. The handler probably should attempt each gamble straightaway. If the dog completes one of them, the dog earns the full points. If the dog fails at one, then he needs to fill the 21 points after the dust settles on the two gambles. This means the handler is going to have to be both pretty quick on his feet and a whiz at doing math in his head.

Qualifying and Titles

Blackjack is eligible as a qualifying game under JFF and TDAA rules. Since all dogs must earn 21 points, the point schedule should be based on a reasonable standard course time in which 21 points might be earned. In the sample JFF course, for example, the qualifying criteria were set as follows:

- Games I—21 points in 60 seconds or less
- Games II—21 points in 50 seconds or less
- Games III—21 points in 40 seconds or less

In Becky Dean's Vegas variation of Blackjack, there was no SCT. The qualification criteria were:

- Games I—21 points
- Games II—10 points + the Ace gamble; or 11 points + the Blackjack gamble
- Games III—Both the Ace gamble and the Blackjack gamble

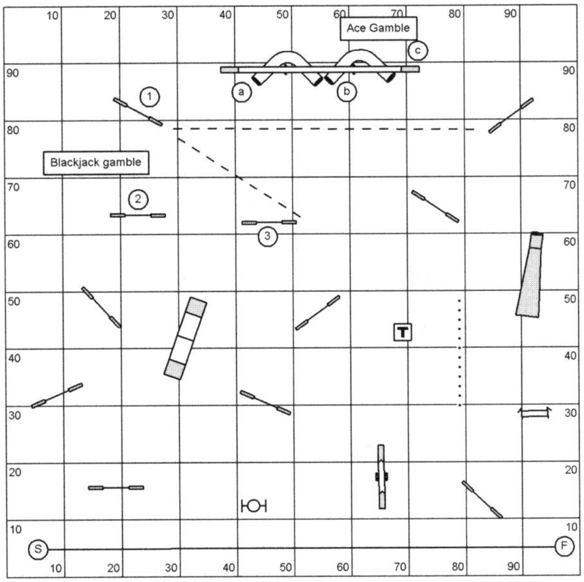

Becky Dean designed this example of the Vegas variation of Blackjack.

Variations

- **Vegas variation**—The invention of Becky Dean, this version includes two gambles. Gambles can be completed at any time during the run.
  - The Ace gamble, worth 11 points, is noted on the course in letters (tunnel, tunnel, dogwalk). USDAA Advanced rules will be used to judge the Ace gamble (only refusals on the contact obstacle will be called).
  - The Blackjack gamble is noted on the course with numbers (jump, jump, jump). USDAA Masters rules will be used to judge the Blackjack gamble (refusals for any obstacle).

If the dog incurs a fault during the attempt of either gamble, he'll earn simple points for the obstacles completed to that point, but will not earn the gamble bonus.

No more than one obstacle in either gamble can be performed back-to-back except when attempting the gamble. However, one obstacle from the Ace gamble could be performed in conjunction with one obstacle from the Blackjack gamble without incurring a penalty. If more than one obstacle in a gamble is taken back-to-back, the team will not be eligible to earn the gamble points.

When playing the Vegas variation in league play, Blackjack should be scored points by level, then time. It's given that advanced dogs will probably have a score of 21points. Leveling for placements will take into consideration successful performance of on-course gambles using this order of precedence:

1. Both the Ace gamble and the Blackjack gamble
2. 11 points + the Ace gamble
3. 10 points + the Blackjack gamble
4. 21 points no gambles

- Ace Fault—In a variation on the Vegas variation, if the dog faults the Ace gamble, he gets only one point (providing the dog succeeds in performing the first obstacle without fault), regardless of the number of obstacles completed in the gamble.

blindman's bluff

This game was concocted as a training game for Bud Houston's competition class at Dogwood Training Center in Ostrander, Ohio. The game is intended to promote visualization skills and provide a way out when you show up at the trial finding that you have missed both the briefing and the walk-through and have nothing but the course map to guide your running strategy!

Briefing

Dogs will run a standard agility course. The dog is required to perform each obstacle on the course at the handler's direction in the sequence designated by the judge. However, here's the challenge: Handlers are not allowed to walk or even see the course until they are called into the ring.

All exhibitors will be sequestered from the course area. At least 30 minutes before each handler runs, he will be handed a numbered course on paper. He must devise his handling strategy solely from the diagram.

Scoring

Blindman's Bluff is scored faults then time. The winner is the dog with the fewest faults. If two dogs have the same number of faults, then time breaks the tie.

Any rules system to determine faults can be used, but the skill level of the players should be kept in mind.

Course Design

There are no particular required obstacles or forbidden obstacles. The judge may use whatever obstacles are available in whatever space is available. A course will typically consist of 15 to 20 obstacles.

There should be a means to keep exhibitors from seeing the course, for instance, by setting up the course in a building from which the exhibitors are excluded until time to run. Or the course could be outside and the exhibitors inside.

Strategies

- The two most important elements in this competition are for the handler to remember the correct sequence and to determine a handling strategy without ever having walked the course.
- The handler should spend every available moment before the run visualizing being on course and working with the dog.
- Please note that groaning and complaining only serve to break other people's concentration.

Qualifying and Titles

Blindman's Bluff is eligible as a qualifying game under JFF and TDAA rules. It should only be used when the conditions of the game can be met. That is, the course should somehow be segregated from the field of exhibitors.

Courses should be designed appropriate to the class level in competition. Qualifying should be based on the JFF schedule of faults (with no standard course time) for competition for both JFF and TDAA.

Variations

- **Cold Turkey**—This variation has been played in competition. Rather than requiring the handlers to be sequestered away from the course, the judge renumbers the course at regular intervals. This minimizes the disadvantage of running early in the class. Cold Turkey is judged under Starters/Novice rules.
- **Blindman's Bluff games**—Blindman's Bluff can be played using nearly any game. Consider it as a basis for Snooker or for Pole Jacks! It's a scary thought!

blitzen's sunday picnic games

Pam Juliano founded Blitzen Agility Club of Chicago as an AKC-recognized club in 1995. This AKC-sponsored club of like-minded agility folks of all different ages, shapes, sizes, temperaments, and personalities has one common goal—having fun together and with their dogs. Lee Zerbian and Lisa Schmit designed the following picnic games for Blitzen's events, including camping outings, an annual awards banquet, a winter get-together, trials, and a summer picnic.

Water Balloon Toss

Form teams of players. They start close together and everyone tosses the balloon to his partner. Everyone takes a giant step back and repeats. Everyone then takes two giant steps back and the game continues. Players are eliminated for dropping balloons or balloons breaking. Last team standing and dry wins.

Lifesaver Relay

Everyone gets a swizzle stick and a lifesaver. Form two teams. Each player must carry a lifesaver on a swizzle stick to the teammate and hand off without dropping or go back and start again. Before the next player goes, he must drop the lifesaver just given him into a bucket, put the lifesaver on the stick, and then go. The twist is that you must have your dog on lead and the handle of the leash must be around the wrist of the swizzle stick hand. In addition, your opposing team is allowed to call and invite your dog to come and visit from the other side of the line! (No correcting of the dog is allowed in this game since opposing team members will be calling the dog to them.) Game ends in three minutes, and the team to have the most total lifesavers wins. (Play again with a twist... opposing team members switch dogs and then the real handler gets to call his dog as that player is trying to carry the lifesaver).

Doggie Hula Snake

Volunteers hold up 6 hula-hoops as the ribs of a tunnel, so that the aperture of each hula hop is fairly presented to the dog. With each pass, the hoops get farther apart and start to snake around (not a straight line). Handler must stand at the end of the line and call his dog to him. Winner is the dog that can do the whole snake without going outside the hula-hoops. By the end, the line of hoops should look like a snake.

Blindman's Doggie Bluff Relay

Two teams are formed with an even number of dogs/people on each team. Dog is on lead. Handler is blindfolded. Teammates call the handler's dog and the handler must follow the dog's lead. In the middle will be a water balloon. Handler must stop when teammates say, pick up the water balloon, and then continue to the end, still being guided by the dog. First team to finish wins, or if the opposing team should step on and break or drop their water balloon, the other team wins.

Bring Me That!

Handler sits in a designated spot and sends a dog to pick up and bring back three articles 5' away. Next player goes. Keep repeating, moving the articles farther and farther away. Players are knocked out each time the dog gets side-tracked, goes off to sniff, or returns without the article. Winner is the last person who can send the dog the farthest to retrieve and return.

Catalog Race Game

Two teams are formed and each player picks a number. Each person must run down to the hula hoop (5' from the catalog), sit or down the dog, and then go over to the catalog and pull the page that matches his number from the draw. Then, the player retrieves the dog and runs back for the next player to go. While the handler is pulling the page from the catalog, the dog must stay in a sit or a down. If the dog gets up, the handler must run back to the start line without the page, losing his turn, and the next player must go. First team to successfully pull their pages wins.

boston bowling

Tammi Stone invented this game, first played at a three-day USDAA trial in Boston, Massachusetts, hosted by ARFF, on December 5, 1997. At this trial, nearly 1300 runs were recorded in a single ring, averaging almost precisely one dog per minute, an American record.

Briefing

Boston Bowling consists of two short courses, each starting with a specific entry to one of two tunnels, set side by side in a "U" shape. The handler "bowls" his dog by sending the dog ahead into a tunnel entrance. Each dog-and-handler team has two bowls. The handler may not step over the penalty line as he bowls his dog into one of the tunnel entrances.

Each tunnel will have one entrance, designated the first obstacle in one of two courses. The opposite entrance, of the same tunnel, will be designated the gutter lane. The course the dog must run depends on which tunnel the dog enters. One tunnel will be designated the beginning of course A, and the other tunnel designated the beginning of course B.

Both courses consist of obstacles totaling 10 points or more. The team earns points for each obstacle performed and continues the course so long as no obstacle has been faulted. If an obstacle is faulted, then scoring ceases.

If a ball is a gutter ball, then the ball is considered used and no additional points may be earned. If the team has a ball remaining, they may return to the line and bowl again. If no ball remains, the dog must cross the finish line designated by the judge to stop the clock.

A strike is earned if a team performs an entire course without fault.

The second bowl must be to the tunnel that begins the course not yet bowled. If the bowler selects the same lane as previously performed, the bowl will be considered a gutter ball.

Scoring

Boston Bowling is scored points then time. If two or more dogs have the same number of points, then time breaks the tie.

The team earns points for each obstacle successfully completed:

- Jumps and tunnels—1 point
- Weave poles and contacts—2 points

Each strike bowled by the team earns 5 bonus points.

The maximum score possible is 30.

Course Design

The Boston Bowling course traditionally begins with two U-shaped pipe tunnels set side-by-side with clearly marked send lines for Novice and Advanced competitors. The correct entries to the tunnels will be clearly marked, leaving the opposite tunnel entries as the "gutter ball" lanes. Each correct tunnel entry will mark a unique sequence on the course.

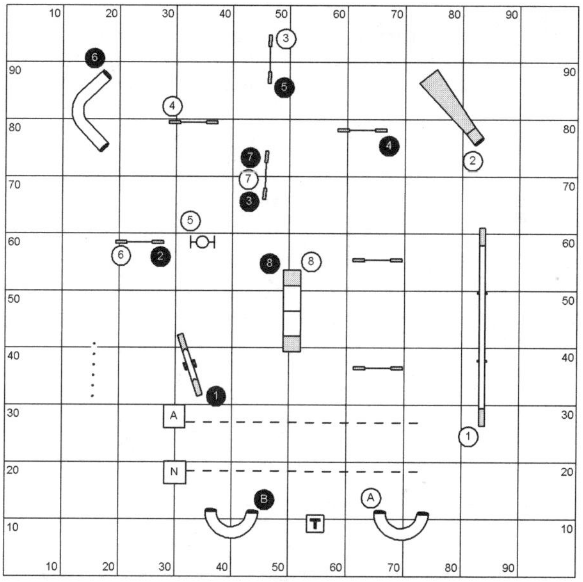

In this example of a Boston Bowling course, the "A" on course indicates the advanced send line; the "N" indicates the novice send line. It's not clear whether the table is a benefit to the bowler or a liability. It certainly creates some separation between the two tunnel lanes. But it also presents a "gutter-ball" possibility should it entice the dog into an off-course in the send.

Strategies

The key to Boston Bowling is, first, to memorize both courses. Second, be prepared to run whichever course the dog initially chooses.

Qualifying and Titles

Boston Bowling is eligible as a qualifying game under JFF and TDAA rules. All classes can run on the same course. Qualification criteria will be:

- Games I—20 points
- Games II—30 points
- Games III—40 points

Variations

- **League play variation**—In league play, the scoring works a bit differently. The first bowl is the more important of the two. If the dog is successfully sent and performs the short course with no faults, then the dog will score 10 for the bowl, plus an additional 10 to carry forward to the next bowl. If the dog faults, however, the dog earns only a point for each obstacle performed before the fault. The second bowl must be to the tunnel that begins the course not yet bowled. If the dog does the same lane as previously performed, the bowl will be considered a gutter ball. If successfully sent to both tunnels from behind the containment line, without regard to subsequent faults, the dog will earn a 10-point bonus.

  In the league play variation, Boston Bowling is scored points then time. The maximum score possible is 40.
- **More bowling rules**—Boston Bowling can be played by a small group of agility enthusiasts (fewer than 10 people) more strictly according to the rules of true bowling. Play ten frames rather than only two.

boxed pairs

On first glance, Boxed Pairs looks like a standard relay with batons, course times, exchange areas, and so on. In fact, providing nothing goes wrong, this game works like a standard relay. But if something does go wrong, well, that's when the fun begins.

Briefing

The Boxed Pairs course is divided into two separate sequences. One dog will be designated to run the first sequence and the other dog the second sequence. Handlers are required to carry and exchange a baton. The first handler can choose to lead out or start with the dog. The second handler is not allowed to lead out. While performing the

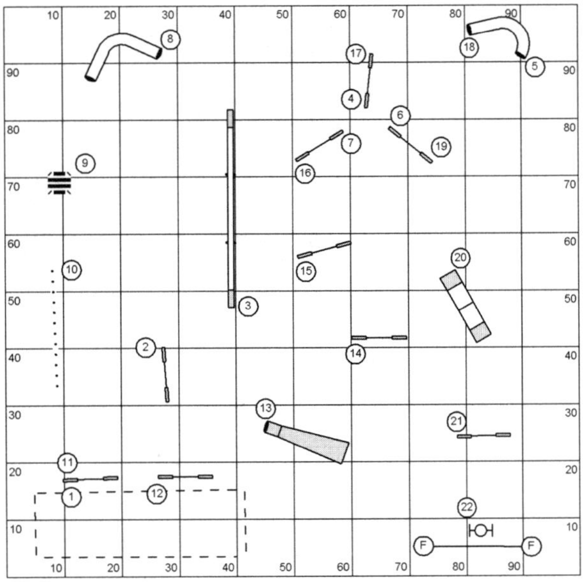

This is a Boxed Pairs relay course designed for competition by ADAA judge, Lyndal Nichols of Queensland, Australia.

exchange, both dogs and handlers must be in the exchange box. Failure to do so results in a disqualification for passing out of the zone.

Both handlers should become familiar with both parts of the course.

If the first dog faults an obstacle, that team must return to the exchange box, exchange the baton, and the second team continues the course beginning with the obstacle at which the first dog made the error. The second dog continues on until he has run the first half of the course. Should the second dog fault any obstacle, that team must return to the exchange box and again exchange the baton. The alternate team must then resume the course from the point of the fault.

When the first half of the course has been successfully run, a scheduled exchange of the baton takes place. The relay continues as in a standard relay with the second side of the course, except that faults force baton exchanges in the exchange box.

Every time an obstacle is faulted, the judge will signal the handlers to change places.

The active dog (the dog that is supposed to be running at any time) will be faulted for taking an obstacle out of sequence. If the exchange dog performs an obstacle on the way to the obstacle faulted by the other team, that dog, too, is called for a fault and must immediately return to the exchange area to hand off the baton to the other team. The inactive dog may perform any obstacle going back to the box.

Scoring

Boxed Pairs is scored time only. The team with the fastest time wins. Since every obstacle must be successfully completed, no faults are assessed. The time it takes for the teams to exchange places is penalty enough.

There is no standard course time. However, a maximum course time should be established.

The stiffer the rules, the more difficult it is to get through clean. If refusals are faulted, this relay gets downright hectic. Most judges use modified USDAA Starters/Novice rules to cut down on the number of potential baton exchanges.

Course Design

The layout of a Relay course is similar to that of a standard agility course. The course is made up of at least 11 obstacles and often many more. Each team performs a sequence of obstacles as designated by the judge. The course can be designed so that one dog will run part of the course and the other dog the remainder, or so that each dog runs the entire course. Each sequence should contain at least one contact obstacle.

Strategies

Sequences should be assigned between the two dogs so that the relative strengths and weaknesses of the two dogs allow them to attack the course with the smallest possibility of any errors.

However, each team member should be familiar with the other course.

In running the game, it's important that the handler of the inactive dog pay keen attention to the performance of the dog on course. The game will get sloppy if the second dog and handler don't know where to resume the course. A keen competitor would be constantly recalculating his route to pick up the active dog's course just in case there is a fault.

Variations

- **Boxed Pairs Dress Up**—Darlene Woz decided that traditional Boxed Pairs was boring and livened it up by creating Boxed Pairs Dress Up. Rather than exchanging a baton when a change of dogs is made, the handlers have to get dressed up. A box containing multiple articles of clothing is placed in the exchange area. Upon return to the exchange area, the incoming handler chooses an article of clothing from the box for the outgoing handler. The articles of clothing may range from hats and underwear to dresses and skirts.

- **Alternatives to batons**—Darlene Woz has also varied the game by using other objects in lieu of a baton. At one event, there was a choice of three exchange items: a can of pears, a pair of mittens, and a pair of socks. Each item was worth bonus points that would be subtracted from the team's total time. The most difficult item to exchange, in this case the socks, was worth the most bonus points. This variation would be suitable for a special event such as Halloween or Christmas—all the exchange items could be related to the event.

box game

USDAA judge, Brian McGunigle conceived the Box Game for a USDAA Starters/Novice-only trial held by ARFF in Massachusetts in 1999. People said they had fun running the game, and a club members later told Brian he had subsequently used it in class for training.

Briefing

Like a typical Jumpers course, the dog is required to perform the course in the order and direction specified by the judge.

Once the dog clears hurdle #1, the handler must stay within a containment area specified by the judge until the dog completes the course.

Scoring

The Box Game is scored time plus faults under USDAA Starters/Novice rules. A special 5-point fault is assessed for each time the handler leaves the containment area before the dog completes the course.

When designing the game for use in JFF or TDAA, a time bonus should be given for each "send." This will offset any failed sends.

Course Design

The design of the Box Game course is fairly simple. The course should use simple distance challenges and include a large containment area in its center. The containment area specified by the judge is a large "box" which could be marked with chalk or tape on the ground.

Strategies

If the handler assumes his dog will not send away for the performance of the tunnels in this game, he should take the faults and forget about even trying to send and simply run with his dog through the course.

The handler might also use the first couple of sends to condition the dog to go away to perform the tunnels, making each send from slightly further away. This strategy might allow the handler to balance faults with bonuses.

If the handler is highly confident of the dog's ability to work away, he should boldly stand in the box and send his dog for each tunnel performance.

Qualifying and Titles

The Box Game is eligible as a qualifying game under JFF and TDAA rules. When using this game as a TDAA qualifier, the judge should establish a baseline for the standard course time that reflects the yards per second in the standard classes. Thus, when the handler steps outside the box, earning a 5-point penalty, the dog's ability to earn a qualifying score is significantly affected, but not eliminated.

When bonuses are used for successful sends, the criterion for qualifying scores should be based on a realistic time and an assumed success/failure rate in sending the dog to the tunnel, reflecting the intermediate skill level of the game participants.

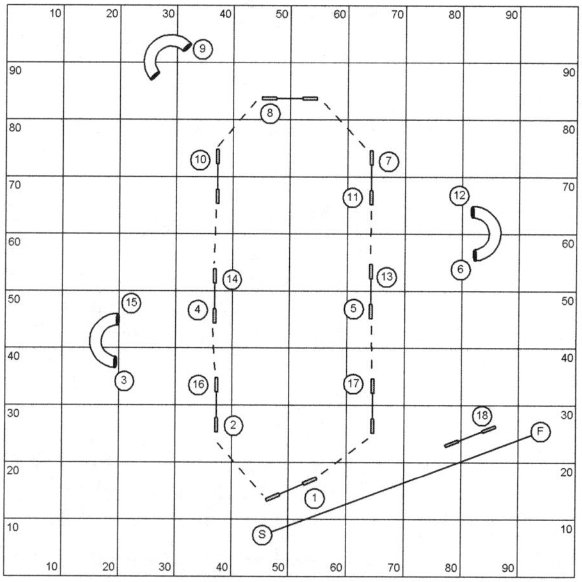

This is the original Box Game course designed by Brian McGunigle that uses the "classic" Starters/Novice gamble of jump-tunnel-jump as the essential challenge on course.

- Games I—Should be based on the standard course time, taking all the faults for stepping outside of the box
- Games II—Should be based on the standard course time, balancing faults and bonuses for sending outside of the box to be equal
- Games III—Should be based on the standard course time, figuring that the dog will go away and earn all the eligible bonuses

brace

Brace is traditionally a USDAA silly game. While it is well-loved for the sometimes-hilarious mishaps that beset a handler attempting to negotiate an agility course with two dogs, the game also showcases the inspiring skill of the occasional two-dogs-with-one-handler-team that compete superbly under these rules.

Briefing

The objective of Brace is for two dogs to run an agility course at the same time. A single handler runs both of the dogs on the sequence indicated by the judge.

The dogs can perform the obstacles simultaneously or the handler can direct one dog to perform an obstacle first and then the other.

Refusals are not faulted. A handler may put either or both dogs on a stay between obstacles.

Two judges are required, one for each dog. Two scribes are also necessary. Only one timekeeper is needed. The timekeeper should start the watch as the first dog crosses the start line and stop the watch as the second dog crosses the finish line.

Scoring

Brace is scored time plus faults. The lowest score wins. After the run, the faults for the two dogs and the team's course time are combined to form the team score.

The traditional judging system used for this class is USDAA Starters/Novice rules. Occasionally, a fault is assessed when the first dog gets too far ahead of the second dog.

This scoring basis is adaptable, depending on the variation of the game played and the whim of the judge.

Course Design

The teeter, dogwalk, and tire are usually omitted from the Brace class, since these obstacles are generally deemed unsafe to perform by two dogs simultaneously. The A-frame should be lowered to 5'.

Jumps are set at the smaller dog's jump height when teams of mixed heights are running.

Strategies

The difficulty in Brace is running two dogs that work uniquely and possibly at different speeds. The handler is often required to gather the dogs to close the gap between them. When performing a complex obstacle, such as the weave poles, a handler might choose to leave one dog in a stay while the other completes the performance. The bolder handler will attack the poles with both dogs, one immediately after the other, possibly leaving the dogs to sort out which will go first and which will follow.

Variations

- **Two handlers**—Brace can be played with two dogs and two handlers. In this variation, the two dogs and handlers begin the same course in the same place at the same time. Ideally the two dogs will work in close conjunction. However there is no requirement that they do so. The overall time of the dogs shall be taken as the time from which the first dog starts until the time that the second dog finishes.
- **Two-handler braced dogs relay**—In this variation a single handler begins by running two dogs in brace and must hand off the dogs to a second handler at a predetermined place on the course.

- **Scoring variation**—A possible scoring variation would be to have the dogs earn points for obstacles performed correctly (usually 1 point) and accumulate them into a team total. This variation would be scored points then time.
- **Brace games**—It is possible to adapt Brace to almost any other agility game. Consider running Brace in Gamblers or in Snooker.

catch me if you can

This is a silly motivational game used at Bud Houston's Camp Dogwood. Catch Me If You Can is a test of the dog's desire to give chase to his handler. The game is usually played when handlers think their dogs are completely exhausted by a day's training. The handlers are often surprised by the dogs' renewed vigor and excitement.

Briefing

The rules of this game are simple. The handler must try to keep away from his dog for as long as possible, even while he teases the dog and carries on in a foolish fashion.

The handler is not allowed to direct the dog to any of the obstacles. If a dog takes an obstacle, it must be of his own choosing.

Scoring

Catch Me If You Can is scored on the basis of time. The handler who keeps away the longest from his dog wins. As a training game, we don't really care who ultimately wins and don't take the scorekeeping thing very seriously. This game is a test of relationship, among other things. If a dog ignores his handler and has no desire to chase, it's ludicrous to suggest that the team has "won" anything.

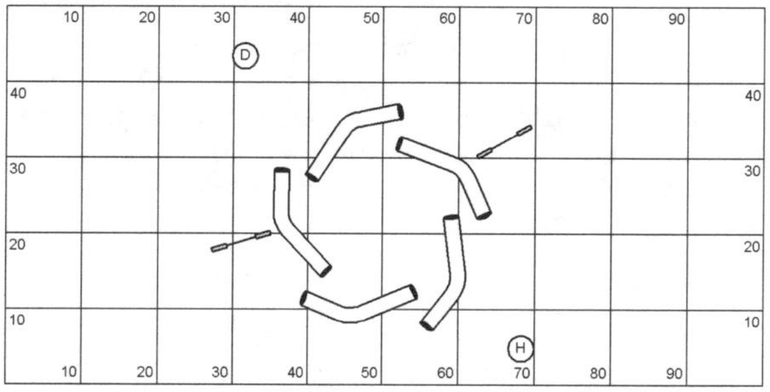

This is a typical design for the Catch Me If You Can game. The tunnels are arranged so that in the counter-clockwise direction, the dog will be tempted to take them, without gaining a real advantage. If the chase goes the opposite direction however, the handler is faced with having to outrun his dog in a foot race.

Course Design

The obstacles used in Catch Me If You Can should be formed into a circular pattern that allows the handler to run around the outside and perhaps step into the circle if the dog is giving chase on the perimeter. Some care should be taken to make the core obstacles safe for the dog. For example, an A-frame might be used, but some dogs might be tempted to leap off the side in their eagerness to catch up with the handler.

Strategies

The handler had better run! The handler might also try switching direction while the dog is in the tunnel. Face it. Dogs are a lot faster than people. The only advantage people might have is that they are, maybe, smarter than the dog. The handler should try to use that advantage.

The best strategy for the dog is to jump straight over the tunnels rather than run around. There's no beating a dog that is both fast and smart.

In the sample course, take note of the "grain" of the tunnels. The handler may do better with a counterclockwise strategy than a clockwise strategy. Note also that the handler is allowed to step inside the circle of obstacles.

Karen Maillioux created Chutes and Ladders and named it after the popular children's game. This game consists of just two types of obstacles: the chutes (tunnels) and the ladders (contact obstacles).

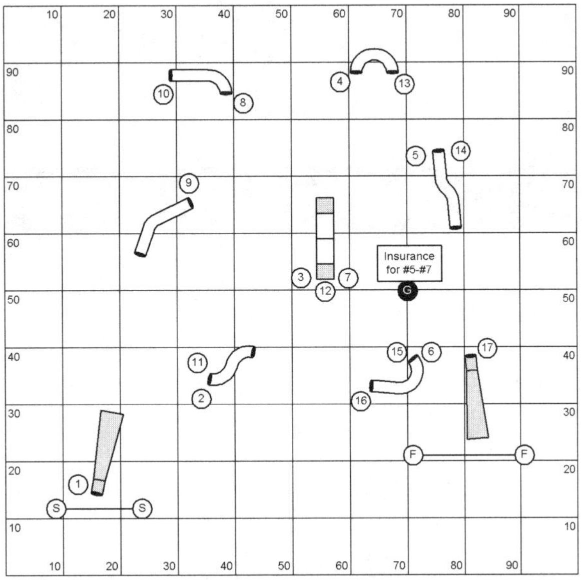

As this example illustrates, Chutes and Ladders is suitable only for an agility community rich in tunnels. The challenge sequence, where an off-course is possible, is from the tunnel at #5 to the A-frame at #7. Presumably the gong will save an off-course penalty if the dog goes into the collapsed tunnel rather than the pipe tunnel at #6. The most logical time to strike the gong would probably be while the dog is engaged in performing the A-frame at #3.

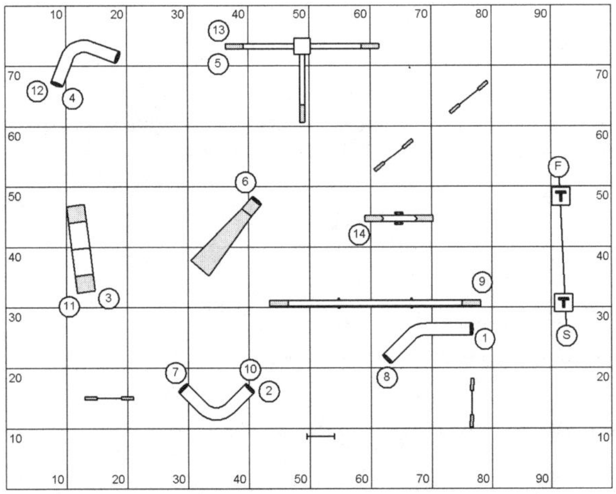

This example of the League-play variation of Chutes and Ladders was designed by Bud Houston and originally run in league play at Dogwood Training Center. The handling isn't inconsequential.

Briefing

The objective of Chutes and Ladders is to negotiate the course of tunnels and contact obstacles. Traditionally, only the A-frame was used, and teams were required to perform it three times during the course run. More recently in game play, all contact obstacles, including the crossover or the dogwalk and the teeter, have been used in Chutes and Ladders.

A gong or chime is placed on the course, which the handler may strike for insurance against faults on a challenge sequence designated by the judge. Insurance will not cover an off-course before the challenge sequence.

The handler must strike the gong before beginning the first obstacle designated as the challenge sequence and must strike the gong while the team is under way (and not while the dog is sitting at the start line on a stay).

If the handler strikes the gong and the dog does not fault in the challenge zone, 25 seconds will be subtracted from the dog's course time.

Scoring

Chutes and Ladders is scored time plus faults. The dog with the lowest score wins the game.

Modified USDAA Starters/Novice rules apply. However, some performance faults are scored uniquely in this game:

- First missed contact—5 faults
- Second missed contact—20 faults
- Third missed contact—Elimination
- Off-course—5 points
- Failure to Perform—Elimination

Course Design

Traditionally, the Chutes and Ladders course is composed only of tunnels and the A-frame. Any or all obstacles can be used several times in the overall course sequence. The "gong" should be placed at a spot on the course that prefaces the most challenging part of the sequence.

Qualifying and Titles

Chutes and Ladders is an eligible qualifying game for both JFF and TDAA games titles. Under JFF rules, the course would have no standard course time. Under TDAA rules, the standard course time should be based on the rate established for each class, as set forth in the TDAA rules and regulations.

Variations

- **Everything but jumps**—The dogwalk, teeter, weave poles and table can be used when designing the course, especially if tunnels are not readily available. However, do not use jumps.

- **League play variation**—In this variation, no "gong" is used and no other concession for "insurance" is used. Modified USDAA Starters/Novice rules apply. That means that all upside contacts will be judged. However, some performance faults are scored uniquely in this game. The first fault will be scored 5 faults. On each subsequent fault, all faults will be doubled: first missed contact or off-course, 5 faults; second missed contact or off-course, 10 faults (cumulative); third missed contact or off-course, 20 faults (cumulative); and so forth. Failure to perform, 50 faults.

clockwatchers

Clockwatchers is an old favorite in Europe, Australia, and New Zealand and is a guaranteed crowd-pleaser. If two dogs and handlers are at the same level, this competition can be cruel (to the handlers!). This is one of the rare formats in which two dogs are competing on the same course at the same time.

Briefing

Two dogs run the same course at the same time, chasing each other around the obstacles that are laid out like the face of a clock. The two dogs start in the middle of the circle, preferably on tables. They both go forward over a hurdle and then both turn right into the flow of the circular course. The dogs go around the course clockwise until each dog returns to the side on which it started. After taking the last hurdle in the circle, each dog must turn right, go back over the hurdle at which it started, and finish on its starting table.

On course, a slower dog must give way to a faster dog.

Scoring

Clockwatchers is run as a knockout (a single elimination game) with the winner of each round going forward to compete against the winner of another round.

The game is scored time plus faults. The dog with the lowest score wins, regardless of which dog makes it back to the finish first. In case of a tie in score, time will decide the winner.

Any rational system for defining faults can be used so long as the winner of each round can be clearly differentiated. A modest system would be the USDAA Starters/Novice and JFF scoring system:

- Knocked bars—5 faults
- Off-course—5 faults
- Failure to perform—20 faults
- Refusals are not faulted

Each dog has a judge, one of whom blows the starting whistle for both teams to begin. Each dog has a separate timekeeper and scribe.

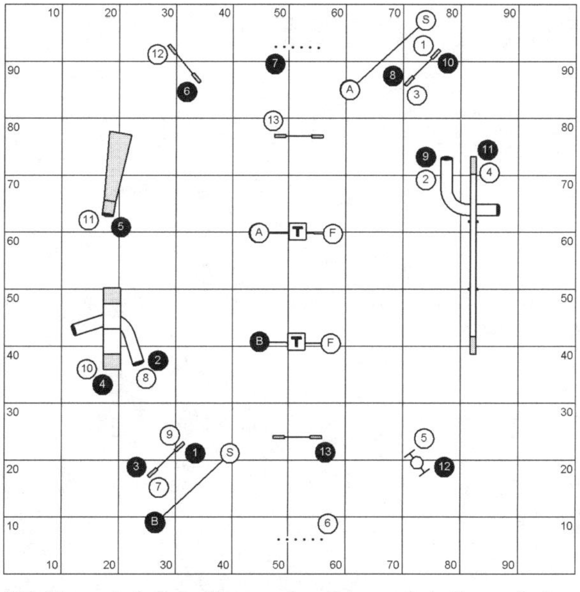

While this example of a Clockwatchers course is mostly loopy or circular, there are clearly handling challenges that break up what would otherwise be a scorching speed course.

Course Design

Place 12 obstacles in a circular course that is 75' to 90' in diameter. Place two tables in the middle of the circle with jumps in front of each table, which will be used to introduce the dogs onto the course. These introductory jumps are not numbered. Each dog will take the first hurdle and then make a right turn onto the course.

Each start/finish is a mirror image of the other. After the first hurdle for each dog, the course can change according to the judge's fancy.

Although start/finish poles can be used instead of tables, the preference is for tables since they are far more visible to spectators. Clockwatchers is very much a spectator event. If start poles are used in lieu of tables in the middle, then ensure there is plenty of distance between the two separate start/finish lines. If the poles are too close, two excited dogs could cross the finish at the same time and run into each other.

Variations

- **Chasers**—In the Chasers variation, by Tara Choate, two dog-and-handler teams run a figure-eight course. The goal is to catch the other team and, at the same time, avoid being caught. Each dog continues running the course until: 1) A team is caught; 2) 3 minutes elapse; or 3) A team earns 20 or more faults. If course time has elapsed and neither dog has been caught or earned 20+ faults, the dog with the fewest faults wins. The scoring of faults is the same as for the basic version of Clockwatchers.
- **Move Over Rover**—This variation is called Circular Knockout in the U.K. The Move Over Rover course consists mainly of jumps, with tunnels or weave poles thrown in occasionally for good measure. Competition is generally on a single elimination, pyramid-type basis.

colors

Colors is the invention of Linda Eickholdt and Rob Robinson and is a titling game in Canine Performance Events (CPE). Colors is also a cornerstone game used in agility league play.

Briefing

The objective is to successfully negotiate one of three overlapping agility mini-courses. The handler may choose which course to run.

Colored markers label each course: red, blue, and yellow. The handler informs the gate steward which course he will be running; the gate steward conveys the choice to the scribe and judge.

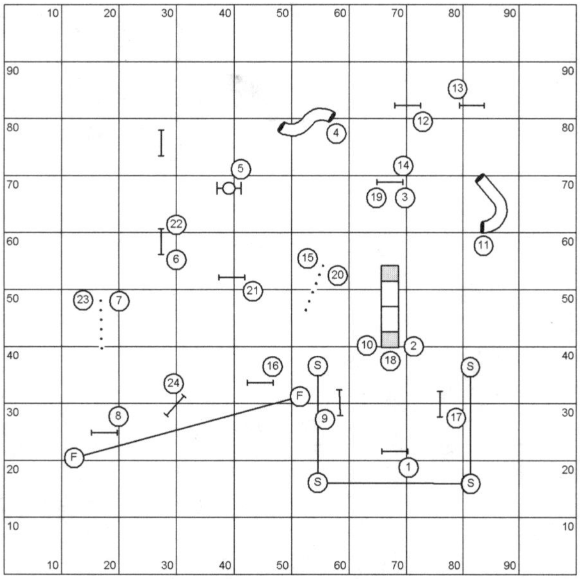

In this rendition of the CPE game Colors, the three courses of choice are numbered #1-#8, #9-#16, and #17-#24. The mini-courses are roughly equivalent in length and complexity. Notice that obstacles can be reused as the mini-courses intertwine and overlap.

Scoring

Colors is scored faults then time and judged under CPE rules. The winner is the dog with the fewest faults. If two dogs have the same number of faults, then time breaks the tie.

Course yardage is determined by measuring for 16" dogs, with 3 seconds added to the standard course time for 8" and 12" jump heights.

Time faults are assessed for the dog going over standard course time. One second equals one fault. Fractions are dropped for scoring. The timekeeper will report time in 1/100th of a second for placements.

Course Design

In CPE, the field will contain 12 to 24 obstacles divided into three relatively equal mini-courses of 4 to 8 obstacles each. Each mini-course will contain the following: one set of 5 to 8 weave poles (substitute another obstacle for Level 1 and 2), one contact, up to two tunnels, jumps, and one or more traps.

The course can be designed in two different ways:

1. The judge will do his best to make each course length the same; however, the course time will be determined by the average of the three courses together.
2. The judge can design three different course lengths and levels of difficulty on the same field. Course times would be shortest for the easiest mini-course and longest for the hardest mini-course with an average time mini-course between.

Strategies

In CPE, the handler should choose the course on which his dog is most likely to have success, or on which the handling is most straightforward.

In league play, the team must report a score at each of the three levels. When team size exceeds three members, the handlers running later with their dogs must know which scores are most in need of mending. If a dog is in the running for MVP (Most Valuable Puppy) honors, running the dog at a lower level might jeopardize the dog's standing in MVP points. The handler is challenged with doing the right thing for his team while being tempted to play for individual honors.

Qualifying and Titles

CPE

To earn a qualifying score under CPE rules, all obstacles must be performed successfully. However, off-courses are allowed in Levels 1 and 2. Time faults are allowed through Level 5.

A title can be acquired at each of the four different levels of competition—Level 1 (CL1-H), Level 2 (CL2-H), Level 3 (CL3-H), and Level 4 (CL4-H)—by earning two qualifying scores under two different judges.

To acquire the CPE Champion Title, a dog and handler must earn four qualifying scores in Level 5 Colors under at least two different judges.

JFF

JFF allows a course to be judged under the rules of any organization or the distinct rules of JFF (no refusals, no standard course time, and so forth).

In league play, Colors is a "standard" course. The dog earns a qualifying score respective to the level of course that he elects to run. A clean round with zero faults is required to qualify. No standard course times should be used.

TDAA

Colors is a qualifying game under TDAA rules. Using CPE course design criteria, Colors is designated a "game." Using JFF course design criteria, Colors is a "standard" course but should use the standard course times set forth under TDAA rules for the respective class.

Variations

- **Pairs relay**—Colors may be run as a pairs relay. The pair must consist of two dogs in the same level and at the same jump height. Dogs are required to run different color courses. Both dogs must qualify for the pair to qualify.
- **Separating the class**—If the class is very large, the judge may separate the class by the color of the course each team is running. This makes the game easier to judge and enhances ring efficiency.
- **JFF League variation**—When Colors is played in a league format, the three courses are both nested and layered. That means that there will be a Beginners course, an Intermediate course, and a Superior course. The judge may stipulate that a team in league play must report a score for each of the three colors or levels.

  In a league with more than three members on a team, each of the first three members should run a separate color (though this is not required). The remaining member must decide which colored course will improve

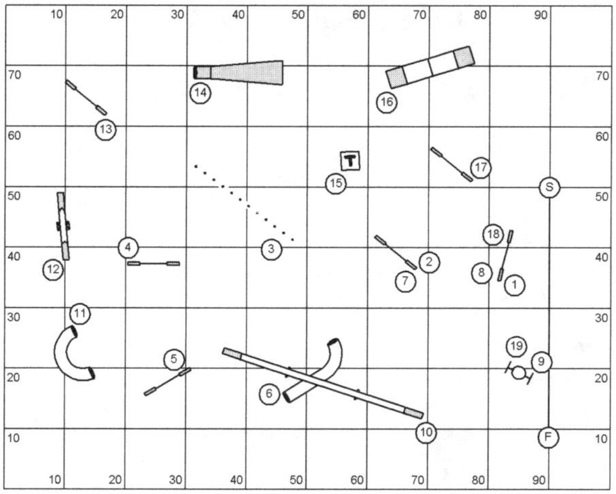

This final example is of the green course for Beginners.

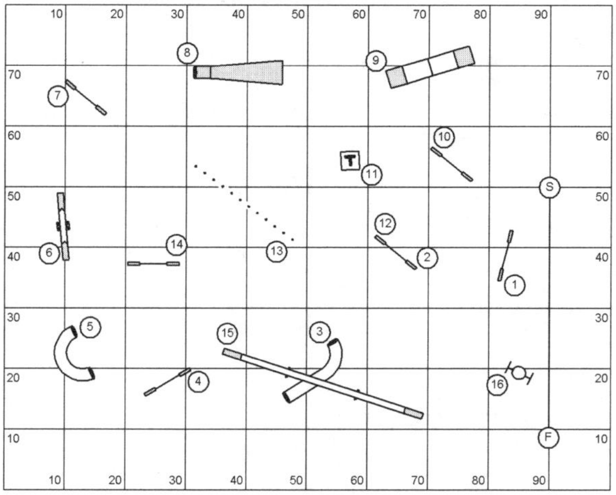

In the JFF league variation, the courses are leveled in complexity. The red course is the Superior course and provides the greatest challenge to competitors.

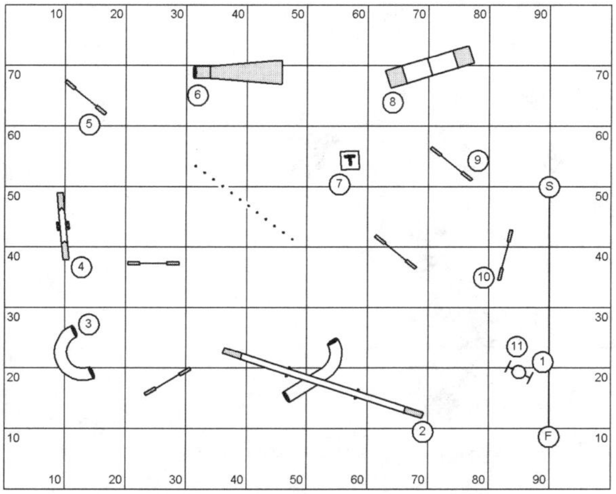

This is example of the blue course designed for Intermediate dogs.

Colors Faults Chart

Missed contact	15 faults
Fly-off, teeter	15 faults
Failure to perform or unsafe performance	15 faults
Missed weave pole	5 faults
Dropped bar	5 faults
Off-course	5 faults

Colors is scored faults then time and judged under CPE rules. The winner is the dog with the fewest faults. If two dogs have the same number of faults, then time breaks the tie.

the team score. Whatever the result (improved or not), the "best" of two scores on the same course will be used to determine the team's final score.

In JFF, the field should contain 18 to 24 obstacles, divided into three courses at the levels of beginners, intermediate, and advanced. There is no attempt to make the three courses the same level. The sample courses show a leveled and nested JFF League Colors course.

comin' and goin'

Comin' and Goin' is the invention of Ilze Rukis. Her club, Northwoods Agility Group (the NAGs), in Northern Wisconsin played the game at a humane society walk on September 15, 2001. She writes that it was interesting to watch the dogs switch from agility to obedience mode. The winning dog earned 200 points and a time of 1:36.

Briefing

Comin' and Goin' is a three-part game that tests various skills of the dog-and-handler team. Total time allotted to complete all three parts is 90 seconds.

- Part 1 is a send around a barrel from a distance. Deductions may be earned if the dog does not do the exercise or the handler must cross the containment line to show the dog the way.

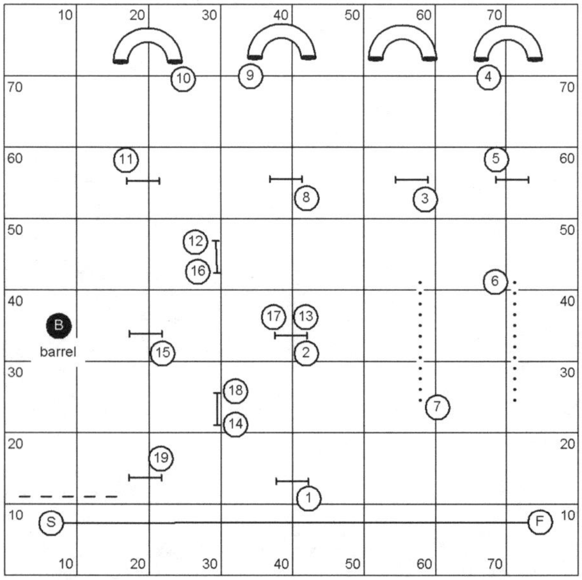

Ilze Rukis designed this Comin' and Goin' course using a jumpers course and two sets of 12 weave poles.

- Part 2 is an agility sequence. Deductions may be earned if the dog faults any of the obstacles in the sequence.
- Part 3 is an obedience routine that follows the judge's call. The obedience pattern will be the same for all dogs and will include heeling, at least one turn, a sit-stay, and a recall. Optionally, the judge may specify that the handler direct the dog to perform an agility obstacle on the recall.

The judge calls the obedience exercise.

Scoring

Comin' and Goin' is scored points then time. Each dog starts with 200 points. High score wins. Time is a tiebreaker only.

Deductions: Forget true precision. Don't score crooked sits, perfect heel position, and so on. This is supposed to be fun, after all.

- Crossing the line for the send to barrel—10 points
- Each knocked bar—5 points
- Wrong course—5 points (optional)
- Dog completely leaves heel position at any time during part three—5 points
- Dog does not sit at heel without a command—5 points
- Dog does not sit with command—5 points
- Dog does not hold stay—5 points
- Dog does not come—5 points

Course Design

The Comin' and Goin' course begins with a send to a barrel. The send line should be clearly marked with the barrel set back 25' or so. The agility course used for the second part of the game could be a standard agility course, though it is usually a jumpers course. The obedience portion requires a large area on the flat, which is ideally positioned beyond the final obstacle on the course.

Strategies

The teams that promise to be most successful are those that manage transitions well from one part of the game to the next. They take a few seconds to collect themselves and their dogs before proceeding to the next portion of the game.

A team might incur the 10-point send-out penalty with the hope of being fast and accurate for part two, with a solid lead-out for part 3 and still be high score. The faster parts one and two are completed, the more time there will be for the third part.

concentration

Concentration is the invention of Stuart Mah. It was originally used as a training exercise to help promote a handler's ability to quickly memorize a changing course. This game is also known as Follow the Leader and Simon's Horse.

Briefing

Players randomly draw numbers to see who goes first. First jump heights are drawn, and then players within each jump height. There might be an advantage to being one of the first to go in this game.

The objective of play is to perform obstacles in the proper sequence and direction. The first player starts by picking any obstacle and performing it. His turn is then complete. The second player must now perform two obstacles. He starts by performing the same obstacle as the first player. If successful, the second player can add a new obstacle of his choosing. His turn is now complete. The third player must now perform three obstacles. He starts by performing the obstacle of the first player and the obstacle of the second player. If successful, the handler then performs an obstacle of his choosing. Play continues in this way until each handler has had a turn. The round is then over.

If a dog faults any obstacle or takes the wrong obstacle, the team is eliminated and must sit to watch the rest of the competition. The player following another who has faulted must run the sequence that was intended for the faulted player.

If, after each complete round there are still players, the cycle begins again. The original player performs all previous obstacles then adds one of his own choosing to the growing sequence.

If after three complete rounds there are still several players remaining, the competition proceeds to the Lightning Round.

In the Lightning Round, the first player must perform the course in 60 seconds or less. If the player succeeds, he can add an obstacle of his choice. The next player must then perform the new sequence in 60 seconds or less. If successful, that player can add an obstacle of his choice. This goes on until only one dog and handler remain. If none of the handlers get through the course in 60 seconds or less, the handler and dog team that completes the most obstacles on the course wins.

Any obstacle can be performed back-to-back, but, if so, a different obstacle must be performed before the obstacle can be used again.

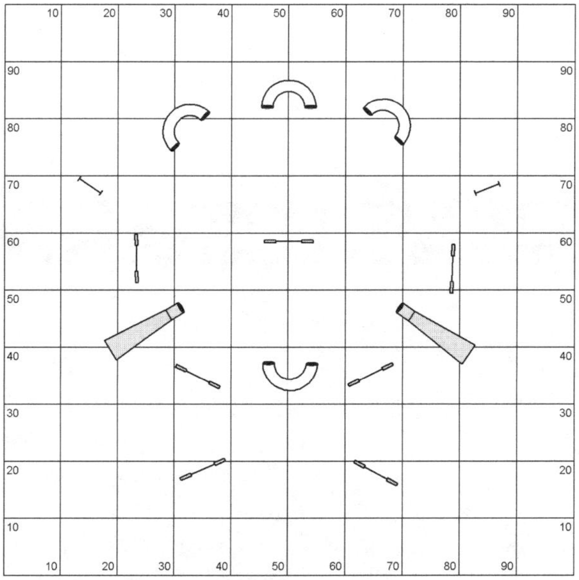

This sample Concentration course uses no contact obstacles, but contact obstacles could be included in a training context to provide work on contact performance.

Scoring

Concentration is scored as a puissance. Players stay in the game until they have faulted out and until there is only one dog remaining. That dog is the winner of the competition.

Players are eliminated if they break the concentration chain (failing to remember the course or going off course), fail to perform an obstacle successfully, or take an obstacle in the wrong direction.

The system of faults might be any rational system. A rational method might be to change the system in each round using progressively more stringent standards. A good model for this would be to use progressive USDAA levels:

- Round one, USDAA Starters/Novice: Faults incurred for dropped bars, missed contacts, and off-courses.
- Round two, USDAA Advanced: In addition to the faults in round one, a missed weave pole will be faulted, and refusals will be faulted at contact obstacles only.
- Round three and the Lightning Round, USDAA Masters: In addition to the faults in round two, refusals will be faulted on all obstacles.

This progressively more stringent system will help limit the length of sequences so that the dogs aren't overworked.

Course Design

In Concentration, 12 to 16 obstacles are best for the course design. Jump heights are set at the lowest height to accommodate all dogs. Only short sets of weave poles are used.

A design for a Concentration course suitable for more advanced handlers and their dogs might include weave poles. The obstacles should be arranged so that it's difficult to put together long straight lines in a sequence to ensure frequent changes of direction and increase handler confusion.

Strategies

The most important skill a handler can develop and use in this game is to carefully watch the dogs running to learn and memorize the course as it develops. The handler must rely solely on visualization to determine a handling strategy. As a handler stays in the competition longer, parts of the sequence will become familiar and can be performed with more speed and gusto. For new elements, the handler might be wise to handle carefully and slowly, babysitting the dog through the new sequences.

Variations

- **Adding a new obstacle**—The handler whose turn it is to add a new obstacle to the sequence may choose to add the obstacle to the beginning of the sequence rather than the end. The next player must then perform this new obstacle first.
- **Alternative obstacles**—Not every club is rich enough in tunnels and weave poles to set the types of courses shown here. Concentration can be played with any configuration of agility equipment and any currently available equipment. In fact, this is an ideal game for the end of a training class. You can just leave the equipment where it sits and start your game.

connect the dots

Connect the Dots is a marvelous game invented by Heather White-Cotterman of Delaware, Ohio. This is an easy game that can be used with nearly any obstacle placement from a standard course and without much obstacle movement.

Briefing

The purpose of this game is for the dog to accumulate as many points as possible in the allotted time by connecting the dots. The "dots" are the contact obstacles on course. These are also the highest-valued obstacles on the course.

The dog earns points for each obstacle performed in a "line," which is the series of obstacles from dot to dot. These obstacles may be performed only once for points between the dots, and may be performed only twice for points overall.

If an obstacle in a line is faulted, then all points in that line are lost from the last dot, through the faulted obstacle. At least one point must be scored from dot to dot. After faulting an obstacle, the handler must direct the dog to perform at least one eligible obstacle to earn points before attempting the next dot.

If the dog faults a dot—one of the contact obstacles—he must be directed to repeat that obstacle until it is performed correctly, or until the expiration of course time.

Time starts and stops on the table. Each dog will have 50 seconds. The timekeeper will blow a whistle at 50 seconds to indicate the end of scoring. The dog will lose a point for each second, or fraction thereof, over 50 seconds. The dog can be directed to the table before the expiration of standard course time for no penalty.

Scoring

Connect the Dots is scored points then time. Points are awarded on the following schedule:

- Dots—10 points
- Jumps—1 point
- Tunnels, Tire, and Weave Poles (6)—3 points
- Weave poles (12)—5 points

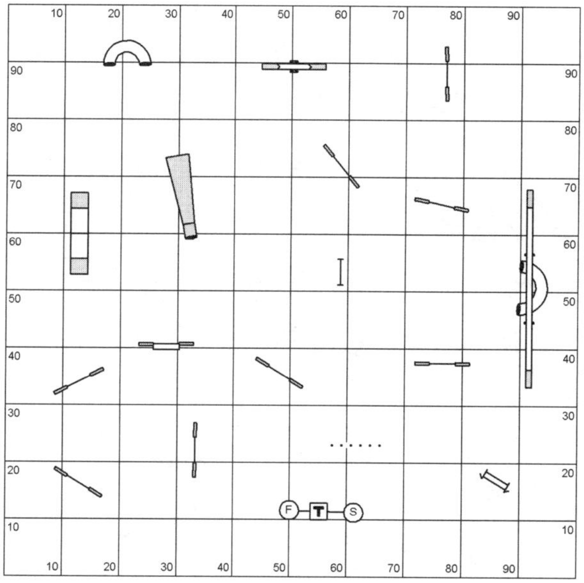

This example of a Connect the Dots course was designed by the game's inventor, Heather White-Cotterman.

Course Design

With only modest tweaking or movement of equipment, a standard course can easily be adapted to a Connect The Dots game. The table is used as the start and finish in the game. It should be positioned at the front of the ring to make a timely transition between competitors.

Strategies

All "dog's choice" games with timing implications require the handler to understand the rate of speed at which his dog will work. This is information that is given to the competitor every time he steps onto a standard course. The judge will stipulate the course distance; the timekeeper will give the competitor the time that the dog stayed on course. Subtracting the time spent for any table performance will give the exhibitor the numbers required to extrapolate the dog's rate of travel.

In Connect the Dots, there are two conceivable point-accumulation strategies worth noting. The handler might attempt robust point accumulation in the lines. In this strategy, the handler tries to do as many obstacles as possible between the dots with the idea in mind that he will arrive at the table with the completion of only the three basic dots at precisely 50 seconds. The downside of this strategy is that the handler's points in a line are constantly at risk on any dropped bar (the only fault that can be made in a line).

The second strategy would have the handler directing the dog in the shortest possible line between the dots to maximize the number of dots performed on the course (which are the most valuable obstacles on the course), and to minimize the potential for lost points if a line is faulted.

Qualifying and Titles

Connect the Dots is an eligible qualifying game in both TDAA and JFF. In JFF, the following point schedule will be used to determine qualifiers.

- Games I—40 points
- Games II—53 points
- Games III—67 points

In TDAA, the standard course time should be expanded to 60 seconds, or the point schedule should be reduced by 15 percent to :

- Games I—34 points
- Games II—45 points
- Games III—57 points

contact donut

An exceedingly simple game that tests reliable contact performance at speed, Contact Donut is the invention of Linda Northrop. Appropriate as a training tool at the intermediate level, the game also allows the handler to experiment with working his dog at a distance.

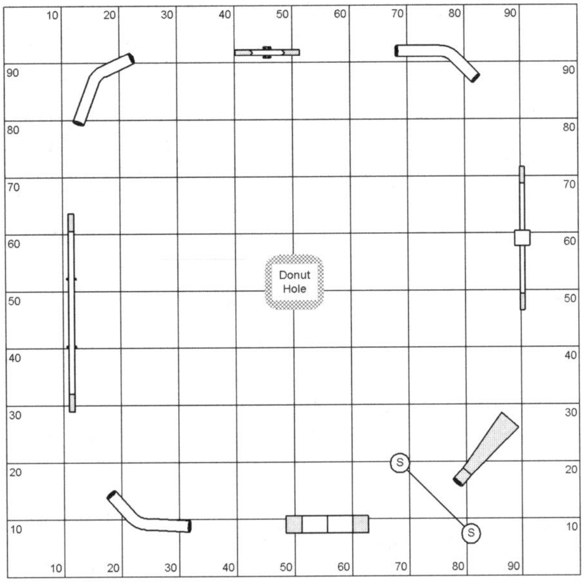

This Contact Donut course uses the traditional three contact obstacles, plus the crossover with straight-over planks. This game allows the handler to work closely on the dog's contacts, or for a more advanced dog, to work the dog at a distance.

Briefing

The objective of Contact Donut is to accumulate as many points as possible by running a circular course composed of tunnels and contacts in a period specified by the judge, usually 30 seconds.

The dog begins at a designated start line in the circle or donut of obstacles. At the end of the time specified by the judge, a whistle blows and the dog and handler must get to the center of the donut to stop time. The donut is a 10-foot diameter circle marked by tape or chalk.

Bonus points are awarded if the handler can direct his dog to perform the entire course, from the start of the course until the whistle blows, while remaining in the donut hole. If the handler steps out of the donut at any time, the dog will earn no bonus.

Scoring

Contact Donut is scored points then time. The dog with the most points is the winner. Time is a tiebreaker only.

Values are assigned to the obstacles as follows:

- Contacts—5 points
- Tunnels—1 point
- Handling from the donut hole—15 point bonus

Scoring ceases if:

- Time elapses
- A dog misses a contact
- A dog goes off course

Course Design

In the Contact Donut course, the contact obstacles are typically placed on the sides of the course, while tunnels are used to soften or direct the turns in the corners. The "Donut Hole" should be a clearly defined area in the center of the circle of obstacles.

copycat

Copycat is the invention of Trisha Stall from Latham, New York. Trisha designed the game in fulfillment of a test to become a judge for the Teacup Dogs Agility Association.

Briefing

Copycat is a "dog's choice" game. That means the handler can direct the dog through the performance of obstacles in the order and direction of his own choosing, or the dog's choosing, as the case may be.

The team has 35 seconds to gather points.

- Jumps—1 point

- Tunnels, tire, and weave poles—3 points
- Contacts—5 points

The dog can perform each obstacle only twice for points. If the dog performs the same type of obstacle back-to-back, called "copycatting" (for example, two one-pointers, two three-pointers, or two five-pointers) he will lose 5 points.

Every second over 35 seconds that it takes the dog to cross the finish line will be penalized two points.

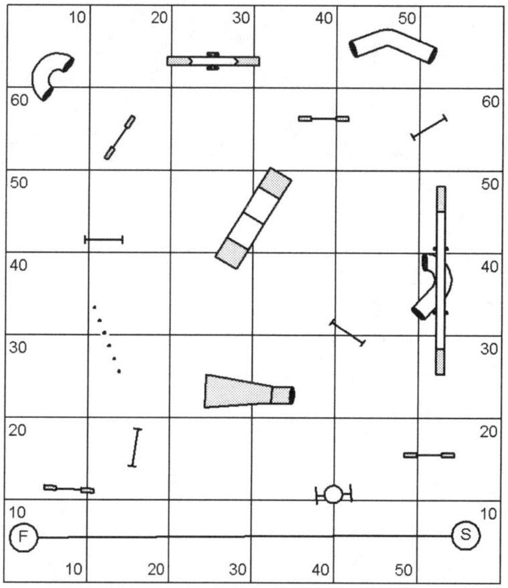

In the original Copycat course, designed by Trisha Stall for play in TDAA, distances between agility obstacles are considerably tighter than in other venues. For venues that allow "big" dogs (over 16"), the course designer should space the obstacles accordingly.

Scoring

Copycat is scored points, then time. The dog with the highest number of points wins. Time is a tiebreaker only.

The scorekeeper is responsible for determining faults for copycatting, repeating an obstacle of the same value in consecutive obstacle performance. The dog is *not* awarded the value of the second obstacle, and will be faulted 5 points instead.

Course Design

The Copycat course should be designed with a somewhat random mix of agility obstacles. However, the course designer should take some care to create copycat dilemmas, a sequence in which the dog and handler are nearly trapped into doing back-to-back performances of obstacles of the same value.

Qualifying and Titles

TDAA

Copycat is eligible as a qualifying game under TDAA rules.

- Games I—score of 15 points or better
- Games II—score of 20 points or better
- Games III—score of 25 points or better

JFF

Copycat is eligible as a qualifying game under JFF rules using the same qualifying criteria as for TDAA.

cowboy dog

Cowboy Dog is the invention of Ilze Rukis from Keshena, Wisconsin. Ilze designed the game in fulfillment of a test to become a judge for the Teacup Dogs Agility Association.

Briefing

Cowboy Dog is based on the barrel-racing game for horses. To qualify, the dog and handler must run the course obstacles in the order marked, under time, with no dropped bars or wrong courses, and no handler-line faults. The handler must send the dog around one or more barrels while remaining behind the handler restriction line. The direction of the dog's turn around the barrel must be clockwise. A counterclockwise turn will be assessed as a wrong course for 10 faults.

Scoring

Cowboy Dog is scored time plus faults. The lowest score wins.

Faults:

- Dropped bar—5 faults

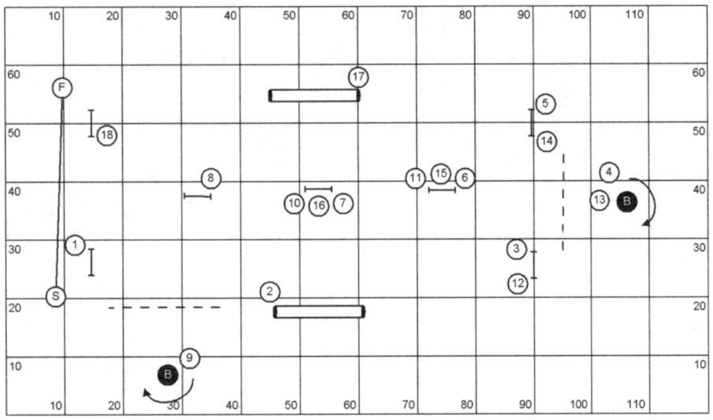

This is an example of a Cowboy Dog course requiring three "send-around-the-barrel" performances. Note that the direction of the dog's movement around the barrel is always from left to right (clockwise).

- Wrong course—10 faults
- Handler line faults—10 faults

Course Design

For Superior dogs, the send distance around a barrel is approximately 10'. For Intermediate and Beginner dogs, the send is approximately 5'. The judge might require a Beginner dog to do only one send around the barrel, then two for Intermediate, and three for Superior.

The course should consist exclusively of jumps and tunnels so that the dog is encouraged to move at a consistent and flowing pace. The handling challenges should not be inconsequential, but should be appropriate to the level of dogs playing.

dare to double

Dare to Double is the invention of Darlene Woz and was the winner of the 1995 Clean Run *magazine games contest. Dare to Double is a game of strategy and daring. This game is sometimes called Double Dog Dare Ya.*

Briefing

Dare to Double is a simple dog's choice game, which means that the dog will earn points for taking obstacles in the order and direction of his, or his handler's choosing. The team has 50 seconds to accumulate as many points as possible. The game begins at a start line designated by the judge and ends at the table or a designated finish line.

To keep all points accumulated on course, the team must get to the table before course time elapses. If the team fails to get to the table before time expires, it loses half its points.

The value of scoring obstacles is based on a simple 1-3-5-7 system:

- Jumps—1 point
- Tunnels and tire—3 points
- Teeter, dogwalk, and weave poles—5 points
- One obstacles in the 5-point list, usually given to an obstacle in a difficult placement—7 points

Scoring obstacles can be taken only twice for points. Back-to-back performances are allowed. Knocked jumpbars will not be reset.

The A-frame has a special value (note that the A-frame was not listed above). It is the doubling obstacle. During the run, a handler may double his current points by performing the doubling obstacle. A successful performance doubles all points earned up to that time. If, however, the dog faults the A-frame, the dog loses half his existing points.

A handler may double points any time he wishes, as many times as he wishes. The only restriction on doubling is that the A-frame cannot be performed back-to-back. Thus, the handler must do another obstacle, for points, before attempting to double point values again.

A warning whistle is blown 15 seconds before time runs out.

Scoring

Dare to Double is scored points then time. The winner is the dog finishing with the most points. In case of a tie, time is the tiebreaker. The table is live during the entire run. If the dog gets on the table at any time, scoring ends.

The scribe's notations must be made in streamlined fashion so that the scorekeeping table can easily decipher when to apply doubling, when to add points, and when to halve the score. For example, the scribe might write:

1 2 3 D 5 4 6 F 6 7 5 D 3 D

The scorekeeper would score this as 132 points. Note that the value of the doubling obstacle is recorded as "D," which means to double the previously accumulated points. "F" indicates that the dog faulted the doubling obstacle and half of the total points accumulated (up to that point) will be lost.

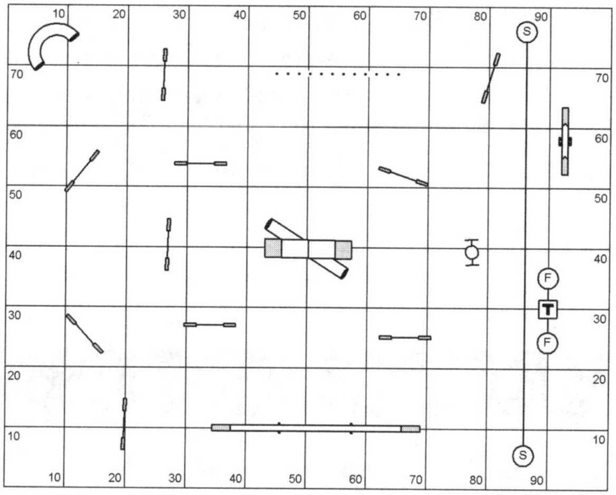

Dare to Double lends itself to virtually any configuration of agility equipment and is a fine choice for a game that can be played on an existing standard course.

Course Design

In the original design concept for Dare to Double, the doubling obstacle (the A-frame) was placed at the back of the ring. Forward, at the front of the ring (and consequently farthest away from the A-frame) were the jumps. Immediately surrounding the A-frame were higher-point obstacles, including the contacts and the weave poles. The tunnels and tire were placed in an intermediate area between the jumps and the contact obstacles.

More recently the designs of Dare to Double use the A-frame more to the center of the course with jumps placed in positions that are more accessible. Dare to Double is an ideal game to be played on an existing standard course with a minimum of movement and tweaking of obstacles in their original positions.

Strategies

The doubling obstacle is the key to accumulating the most points and winning the game. Consequently, performing the doubling obstacle as often as possible is desirable. Double early, double often is the key to the game.

Since scoring obstacles can only be taken twice for points, the handler should make judicious use of those obstacles near the A-frame. It doesn't make much sense to do all the obstacles around the A-frame before doubling. It's a better strategy to do an obstacle once, and then double on the A-frame—do the single obstacle again, and then double on the A-frame, and so forth.

When playing with a 15-second warning whistle, the handler might think about the implications of being able to double three more times and taking the time fault, rather than racing on to the table to stop time and scoring.

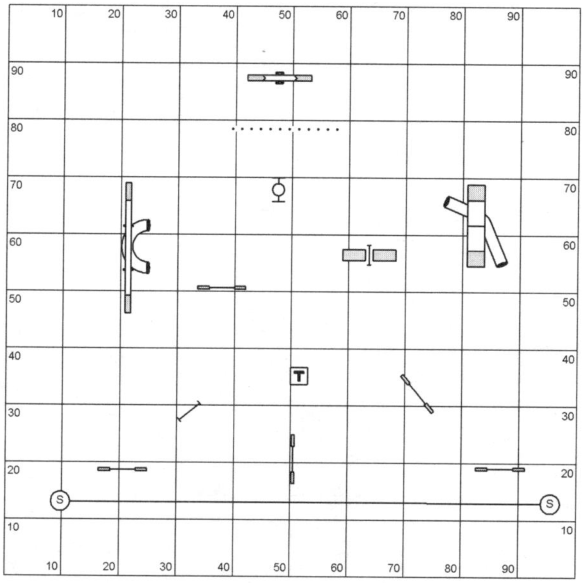

Qualifying and Titles

Dare to Double is an eligible titling game in JFF and TDAA. The qualifying criteria reflects the "doubling" nature of the game:

- Games I—A score of 40 or better
- Games II—A score of 80 or better
- Games III—A score of 160 or better

Variations

- **Placement of obstacles**—Surround the A-frame with low-point obstacles and place high-point obstacles away from the A-frame.
- **Change the doubling obstacle**—As a training exercise especially, use an obstacle other than the A-frame as the doubling obstacle to focus on the performance of that obstacle.

- **The Flanigan variation**—In Amy Flanigan's variation, the A-frame can only be taken twice, whether taken successfully or faulted. As a consequence, the handler has to decide at what point in the run the two doubling trips should be taken over the A-frame, but should not tarry so long that an opportunity is lost. Note that the dog can do the A-frame only twice, and it may not be taken back-to-back whether or not the first performance led to a fault.
- **The Masters variation**—In the Masters variation, there will be no warning whistle. Also, if the dog does not get to the table at the expiration of course time, all points are lost.
- **The Four Paws variation**—In this variation, the time limit is 45 seconds, with a warning whistle at 40 seconds to alert handlers. Any points accumulated on the way to the table are valid, provided the dog makes time.

  The weave poles are designated as the doubling obstacle. No penalty (half score) is assessed for any bobble in the weave poles as long as the dog completes the obstacle. If the dog faults any contact obstacle, however, he is assessed a half-score penalty.

dealer's choice

Dealer's Choice apparently comes to us from the U.K., and little is known about the game in the U.S. Agility seminar leaders such as Nancy Gyes have popularized it as a training exercise. This game could be used in competition when you want to do something just a little bit different.

Briefing

Dealer's Choice is like standard agility in that the course must be completed in numerical order. However, unlike standard agility, a Dealer's Choice course contains options. In several places on course, the same number appears on more than one obstacle. In these cases, it is the handler's choice or the dog's choice as to which path to take. The obstacles may be performed in any order and in either direction if they are bi-directional obstacles, but no obstacle may be taken more than once. The dog and handler must complete all obstacles with the same number before going on to the next number in sequence.

If the collapsed tunnel is part of the course, both the dog and handler may cross the fabric portion of the collapsed tunnel without penalty.

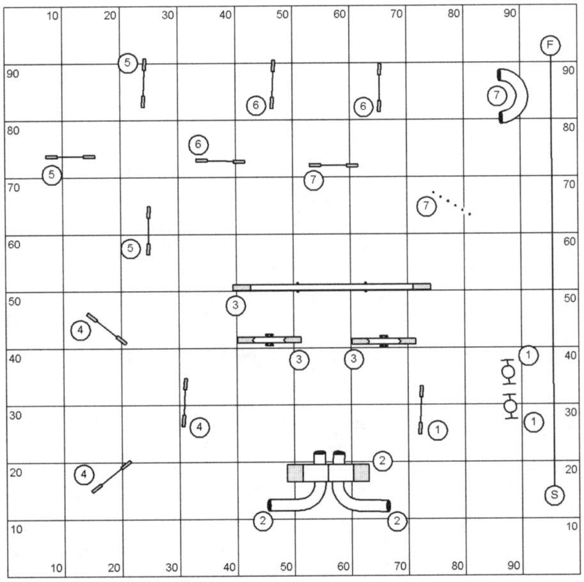

This example Dealer's Choice course was designed by Bud Houston for play in agility league at Dogwood Training Center in Ostrander, Ohio.

Scoring

Dealer's Choice is scored time plus faults. The lowest score wins. USDAA Starters/Novice rules may be used to assess faults since refusals will be difficult to judge because the order of the sequence the dog is attempting is up to the handler.

Nancy Gyes, the American innovator of the game writes: "I play Dealers Choice occasionally at the end of seminars and, occasionally, at class here at home. I really don't have any rules unless I make up silly ones. I normally judge it very loosely, as time plus faults. Five faults for any dog fault, 20 faults for a stupid handler fault, at my discretion."

Course Design

The course designer must give the handler and dog multiple choices throughout the course. Optional sequences of three obstacles are designed into the overall flow. The handler can take these sequences in the order and direction of his choosing. The choices selected must balance risk and reward to make the course an interesting one.

The basics are groups of three obstacles: two jumps and set of weaves, two jumps and the collapsed tunnel, two tunnels and a jump or weave, any contact and two jumps or two tunnels, teeter, and two short sets of weaves, and so on. The sets might be linked by a couple of jumps for speed and flow between sets to keep the course fast.

Strategies

Dealer's Choice relies on the handler's knowledge of his dog's working style to find the most efficient path (the fastest route) for completing all the obstacles on course. The handler should take account of the transitions between groups when solving the order and direction in which obstacles in a group should be performed.

Qualifying and Titles

Dealer's Choice is an eligible titling game in JFF and the TDAA. To earn a qualifying score, the dog and handler team must complete the course without faults. No standard course time should be used, though a maximum course time would keep exhibitors from "heeling" their dogs through the course.

The level of the game qualifier should depend on the complexity of the course. In the sample course shown, the qualifiers were set as follows:

- Games II—Intermediate Course—Two—and only two—obstacles in each group must be performed.
- Games III—Superior Course—All obstacles in each group must be performed.

Variations

Judge's Twist—In this variation of Dealer's Choice, the judge may specify combinations requiring more strategic analysis by the handler. For instance, the judge may specify that only two out of three obstacles in a group be performed, or may even specify that three of two obstacles in a group be performed (one of the obstacles must be performed twice). The judge is urged to remember and be prepared to judge whatever sequence rules he makes up.

dogwood's white elephant

Dogwood's White Elephant is a club get-together game for the New Year. The invitations would go something like this:

Mark your calendars for: December 30 (New Year's Eve's Eve), at 3:00 P.M. We're having an all-Dogwood students and instructors (active and inactive) get-together to play a great new game... and exchange White Elephant gifts. Everyone is invited! This is a great opportunity to meet Dogwood folks whom you don't usually get to see on your training night.

Bring a wrapped gift for each dog you intend to run (Note: the wrapping should be loose; just enough to keep anyone from guessing the contents, but easy to remove). Mark the gift with the name of your dog. A white elephant gift is that special something you got for Christmas that just isn't right for you (and you'd love to get rid of). Note: whoever brings the best gifts will probably wind up running the most.

Briefing

Each handler will have a choice of one of the following:

a) Pick a new, wrapped gift from under the tree. You must run a knockout (parallel) course with the dog and handler who brought the gift. If you lose, the gift remains under the tree. If you win, you keep the gift (lucky you!)

b) Take away (challenge) a gift someone else has already selected and won. You must run a knockout course with the dog and handler who brought the gift. You can only take away the gift if you beat them. If you lose, you have to pick a new gift from under the tree and run a knockout course with the dog and handler who brought the gift.

If you win the knockout, you keep the gift (until, possibly, challenged by someone else). The person who had the gift then has the option of challenging someone else for a gift or taking a new gift from under the tree.

Keep going until all gifts are gone from under the tree!

Course Design

Dogwood's White Elephant game typically uses a knockout format with two identical sequences. The course might also have mismatched obstacles. For example, a teeter in one sequence could be replaced by a short set of weave poles in the other sequence.

Dogwood's White Elephant game might also be played in a Pairs Pursuit format (individual competition variation).

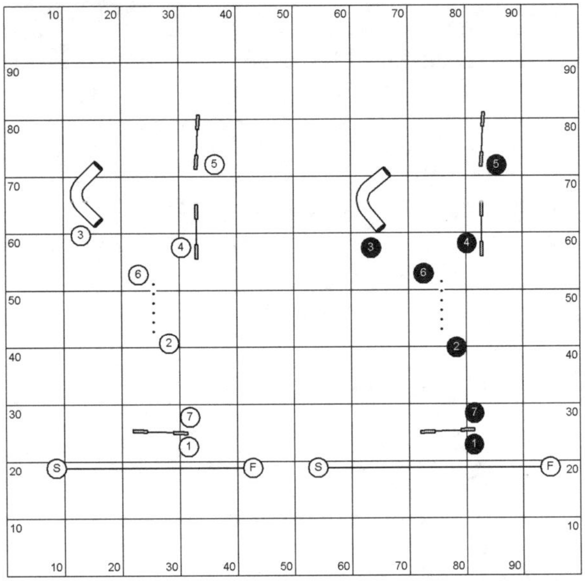

This design for the White Elephant game uses identical side-by-side sequences.

Strategies

Each competitor should make careful note of what gifts other competitors have won and be aware of who brought the gift. To wrest the gift from the current owner, the challenger's dog will have to beat the dog of the handler who brought the gift.

In general, the game runs longer if there are more challenges for gifts that have already been opened. So, if things are going a bit too long, the competitors can speed things up by picking a wrapped gift from under the tree more often.

The competitors should also be aware that they'll probably get a lot more time on the floor and in competition if they bring an interesting and compelling gift that would spark challenges from many other handlers.

don't sit on the dog

Don't Sit on the Dog, sometimes called "Red Roof" is a whimsical suite of games and training exercises documented by Bud Houston for the agility fan holed up in a Red Roof Inn during evening's rest at an agility trial, with contributions from Mary Ellen Berger, Shirley Ann Redl, Nancy Creel, Kathy Helmke, and Ken Ring.

Briefings

- **Doggie Dodge 'Em**—The object of the game is to carry as full an armload of stuff as you can into or out of your room without letting the dogs escape through the door. It's a wonderful twist-and-stretch warm-up routine for the next day's trial. Bonus points if you carry in your dinner at the same time.
- **Doggie Dodge 'Em, Gambler's variation**—A high-stakes variation of Doggie Dodge 'Em, in which you try to maneuver in and out while leaving the room key in the room. Hint: tell the Red Roof Night Manager the "wind blew the door shut."
- **Suitcase Hurdles**—The space between the beds and the dresser is just wide enough to squeeze in luggage. Have an impromptu game of straight-line hurdle jumping for dog treats. Be alert for possible concussion activity with the door when the enthusiasm starts to rise, however.
- **Go for a Run**—Let four- to six-year-olds (other ages optional and just as effective) explore all the hallways of the hotel. Track where they are by the sound of muffled feet and scampering paws. In the event a child is "lost," let dogs go find the child. Warning: all stairwells and all hallways will be investigated before the dogs find the child in a hotel room (yours).
- **Automatic Loader**—Throw the tennis ball only when the dog actually puts it in the hand, flopped out to the side of the bed; bonus points if done while you watch television. Five a minute is considered a pretty good rate.
- **Bed Jumping**—For exercise, jump the dog back and forth from bed to bed. The game is over when all the pillows and bed covers have been spilled on the floor. Variations include: bed jumping in brace, and bed jumping by the pack.
- **Kick the Bucket**—Throw the Frisbee® over and over into the bathroom alcove until one of the dogs kicks over the Red Roof ice-bucket dog water dish. Easy to repeat: fill the bucket back up and play again.

- **Intruder Alert**—Try to guess which late-night guests are causing your hyper-vigilant-guard-dog-wannabe to growl and yip. Not too popular with the humans but provides hours of entertainment for the dogs.
- **Teach the Sheltie to Bark on Command**—Clever people who are annoyed by barking dogs have determined that the thing to do is to teach the dog to bark on command. Tell the Sheltie to "speak." When he barks, give praise and a cookie.
- **Teach the Sheltie to Stop Barking on Command**—This isn't actually possible.
- **Find the Door**—This is a form of variable surface tracking. Allow the dog to run ahead to find the room, which he'll do by magical scenting skills. Praise and reward the dog for indicating the right door.
- **Recall Practice**—Practice and proof recalls when the entire pack of dogs has run into some strangers' open door while playing "Find the Door."
- **Aussie Earthdog**—The dog's owner gets under the bedcovers, tucking them tight all around with no parts of him showing. Yell and cry and make pitiful cries of pain to tease the pups from this superior entrenched position. This game ends when the owner is in great physical discomfort from being scratched and clawed at and getting groin, chest, stomach, and face well used as a trampoline.
- **Pillow Fights**—Just like the kids play. Belabor the dogs with a pillow or two. Whack 'em good. The charming part about this game is they can't hit back. This game ends when it becomes apparent that Red Roof is probably going to charge for the shredded pillows.
- **Who Ate the Rollover?**—As scientifically as possible, using deductive reasoning, figure out which dogs ate the entire 5-pound log of rollover. (Hint: feel the tightness of their bellies).
- **Who's that Barfing?**—Wake to the sound of retching in the middle of the night. Figure out which dog is barfing before rolling out of bed. A whole mess of penalty points is earned for stepping in it. (Hint: see Who Ate the Rollover?)
- **Who's the Loudest?**—See which dog can bark the loudest when the drunk knocks loudly on the door at 2 A.M. (Insider info for betting odds: JRTs will beat out the GSD-cross!)
- **Handler Demolition Derby**—See which person comes out unscathed as they rise from a dead sleep to dive for dogs in the dark when the dogs are playing "Who's the Loudest." This game works best when each handler has more than one dog and all the dogs are allowed to sleep uncrated on the beds with the people!
- **Who Knocked Over the Water Bowl?**—Best played in the middle of the night. Bonus points for spilling the water bowl on the carpet instead of the tile and for getting your suitcase or towels soaked as well.
- **Who's Drinking From The Toilet?**—Played after the water bowl has been dumped. Figure out which dog to yell at in the middle of the night just from the sound of the drinking.
- **Wake-Up Call**—Teach your dogs to wake you up in the morning. This can be very useful when the game of "Automatic Loader" displaced the phone from the cradle the night before.
- **Don't Sit On the Dog**—This is a foundation exercise for Tunnelers, geared especially for the small dog (8 lbs. and under is optimal). Let the dog crawl under the covers of a king-size bed. Go about your business of unpacking. Time to set down and rest… ah… Just where is the dog? Do not pass go and do not collect $200 if the small dog disagrees with seating arrangements.

double joker

Double Joker is the brainchild of Bud Houston, who didn't so much invent the game as free it from the rules of the traditional Gamblers game. Inspired by Darlene Woz and Sharon Nelson, agility pioneers who remember that fun is the number one goal in dog agility, the AKC considered this game briefly as a sanctioned game. Ultimately, a game without rules was of no interest in a titling program. Double Joker survives today as the essence of pure fun.

Briefing

The objective of Double Joker is for the dog and handler team to accumulate as many points as possible in a specified time and then to perform a designated joker, a sequence of obstacles with the dog and handler working some distance apart.

At any time, points may be doubled if the handler is in the doubling box designated by the judge. This can be an area marked on the course or it can be a portable base that is carried with the handler from the start line so that he can choose the location of the doubling box.

If the handler is in the doubling box and leaves, points will be awarded at the regular values. If the handler returns to the doubling box, points will be doubled. If a portable base is used as the doubling box, scores will not be doubled if the handler is carrying the base. The base must be resting on the ground and the handler standing on it for double points to be earned.

Double Joker is a two-part game: the point-accumulation period and the joker period.

Point-accumulation period—The judge decides the length of this opening period. Time begins when the dog crosses the start line or leaves the designated starting position. The handler may lead out. The dog earns points for each obstacle successfully performed. The judge will typically call out the point value for an obstacle when it's successfully performed. Point values are doubled whenever the handler is in the doubling box. The timekeeper will blow a whistle at the end of the point-accumulation period, announcing the beginning of the joker period.

Joker period—This closing period requires the dog to perform a sequence of obstacles, the joker, in the order indicated by the judge. If the handler stays behind the specified containment line, point values are doubled. If the joker is successfully completed in the time allotted by the judge, the team may attempt the joker a second or a third time. The timekeeper will blow the whistle again at the end of the specified joker period. Points for the joker are doubled again if the handler is in the doubling box.

The following rules should be observed in running the class:

- Back-to-back performance of any obstacle during the point-accumulation period is allowed. Indeed, the dog may perform the same obstacle for the entire period. This is known as the Koukkari Strategy.
- No table or finish line is used on the course to get a time for the dog. The clock is not stopped at the second whistle. That whistle merely signals the end of the joker period.
- Practicing the joker during the point-accumulation period is permitted. Points may be doubled during joker practices if the dog successfully completes obstacles while the handler is in the doubling box.
- If the dog knocks down a jump bar, the dog cannot earn any more points for that obstacle unless the handler resets the bar.
- More than one joker can be used in the joker period.
- There is no penalty for loitering near the joker.
- No points are awarded for performance of the dogwalk, if one is used. This is an exceptional test of the handlers' ability to listen to and understand the judge's briefing.
- Points may be accumulated for non-joker obstacles in the joker period, providing the obstacles are on the way to performance of the gamble.

Scoring

Double Joker is scored points then time. The team with the most points wins. Time is a tiebreaker only.

A 1-3-5 point system is recommended with point values as follows:

- Jumps—1 point
- Tunnels, Tire, and Weave poles (6)—3 points
- Weave poles (12), A-frame, and teeter—5 points
- Dogwalk—0 (zero) points

The value of the each joker is double the sum of the regular values of the obstacles included in the joker, provided that the handler remains behind the containment line. If the handler is in the doubling box and performs the joker, the value of the joker would be the sum of the regular values of the obstacles doubled for proper performance of the joker, then doubled again because the handler was in the doubling box.

The entire joker does not have to be completed. If the final whistle blows while the dog is engaged in the performance of the joker, the dog will get credit for those obstacles performed.

Course Design

In the Double Joker course, the obstacles are usually arranged without much thought to an overall flow. However, the course should consist of two or more distance challenges of varying complexity and difficulty. All containment lines for the individual jokers should be clearly marked.

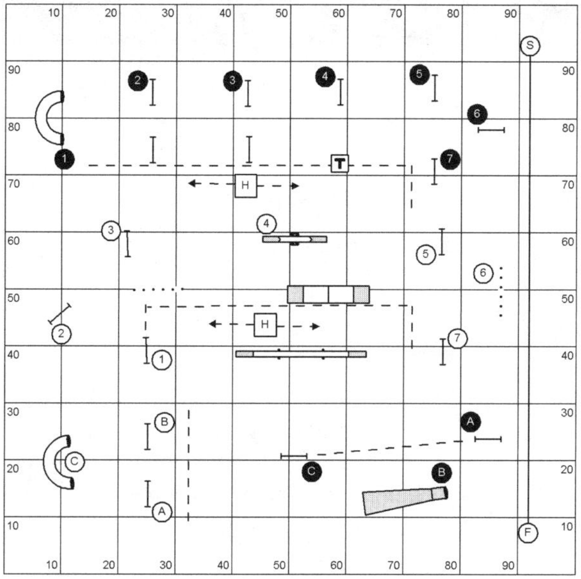

In this Double Joker course, there are actually four jokers that the handler might choose for his dog to work in the final 20 seconds. An efficient dog might accomplish two or more.

Strategies

Since this game allows training or patterning the joker or any other sequence, it would benefit the handler to do so with his dog.

If the course provides a nice flow of obstacles around the doubling box, the handler could work the sequence once, close to the dog, before committing to the box.

When playing the Sterling Wildcard variation of the game, determining a strategy for the placement of the portable doubling base is very important. Place the base in a location from which the dog will willingly work, and from which the dog will accumulate enough points to make the positioning worthwhile. The doubling base isn't active until the handler steps on it. Hence, it is a good strategy to throw down the base and run with the dog around the desired sequence once to pattern the performance, before stepping onto the base to double subsequent points.

Another good strategy is to position the base in anticipation of the performance of the joker in the joker period, allowing the handler to rehearse the joker at double point value and ultimately to double the point value of the joker itself when the joker period begins.

Qualifying and Titles

Double Joker is an eligible titling game in JFF and TDAA. The qualifying criterion reflects some success in the performance of jokers during the game:

- Games I—A score of 25 or better
- Games II—A score of 40 or better
- Games III—A score of 55 or better

Variations

- **Sterling's Wildcard**—In this variation, concocted by Bill Sterling, a portable base is used rather than a stationary doubling box. Bill used a 1-3-5-7 point system, giving 7 points for performance of a technical obstacle designated by the judge. His variation also used a table to stop the time, which would be used for breaking ties, and, perhaps, for more efficient ring administration.
- **Boring rule**—The Koukkari Strategy, doing the same obstacle throughout the point-accumulation period, can be dreadfully boring to spectators. Therefore, you may choose to use the "Boring" rule. If the spectators chant "Boring! Boring!" and the judge agrees, the judge can subtract the points for performance of the obstacle from the dog's score.
- **No negatives**—Another twist for this game is to include a prohibition on negative words. The handler loses 5 points for every verbal "No," "Aack," or other negative word or sound. The judge's decision as to what constitutes a negative word is final. Note: if the handler is in the doubling box when the penalty is received, then the penalty is likewise doubled.

double or nothing

Double or Nothing is the invention of Sharon Nelson with refinements made by Stuart Mah. This game originated when judge Nelson, unhappy about the success rate of a Gamblers class in Arizona, decided to offer handlers a second chance at the gamble, changing the gamble itself only slightly. Needless to say, several people took her up on it.

Briefing

Double or Nothing is similar to the standard Gamblers game. Time allotted, obstacle performance, and the scoring system are all the same. There is also a point-accumulation period and a gamble period (sometimes called a joker period) as in Gamblers. The chief difference is that during the gamble period in Double or Nothing, there are two gambles. However, the team only needs to perform one of the two gambles. Successful completion of the chosen gamble gives the standard bonus points for the gamble.

If a handler is very daring and wants to win the class hands down, he goes for double or nothing. Upon completion of the first gamble, the handler must declare, "Double!" and attempt the second gamble in the remaining gamble time. Successful completion of the second gamble automatically doubles the total score accumulated. Failure to complete the second gamble results in the loss of all accumulated points.

Point accumulation should be set at 40 seconds, with 20 seconds for the performance of one or both gambles.

Double or Nothing Points Chart

Obstacle	1-2-3-5 system	1-3-5-7 system
All jumps	1	1
Tunnels, Tires, Weave poles (6)	2	3
Contacts†	3 or 5	5 or 7
Weave poles† (12)	3 or 5	5 or 7

† *Only one high-point obstacle should be used on a Double or Nothing course.*

Scoring

Double or Nothing is scored points then time. Time is used only to break a tie in points. The winner is the team with the most points, or in the case of a complete disaster, the fastest team to get 0 (zero) points.

The point value for each obstacle is up to the judge. The standard Gamblers point system defined in the table below can be used.

Course Design

The Double Joker course is designed much like a regular Gamblers course except that it will include two distance challenges. These two jokers should be set in proximity so that the dog can make a quick transition between the two if the team decides to go for the double or nothing joker.

Strategies

For the savvy field general, point accumulation is a huge part of this class. Winning or losing is often a matter of how well the point-accumulation period was conducted. Plotting a path through the obstacles is a puzzle to be solved. The handler must determine the maximum number of points that can be earned. This often means performing high-value obstacles back-to-back and running a smooth, short path through the field. This strategy should be devised so that the dog is on the approach to the first joker when the opening period ends.

Timing is everything in this game. To go for the double-or-nothing gamble, the handler must be in an excellent position to perform the first gamble when the whistle blows. The handler must also have the presence of mind to measure the dog's speed through execution of the first gamble to ascertain whether there is enough time to perform the second gamble. If there is likely to be enough time, if the dog is performing smoothly and at considerable speed, and if the second gamble is in reasonable proximity to the first, then the bold handler should go for it.

Qualifying and Titles

Double or Nothing is an eligible titling game in JFF and TDAA. Qualifying criteria depend on the complexity of the jokers. In the sample course shown above, the first joker is a clearly a beginners challenge; yet the second joker is a superior joker.

In this case, qualifying might be set for the different levels requiring a combination of points earned and performance of the two jokers. For example:

- Games I—Successful completion of the first joker and 20 points earned in the point-accumulation period
- Games II—Successful completion of the first joker and 30 points earned in the point-accumulation period; or successful completion of both jokers and 20 points earned in the point-accumulation period
- Games III—Successful completion of both jokers and 30 points earned in the point-accumulation period

Note that if the handler risks the second gamble and does not complete it, all accumulated points are lost

Variations

- **Handler gamble**—A second gamble can be specified in which the handler is required to perform a sequence of obstacles while the dog waits in a specified area. It is common to see handlers racing through weave poles or crawling through tunnels. If the dog leaves his stay in the designated area, the gamble is invalidated and no points are awarded.

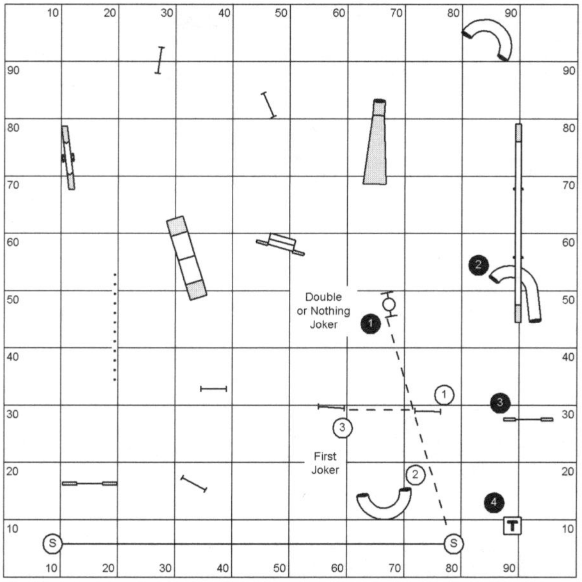

In this sample course, the dogwalk is designated as the 7-point obstacle. The judge stipulated that the first joker, labeled with white numbers, could be taken in either direction. The handler will be sorely tempted to try the second gamble if he has success with the first.

easter egg hunt

Easter Egg Hunt is the invention of John Ostrowski. His agility club has played this game for several years as a holiday favorite at Easter time. It's a good game for practicing control and distance handling.

Briefing

Several plastic Easter eggs are placed in a 10' by 10' marked square in the center of the field. The obstacles are set at random with no discernible sequence. Each obstacle is assigned a point value by the judge.

The handler is provided with an Easter basket at the start of the run. When each obstacle is performed without fault by the dog, the handler earns the point value of that obstacle, picks up an egg, and places it in his basket. The team continues earning points (picking up eggs) by continuing to successfully perform obstacles. Each obstacle on the field can be performed for points only once.

The course time is set at the discretion of the judge and the trial committee. It is usually from 40 to 60 seconds. The timekeeper will blow a whistle when course time has expired, upon which the handler must direct his dog to a designated finish line to stop the clock.

The penalty for traditional performance faults is that the dog must retry the obstacle. The judge will indicate a performance fault by declaring "Fault!" immediately after it occurs. The handler must then reattempt the faulted obstacle. If a bar is dropped on a jump, the handler must reset the bar before attempting the jump again.

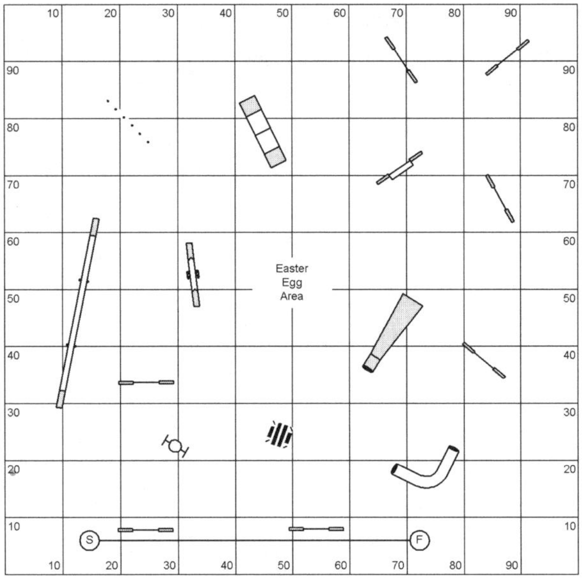

This is a representative example of an Easter Egg Hunt course.

This game has certain unique faults that end scoring before course time elapses. The judge will indicate that the fault is an end-of-scoring fault by blowing his whistle. Faults that will end scoring include:

- Performing two obstacles in succession without collecting an egg in between
- Collecting two eggs without successfully performing an obstacle between
- Taking an obstacle that has previously been performed
- Performing an obstacle in an unsafe manner

Scoring

Easter Egg Hunt is scored eggs plus points then time. The greater number of eggs breaks the first tie. Time is used only to break a second tie.

Any system can be used to award points for obstacles. One of the traditional Gamblers point systems (such as 1-3-5-7) can be used or obstacles can be numbered uniquely (1 through 20, for example).

Points are awarded for the eggs collected by the handler. At the judge's discretion, each egg will be worth 1 point or a point value can be painted onto each egg.

Course Design

In the Easter Egg Hunt course, the obstacles should be arranged with no discernable flow and no more than about 15 obstacles on course. An area with ample room at the center of the course should be designated the Easter Egg area.

Strategies

The handler should keep in mind that trips into the center of the field to collect Easter eggs would often influence the dog's path. With that in mind, the handler should define a strategy that uses the dog's path to the team's advantage for point accumulation.

The bold handler with excellent distance control may choose to stand in the center of the ring and collect eggs while his dog works at the perimeter of the field.

egg-in-spoon relay

This game is based upon a game reported by Kathryn Bayne, Zone 3 Dog Agility Club, in Wellington, New Zealand.

Briefing

The Egg-in-Spoon Relay is essentially played like the kids' Egg-in-Spoon races. Two teams of dogs and handlers will run two elements of a course, with an "Egg in Spoon" exchange in an area designated by the judge. Tennis balls are used as the eggs.

If the egg is dropped, the handler must put the egg back into the spoon before resuming the course. The course must be resumed from the point that the dog had reached before the egg was dropped.

At the exchange area, the first runner will give the spoon and egg to his teammate, who then races with his dog through the second leg of the sequence.

Scoring

The Egg-in-Spoon Relay should be scored time plus faults. Use a simple system of faults, like USDAA Starters/Novice. Before running the game, the judge should stipulate whether faults will be assessed during the "penalty periods" while the egg is out of the spoon. In the quest for a just-for-fun game, it's probably better not to assess faults while the egg is out of the spoon.

Course Design

The Egg-in-Spoon Relay course should be of simple design and give the handler some advantage if taking a lead-out.

Variations

- **Egg-in-Spoon and Hop-in-Sack variation**—In this variation, the handler is also required to navigate the course jumping in a hopsack while balancing the egg in the spoon and directing the dog. Francis Harvey of Australia reports this variation.
- **Pre-Novice**—A pre-novice variation would allow the handlers to work their dogs through the course on-leash. This isn't precisely easier than running with the dog off-leash since the dog may tug on the leash, jerking the handler, who is trying to balance the egg in the spoon.

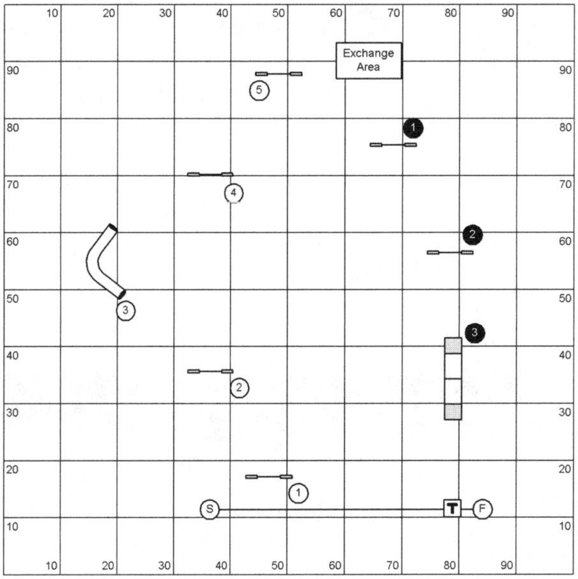

An Egg in Spoon Relay course should be simple in design

extra credit game

Marilyn Steward invented the Extra-Credit Game to engage the students in working and playing with their dogs at home. After teaching a few agility and obedience classes, Marilyn recognized that many students don't practice between class days. Okay, so this isn't the scoop of the century. Before starting a new beginner agility class, she devised a game to motivate the students to do their homework.

Briefing

On the first day of class, the students will have an opportunity to display one trick that they have taught their dogs. Tricks could include the very basics such as sit-stay or down-stay or such standbys as shaking hands, rolling over, and so on. Each week after that, students will have the opportunity to show off a new trick, so potentially they could teach the dog eight new tricks during the course of the class session.

A new trick needs to be displayed every week and must be taught using positive reinforcement. The use of harsh commands will result in no extra-credit points.

Scoring

Keep a list of students who have extra-credit points. Total point tallies should be acknowledged on the last night of class. The team that has accumulated the most points for tricks will receive a prize. If all teams have been motivated to teach tricks, then all will get a prize.

This game probably should be scored on a total-points basis. Winning isn't so much the objective. More rightly stated, winning encourages students to develop a training relationship with their dogs at home.

Outcome

You'll find the outcome of this game most interesting. People who actively played the game and made sure they had a trick every week will have happy and willing dogs. Those people who don't participate in the game will have dogs that are more cautious of the equipment and still have attention problems. Even those people who teach tricks part of the time will have more confident dogs than those who do not play at all.

Strategies

It might be a good idea to develop handouts on teaching dog tricks and behaviors. Step-by-step instructions can guide your students in how to go about training the behaviors and tricks. In the meantime, they will develop a training relationship with their dogs.

flygility

Flygility is a dog sport that comes to us from New Zealand, using some features taken from both agility and flyball. Flygility is a team knockout competition in which two teams compete simultaneously over separate courses that are as close to identical as possible. The best of three runs decides which team proceeds to the next heat.

Briefing

This is a timed-relay performance by a three-dog team over the official course. The course consists of a sequence of agility obstacles. At the end of the sequence, the dog must operate a flyball box, take the ball, and return over the agility obstacles, carrying the ball. When the dog crosses the finish line, the second dog on the team runs the course. When that dog crosses the finish line, the third dog runs.

A dog must rerun the course if he misses any obstacle, does not touch a contact, or is responsible for the ball rolling across the start/finish line. If a dog has started before the preceding dog has reached the start line, does not negotiate an obstacle, dislodges a hurdle bar, does not trigger the box, or does not return with the ball, the judge will immediately flag the dog on its first fault. The dog will be required to rerun after the other dogs have run. If the handler's foot crosses the start/finish line during the dog's run, the handler will be flagged, and the dog will have to rerun after the other dogs have run. If more than one dog needs to rerun, they will rerun in their original running order after all the other dogs on a team have run.

A 5-second penalty is added to the team's score if a jump bar is displaced. No attempt is made to replace the bar during the round. No additional 5-second penalties are added for subsequent dogs. However, dogs must pass between the uprights of the jump. The dog responsible for dropping the bar is not required to rerun. Bars must be replaced before the next round.

Each dog is to negotiate all the obstacles in succession, trigger the box, and return, negotiating all the obstacles in succession with the ball in its mouth. Only when the first returning dog has crossed the start/finish line with any part of its body (on the ground or in the air), and the ball is over the line may the second dog start (and so on). The first team whose dogs all complete faultless runs will be the winner.

A handler may recall the dog to the start line if the dog makes no progress or earns a fault. The judge will immediately raise the colored flag and start a 5-second count. The next dog to run will not cross the line until the judge says "Go," and the flagged dog has returned over the start line. Two dogs must not be on the course at the same time.

Scoring

Flygility is scored time plus faults. A team's score is the total time for the three dogs to run the course, plus any time penalties (5 faults per bar) for displaced jumps. The team with the lowest score wins.

The following rules apply:

- A handler may run more than one dog on a team or different dogs on different teams. However, no dog can run on two different teams.
- Before the teams compete, each dog may have one practice run over the official course. A ball is used in the flyball box as usual. The handler is free to encourage the dog in any way during that practice run.

- The practice runs for a team will be followed immediately by one timed run, including any reruns if necessary.
- A handler may designate the box-loader of his choice.
- The judge will be the timekeeper.
- If the dog starts before the word "Go," the dog will have to rerun.
- The clock will not be stopped until every dog on the team has completed a faultless run or the necessary rerun.
- On the rerun only, if the handler wishes, he may run with the dog to encourage it, press the pedal of the flyball box, or put the ball in the dog's mouth. However, the handler may not carry the ball. The dog must carry the ball over or through all the obstacles and over the finish line. If these conditions are not fully met, the dog (and its team) is disqualified.

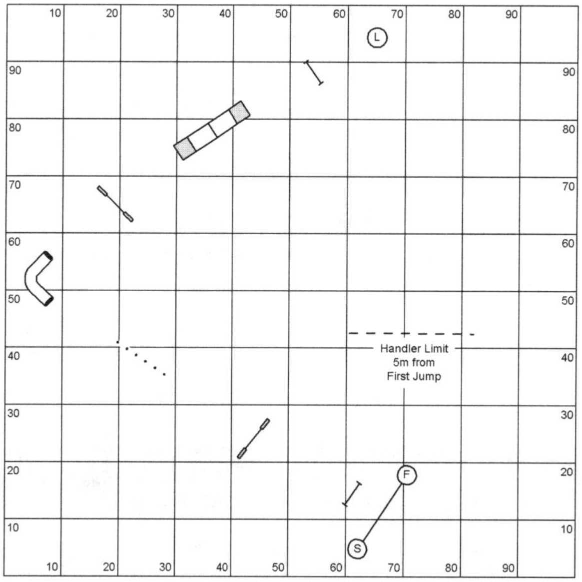

This is a sample flygility course that is appropriate to the Open level (see opposite). The distances between obstacles are carefully measured, according to the judge's specifications.

Course Design

The Flygility course should be designed according to one of four levels of competition:

Beginners: At this level, the course will be straight and will include only jumps.

Intermediate: In addition to jumps, the A-frame and tunnels may be included. One change of direction is allowed but only by way of the pipe tunnel. The change of direction will not be less than 150º.

Open: The weave poles may be included. There may be two changes of direction with or without the pipe tunnel. Any single change of direction will not be less than 120º unless the pipe tunnel is used as the corner, in which case the corner can be as sharp as 90º.

Advanced: The only limitation on the complexity at this level of competition is the equipment available, the practicality of setting out two equal courses, and the safety of the dogs. Dogs that have gained the Flygility Dog Excellent (FDX) title will not be entitled to a practice run.

Novelty Class: Points for heat winners in this type of class will not be credited toward titles.

forty-yard dash

The Forty-Yard Dash is a simple game Sharon Thompson, from Lenexa, Kansas, developed from an even simpler game developed by Matt Skogan of the Overland Park, KS Police K-9 unit for their annual Dog Olympics. The Dog Olympics raises money for the pet adoption side of the kennel that Matt Skogan and Bob Valencia own and operate. Bob is a detective and Matt is a K-9 officer. The game teaches simple matters of motivation, speed, body posture, and movement. As a simple foot race, it might also teach some people to relax and have fun with their dogs.

Briefing

All dogs will run a simple straightaway race in a lane (much like a bowling alley lane), with only a single hurdle at the end of the 40 yards. This lane may be fenced to limit the dog's options to run any direction except forward.

The Forty-Yard Dash is a timed event. The handler can be anywhere in the lane and may use food, a toy or ball, or just about anything to lure or encourage the dog. A person can hold the dog at the start line if the handler desires.

Weight of dogs rather than the height of the dog divide classes.

Scoring

The Forty-Yard Dash is scored time only. The fastest time wins.

A dog that drops the jump bar is eliminated.

Course Design

The lane should measure 35 yards from the Start Line to the hurdle, and 5 yards from the hurdle to the Finish Line.

Strategies

A formal obedience recall is not the best way to get speed from the dog. The handler's posture and movement are important factors in motivating the dog to move as quickly as possible.

For some dogs, if the handler gets too far ahead of the dog, the dog might not want to play the chase game. If the handler stays too close to a dog that won't move on ahead, however, then the dog's speed will be limited to the handler's speed.

Variations

- **Down and back again**—Make it a 20-yard lane, placing a curved tunnel at the end, so that the course goes down and back again.
- **Knockout**—Add a second lane side-by-side so that each dog will race another dog in knockout heats. This really gets the competitive juices going.
- **Team relay**—When two lanes are used, the game can be played as a team relay.

four-leaf clover

This is a directional training game, mostly intended for Novice dogs and handlers concocted by Canada's M.J. Thuot. It can be played individually or in teams of two or three. This is just the ticket for tunnel-enthusiastic dogs. Perfect for a Corgi, eh?

Briefing

The dog performs a numbered sequence. The dog must first perform the weave poles (the stem of the 4-leaf clover) and then perform each leaf of the clover. The handler can earn bonuses for remaining in the containment area that is bounded by the jumps. The sequence ends when the dog makes his way back down the stem to the finish line.

Note that the tunnels all can be performed with the dog going in either entry. At the judge's discretion, a specific entry could be named, which would have serious consequences in terms of handling at a distance.

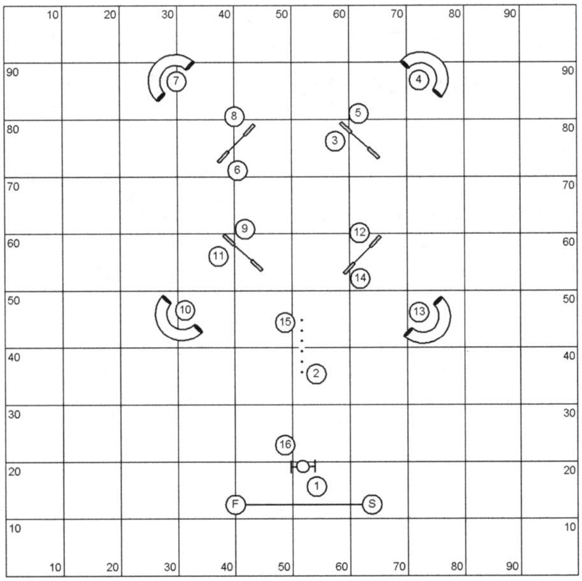

In this sample Four Leaf Clover course, the dog may take either entry of any of the four tunnels to be performed.

The standard course time is 40 seconds. When the whistle blows to indicate the end of time, handler and dog must leave the course. Or, if time has not yet expired, the handler and dog must cross the finish line to stop time.

Scoring

Four-Leaf Clover is scored points then time. Each handler starts with 100 points.

The judge will call out all point deductions. Points lost will be subtracted; bonuses earned, added.

Deductions

- Stepping out of the containment area to help the dog perform the proper tunnel entrance carries a 5-point deduction for each occurrence.
- Knocked bars and wrong courses each carry a 5-point deduction.
- A missed weave pole (not corrected) carries a 20-point deduction for failure to perform. If the performance is corrected, no points are deducted.
- The handler who has to leave the course because of expired time will earn an additional 25-point deduction. The team's time will be recorded as 40 seconds.

Bonuses

- The dog performing a leaf or the stem of the clover while the handler stays in the containment area earns 5 bonus points. All tunnels are bi-directional.
- The dog performing the entire sequence while the handler stays in the containment box will earn an additional 50 bonus points. Note that *only* by staying inside the box for the entire sequence does the team qualify for the 50-point bonus. Thus, a team may have bars down, missed poles and so forth, and still qualify for the 50-points.

Course Design

The course is set up in a shape approximating either a four-leaf or a three-leaf clover. Pipe tunnels should be used to mark the curve of each leaf while the weave poles should be used to mark the stem of the clover. The containment area will be defined as the area between the jumps in the center.

Strategies

When working a dog at a distance, even a modest send into a U-shaped tunnel, the handler should keep the focus of his body on the end obstacle as the dog is sent away. "Focus" implies that the handler's toes and shoulders are facing the desired obstacle and that he is providing some movement toward it, however modest.

In the transitions between leaves, the handler should take care to create a square approach to the jump leading to the tunnel which lines the performance up nicely for the dog. If the handler is indifferent to these corners, then the dog might not be well directed.

Qualifying and Titles

Four-Leaf Clover and Three-Leaf Clover are eligible titling games in JFF and TDAA. To earn a qualifying score, the dog-and-handler team will have to earn more bonuses than penalties and perform the entire sequence in less than the allotted time.

Following is a schedule of points that is adapted from the sample course. Note that all levels of competitors can run the course. Some allowances have been made to enable qualification appropriate to the level of the competitor.

- Games I—A score of 100 or better
- Games II—A score of 120 or better
- Games III—A score of 175

Variations

- **Three-Leaf Clover variation**—In this variation, the clover has only three leaves. Otherwise, the concept of the game is the same.

full house

Full House is the invention of Al Ceranko and replaces Blackjack as a titling game for CPE. The intent of the game is to have the dog in the air to the table when the whistle blows. This is akin to the dog being at the start of the gamble when the whistle blows in Jackpot. The game can be played two ways for a qualifying score or may be used to teach the handler how to plan for opening strategies in gambler-style distance games. Games, after all, are meant to teach skills.

Briefing

The objective of Full House is to successfully accumulate required points, and before time expires, gather the elements of the Full House:

- Three-of-a-kind—3 single bar jumps
- Twosome—2 "circles" (tunnel, collapsed tunnel, tire or window jump)
- Joker—1 contact, weaves, broad, double, or triple jumps

All obstacles may performed only twice for points. Back-to-back performances are allowed.

The timekeeper's whistle will signal the end of the point-accumulation period. At the expiration of time, the team has up to five seconds to stop the clock by going to the table or crossing the finish line. Any delay in heading for the finish line or attempting to perform any obstacle on the way to the finish line will result in the loss of the last point value earned. The team will not lose the last point value earned if the dog takes an obstacle without handler direction.

Point accumulation time differs by jump height:

- 8" and 12", whistle at 35 seconds; total game time, 40 seconds
- 16", 20", and 24", whistle at 30 seconds; total game time, 35 seconds

Fractions are dropped for qualifying purposes. One point is subtracted for each full second over the total game time.

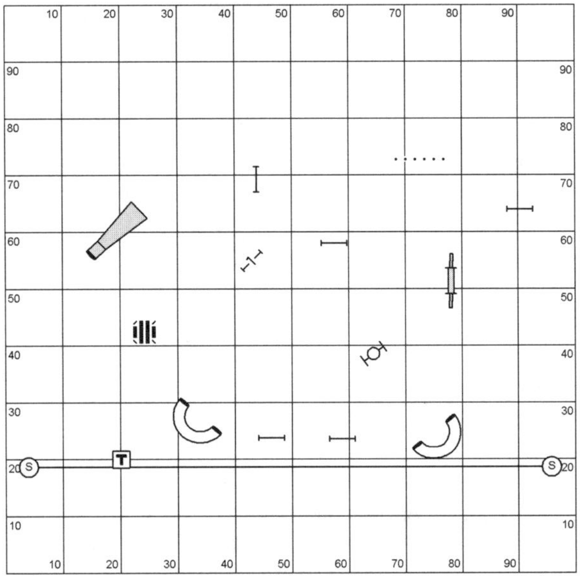

This Full House course was designed for all levels by CPE judge Al Ceranko and used at a Tunnels-N-Tails trial in Ravenna, Ohio on August 19, 2001.

Scoring

Full House is scored points then time.

Points for obstacles are on a 1-3-5 system:

- Jumps—1 point
- "Circles" (tunnel, collapsed tunnel, tire, window)—3 points
- "Joker" (contacts, weaves, broad jump, double, and triple)—5 points
- Table; stops the clock and is live at all times—0 points

Course Design

The Full House course should include:

- Table, on the finish line, which stops the clock
- 6-10 bar jumps (one must be a one-bar jump; panel jump—optional)
- Four "circles" - 2 pipe tunnels; 1 collapsed tunnel, tire, or window jump. Substitute pipe tunnel for collapsed tunnel in adverse conditions
- Three "jokers" - choose two from List 1 and one from List 2:
  - List 1: dogwalk, A-frame, broad jump, double jump
  - List 2: teeter, weave poles (5 or 6), triple jump

Strategies

CPE judge Al Ceranko notes that many exhibitors don't know how long it takes their dogs to perform an obstacle, how to get from obstacle to obstacle, and how to be where they need to be when the first whistle blows for games such as Jackpot or Gamblers. Full House is essentially the opening to a Jackpot run. The twosome (circles: tire, two pipe tunnels, and collapsed tunnel), three-of-a-kind (single bar jumps), and joker (contacts, weaves, and spread jumps) were just a way of fulfilling the need for some kind of requirement. Given that the point accumulation time is slightly less than for Jackpot, the proportion of required points is similar.

Qualifying and Titles

In CPE, the dog must accumulate the elements of the Full House while earning the required points for its respective level:

- Level 1 –19 points
- Level 2—21 points
- Level 3—23 points
- Levels 4, 5, and "C"—25 points

Full House is eligible for qualification for both JFF and TDAA Games titles using these point totals for different classes:

- Games I—19 points
- Games II—22 points
- Games III—25 points

Kenneth Tatsch, president of the USDAA, invented Futbol as an enjoyable wrap-up class and in response to someone commenting to him, "The thing that assures spectator attraction to a sport is having a ball in the game." So he added a ball to the mix. Watching some dogs, even the little guys, go bonkers after the ball will be entertaining, especially when they herd the thing and won't let the handler have it back. Sometimes the dogs will chew at the ball, growl at it, paw it, and so forth. The balls will get some wear and tear.

Briefing

The dog and handler are required to run a jumpers course with soccer balls strategically placed. When the team comes upon one of the placed balls the handler has three options: kicking the ball over the hurdle for a 10-second reduction in score; picking up the ball and throwing it over the hurdle for a 5-second reduction in score; or ignoring the ball altogether, for a 5-second penalty.

The handler is allowed to down his dog before attempting a kick. After the kick or throw, the handler must direct his dog over the jump that served as the goal posts. If the ball drops the bar, the dog will not be penalized for dropping it but the handler will not earn the bonus if the ball went through the standards.

Scoring

Futbol is scored faults plus time, plus penalty, minus bonus. The dog with the lowest score wins.

Futbol is played using USDAA Starters/Novice rules for performance faults:

- Dropped bar—5 faults
- Off-course—5 faults
- Failure to perform—20 faults

In addition,

- Not attempting a kick or throw—5 faults
- Making a successful kick,—10 points
- Making a throw—5 points

The balls used in the game will be awarded as prizes for the contest. First place gets the ball in best shape (it might still be inflated), second place gets the ball in next best shape (partially inflated), and third place gets the third ball (probably DOA).

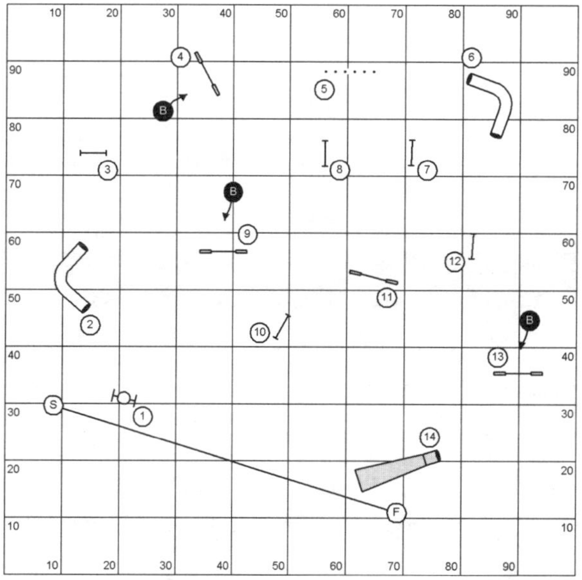

This example of a Futbol course has soccer balls located at jump #4, jump #9, and jump #13.

Course Design

Futbol should be designed as a jumpers course of 14 obstacles or fewer with 3 soccer balls at strategic points. Adequate space should be provided for the handler to have room to down his dog or make the attempt to do so.

Variations

- **Football variation**—In this variation an American-style football is used. The handler is required to throw a football through a tire at a 10' distance.

gamblers

Gamblers is an enormously popular game in the U.S. and Canada. This game specifically showcases a dog's willingness to work at an appreciable distance from his handler and the dog's skill at doing so. Gamblers is intrinsic to the higher levels of titling and accomplishment in USDAA, NADAC, AAC, JFF, TDAA, and CPE (where it is called Jackpot, see page 80). Some form of Gamblers is always included in the Dog Agility Masters tournament.

Briefing

The objective of Gamblers is for the dog-and-handler team to accumulate as many points as possible in a specified time and then to perform a designated gamble (sometimes called a joker), also within a specified time, which consists of a sequence of obstacles that requires the dog and handler to work some distance apart.

Gamblers is a two-part game: the point-accumulation period and the gamble period.

Point-accumulation period—The judge determines the length of the opening period. Time begins when the dog crosses the start line or leaves the designated starting position. The handler is usually allowed to lead out. The dog earns points for obstacles successfully performed. An obstacle can be performed only two times for points. The judge will typically call out the point value for an obstacle when it's successfully performed. The point-accumulation scoring ends when the timekeeper blows a whistle, announcing the beginning of the gamble period.

The time allotted for the point-accumulation period ranges from 30 to 50 seconds, with 40 seconds being the most commonly used. The number of points required in the point-accumulation for qualifying purposes varies among the different organizations. See "Qualifying and Titles" for more information.

Gamble period—This closing period (sometimes called the joker period) requires the dog to perform a series of obstacles, the gamble, in a certain amount of time and in the direction and sequence indicated by the judge. The handler is required to remain behind a containment or handler's line. If the gamble sequence is successfully completed in the time allotted by the judge, the dog will earn points for the gamble.

Gamblers Obstacle Point Values

Obstacle	1-2-3-5 system	1-3-5-7 system
All jumps	1	1
Tunnels, Tires, Weave poles (6)	2	3
Contacts†	3 or 5	5 or 7
Weave poles† (12)	3 or 5	5 or 7

† *In USDAA, only one high-point obstacle can be used on a Gamblers course.*

The time allotted for performance of the gamble is closely related to the standard course time of titling classes for the level at which the dog competes, plus a few seconds to get into position for performance of the gamble. The time will always be greater than 10 seconds and less than 20 seconds.

Gamble points will be lost if any of the following occurs:

- The dog exceeds the time allotted for the gamble period or faults a gamble obstacle. Performance faults are assessed according to the level of the class.
- The handler steps on or over the containment line to aid the dog in performance of the joker. The handler is allowed to extend his hands or arms over the handler's line.
- The handler loiters near the start of the gamble while time remains in the point-accumulation period.
- The dog performs any two gamble obstacles in any sequence during the point-accumulation period.
- The dog knocks down a jump in the gamble sequence during point accumulation, making correct performance of that jump in the gamble period impossible.

Some rules for Gamblers may change from time to time at the discretion of the judge. These rules should be clarified with the judge in the briefing, before the running of the class:

- Back-to-back performance of any obstacle during the point-accumulation period is okay/not okay.
- The table, if one is present, is live/not live during the point-accumulation period.
- The dog must be in the yellow/off the obstacle to get points for a contact obstacle when the whistle ending point accumulation blows.

Scoring

Gamblers is scored points then time. The team with the most points wins. Time is a tiebreaker only.

The judge will call out the point value for each obstacle successfully performed during the point-accumulation period. Obstacle performance in the point-accumulation period uses one of three systems: 1-3-5, 1-2-3-5, or 1-3-5-7. Point values for obstacles are listed in the table on the previous page.

Note: The judge may add up to 4 points to the value of any obstacle in the 1-3-5-7 system or 2 points in the 1-2-3-5 system if the obstacle is placed in a position of relative difficulty. The value cannot exceed the maximum point value in the system being used.

In USDAA, the point value for the gamble is generally arbitrary and set high enough to differentiate a dog that has successfully completed the gamble from the field of dogs. It is possible, however, for a dog that performs the gamble and qualifies in the class to be beaten in placement by a dog that earned more points but failed to perform the gamble (and did not qualify).

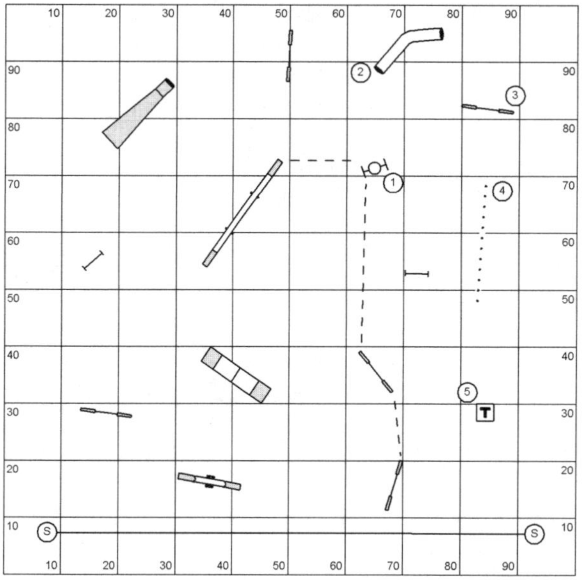

This is an example of a USDAA Masters Gamblers course. The gamble requires the dog to perform a technical obstacle (the weave poles) at a significant distance from the handler. The dog's path through the gamble measures about 110'. The judge would possibly set the time to complete the gamble at something like 18 seconds for 12" dogs, 15 seconds for 16" dogs, and 14 seconds for dogs jumping 22" and 26".

The judge might stipulate that the weave poles are the high-point obstacle (7 in a 1-3-5-7 system) mostly because the poles are trapped in the gamble and may make the handler wary of invalidating the gamble by doing two or more gamble obstacles in sequence.

In NADAC, the point value of the gamble depends on the number of obstacles in the gamble. Typically, there are four obstacles. The judge may include a fifth obstacle as a bonus. Each obstacle is worth 2 points more than the previous one. The first obstacle in the gamble is worth 2 points; the second, 4 points, to the maximum of 5 obstacles, or 10 points, for the fifth bonus obstacle (for a total of 30 possible points).

Course Design

Obstacles are arranged on the field in a random fashion without any discernible flow. The judge will take care to set the higher-point obstacles apart so that they cannot be performed in an easily flowing sequence.

The dog's time is stopped at a designated place at the end of the gamble. This may be an obstacle, a table, or a finish line.

The design of the gamble should pose a challenge appropriate to the skill level of the class. The USDAA makes a distinction in types of distance challenges. These can be grouped into four distinct types:

- Complex obstacle challenge—The dog demonstrates complex obstacle performance (weave poles or contact obstacles) at a distance from the handler.
- Directional challenge—The dog demonstrates directional control at a distance from the handler. This is the measurement of the handler's ability to direct his dog to change direction with verbal and other cues. Typical directional commands are: Left, Right, Turn, Come, and Go.
- Obstacle discrimination challenge—The dog demonstrates the ability to distinguish between two obstacles placed in proximity and at a distance from the handler. The pipe tunnel under the A-frame, for instance, is an obstacle discrimination problem.
- Distance challenge—The dog demonstrates the ability to continue forward and perform obstacles while the handler stays behind or to the side.

When contact obstacles are set in close proximity, as in this sample course, the judge will often stipulate that the handler is not allowed to do two contact obstacles in sequence without doing some other obstacle in between. This stipulation isn't to deprive the handler of quick scoring opportunities; it's a matter of the judge being able to get into position to judge both up and down contacts for two contact obstacles in sequence.

Strategies

When planning course strategy, there are several considerations:

- Plan your strategy before you go into the ring. Find a course path for the opening that will allow you to pick up the minimum number of points required as quickly as possible. You should have a plan for how many points this course plan will earn. You can then start working the dog at increasingly greater distances, allowing the dog to become comfortable working away. This way when the whistle blows, the transition from close handling to distance handling will not be so pronounced.
- Perform obstacles that are farthest away from the gamble area (often the high-point obstacles) first, and then work toward the gamble to be in a good position to start the gamble. If you are too far away from the gamble when the whistle blows, there will likely be insufficient time to complete it.

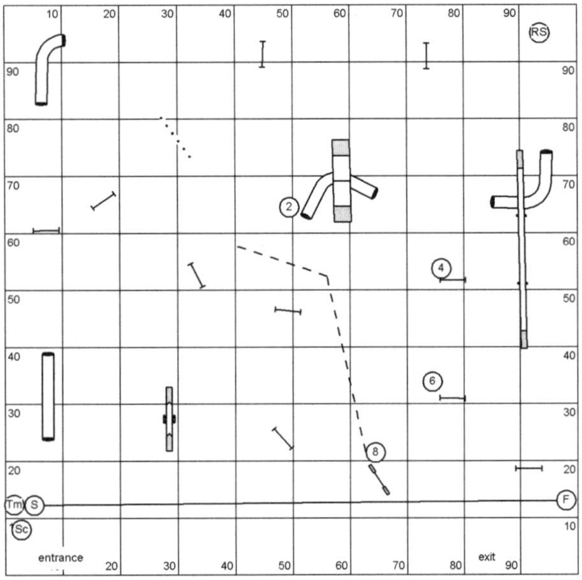

This is an example of a NADAC Elite Gamblers course designed by judge, Ilze Rukis and played in August 2002 at A-1 Dog Training Club, Brooklyn Park, MN. It's worth noting that the chief distinction in gambler challenges in NADAC is the distance between the gamble containment line and the obstacles in the gamble. All exhibitors might see the same gamble, but the line would be drawn ever closer to the obstacles in the gamble as the class progresses from Elite to Open, and from Open to Novice.

- Take the time to set up the dog's path properly for the gamble even if the gamble whistle has blown. If the gamble sequence has a curve to the left, for example, set up the dog so that the curve to the left is the more natural flow for the dog.
- Always keep a couple of simple performance obstacles (jumps and tunnels) near the gamble unperformed until near the end of the opening period. If you find yourself ahead of schedule in the opening period, these obstacles allow you to work close to the gamble area without receiving a penalty for loitering. If you are deemed loitering, no points are awarded for obstacles performed.
- Use the handler's area to maximum advantage. Often a handler restricts his movement, and thus the movement of his dog, more severely than the restriction line warrants. Keep rapid changes of direction to a minimum. Frequent and sharp turns pull the dog's attention to the handler. This can result in the dog turning back frequently to watch you during the gamble. Avoid slamming on the brakes when going into the gamble, since this does nothing but call undue attention to you. It is better to ease into the handler area.
- Occasionally, there is a segment on a Gamblers course that approximates the actual gamble or part of the gamble. It may be beneficial to have the dog perform these sequences so that the dog will have been primed when it's time to attempt the actual gamble.
- Do not get greedy. Often, a handler will try to squeeze just one more point out of his dog toward the end of the opening period. These handlers frequently end up out of position and running like crazy when they hear the whistle for the gamble.
- Some intrepid handlers have discovered that the key to getting on the USDAA Top Ten list is to "place" in the Gamblers class. When there is a particularly wicked gamble set up that is likely to skunk the class, or when the judge has set the value of the gamble so low that it can be outscored in point accumulation, then the handler might make use of sequential performance of obstacles in the gamble itself even though the performance of those obstacles might invalidate the gamble at the end of the run. Also, some judges will allow continued point accumulation after the whistle signaling the end of the point-accumulation period. The intrepid handler can continue to rack up points, with no intention of actually doing the gamble or even qualifying in the class. Placement is what gets a dog on the Top Ten list, not qualifying.

Qualifying and Titles

Several organizations offer titles for Gamblers. NADAC offers Gamblers titles at each level from Novice to Elite. USDAA offers a Gamblers title only at the Masters level. JFF and TDAA allow Gamblers as eligible titling games at all levels. In the United States, only the AKC and the UKC do not offer Gamblers classes.

USDAA

At present the Starters/Novice Gamblers class is for experience and fun and doesn't count toward qualifying for titles. In Advanced Gamblers, however, a dog-and-handler team can earn the right to move up to the Masters Gamblers class by achieving two qualifying scores at the Advanced level. In Masters Gamblers, the team can begin earning qualifying scores toward the Gamblers Master title, which requires five qualifying scores in Masters Gamblers. As we go to press, the USDAA is revamping its titling process in both the Championship and the Performance Programs, making it possible for dogs to earn games titles at all levels, not just Masters. Please consult *www.usdaa.com* for updates.

To earn a qualifying score, the team must achieve a certain number of points in the opening period and also successfully complete the gamble (without faults and under time). The number of opening period points required depends on the time allowed and the point system used. To calculate the number of points needed, the judge will take highest point value in the point system being used (5 or 7), multiply that value by the time allotted, and drop the zero. Thus, if the highpoint obstacle is worth 7 points and there are 40 seconds for accumulating points, the judge will multiply 7 by 40 (280), and drop the zero. This means the team must earn a minimum of 28 points in the opening sequence.

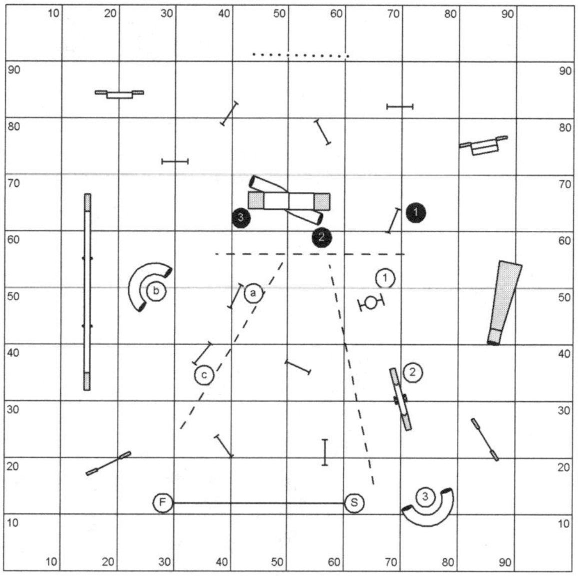

This is an example of the JFF Nested variation of Gamblers. The judge stipulates that the dog's time would be recorded at the moment a foot touched the ground on the dismount of the final obstacle of the respective gamble.
The Beginners gamble is the sequence labeled "a" through "c," which can be taken in either direction. The Intermediate gamble is labeled white #1 through #3. At the advanced level, refusals are faulted on contact obstacles only. The Superior gamble is labeled black #1 through #3. Refusals are faulted on all obstacles.

NADAC

To qualify for a NADAC Gamblers title, the team must obtain a minimum number of points in the opening period and successfully perform the gamble.

The number of opening points required depends on the level of competition:

- Novice .... 20 points
- Open .... 24 points
- Elite .... 28 points

The point-accumulation period varies from 40 (large dogs) to 45 seconds (small dogs).

NADAC Gamblers

Level	Distance of Gamble	Obstacles Permitted in the Gamble
Novice	10'	Jumps, open tunnels, A-frame
Open	15'	Jumps, tunnels (open or closed), A-frame, teeter, short set of weaves poles (6)
Elite	20'	Jumps, tunnels (open or closed), A-frame, teeter, short or long set of weaves poles)

For all levels of competition, the gamble consists of a maximum of four obstacles valued at 2 points, 4 points, 6 points, and 8 points each for a total of 20 gamble points. A fifth and optional "bonus" obstacle worth 10 points may be offered. Scoring is total points (opening plus gamble) with time as a tiebreaker. The difficulty of the gamble between the competition levels is determined by the distance between the dog and handler at the point of the gamble test and by the obstacles that are permitted in the gamble at the different levels.

Adjustments to the base gamble time (14-16 seconds) may be made when the dog must collect itself for a change of direction, for a discrimination, or because the gamble includes certain obstacles requiring additional time for execution, such as the A-frame, the seesaw, or the weaves. Based on any adjustments to the large dog gamble time, additional time (either 1 second or 2 seconds) is added for the other dogs.

A well-designed gamblers course will provide opportunity for various point-accumulation path strategies in the opening period and also provide for various entry points into the gamble, some more advantageous than others.

Two qualifying scores are required to earn the NADAC titling certificate at each level. Additional performance recognition certificates may also be earned at each level.

JFF and TDAA

Typically, TDAA and JFF will observe the specific rules used by other agility organizations in determining qualifying scores for Gamblers classes. The rationale for this is that while playing the game for fun, the experience should also be used to prepare the participants for what they'll see in USDAA and NADAC. It's entirely up to the judge to amend any rule for play in JFF and TDAA. Also, times to complete the gamble should be more relaxed, to acknowledge that many dogs, if not most, tend to slow into a more thoughtful mode when working at a distance.

The JFF Nested Variation or a well-nested NADAC course is preferred for JFF and TDAA so that exhibitors at all levels can run on the same course.

CPE

The game is called Jackpot in CPE (see page 80), and titles can be earned at each level by earning two qualifying scores.

Variations

- **League Play Nested Gamblers variation**—In this variation, gambles are indicated on course for three different levels of competitors: Starters/Novice, Open, and Masters. The exhibitor is allowed to select which gamble to attempt. USDAA rules are observed. The judge will have to be on his toes for changes in rules for the three different levels.

gamblers anonymous

Gamblers Anonymous is the invention of Bud and Marsha Houston who dreamed up this game on the road, returning from a USDAA trial in Indianapolis, Indiana. They wanted to create a game that might depend on the whimsical fortune of a roll of dice. This game is the result.

Briefing

Gamblers Anonymous is a point-accumulation game. All dogs will start on the table and will have exactly 60 seconds to accumulate points. The timekeeper will indicate the end of scoring by blowing a whistle or calling time.

Scoring

Gamblers Anonymous is scored points then time.

Dogs earn points for simple performance of obstacles by the following schedule:

- Jumps—1 point
- Tunnels and tire—3 points
- Contacts and weave poles—5 points

Before a dog can run, the handler must roll the dice, one white, and one red, to determine the High Roller bonus for one of the jokers on the field. The handler will not know until the moment he steps on the field which joker will have a high roller bonus and what that bonus will be.

Joker Points are awarded for successful performance of any of the individual distance challenges on the course. The point value for any of the jokers will be the combined value of obstacles in the joker plus a 5-point bonus. Back-to-back performance of jokers is not allowed. Another obstacle must be successfully completed in between.

For the High Roller Bonus Points, the *White* die will indicate the joker by number; the *Red* die, multiplied by 10, will determine the High Roller Bonus Point value (plus the value of obstacles in the joker).

Super Bonus Points are awarded for performing all six of the on-field jokers. The Super Bonus is 200. The Super Bonus will be awarded *in addition* to all other points awarded.

Faulting an obstacle will negate the point value for that obstacle and will negate any overall gamble or bonus points if the obstacle is an element of a gamble.

Course Design

The Gamblers Anonymous course requires six jokers to be identified with containment lines clearly defined for each. Typically, the jokers increase in complexity from #1 through #6.

Strategies

The roll of the dice tells the tale for the dog-and-handler team. If the dice give a low High Roller bonus for one of the more difficult jokers, it might be worthwhile not to agonize over performances of that joker, especially if the dog is unlikely to successfully perform it.

If the handler rolls a very high bonus for a simple joker, it might be advantageous to do that joker as many times as possible in the time given for the game.

Ultimately, a dog earning Super Bonus Points might win the game. If the handler thinks his dog is able to do every joker on the field, then the handler's walkthrough should be geared to a handling plan that incorporates every joker.

Qualifying and Titles

Gamblers Anonymous is eligible for qualification for both JFF and TDAA Games titles using these point totals for different classes:

- Games I—40 points
- Games II—80 points
- Games III—160 points

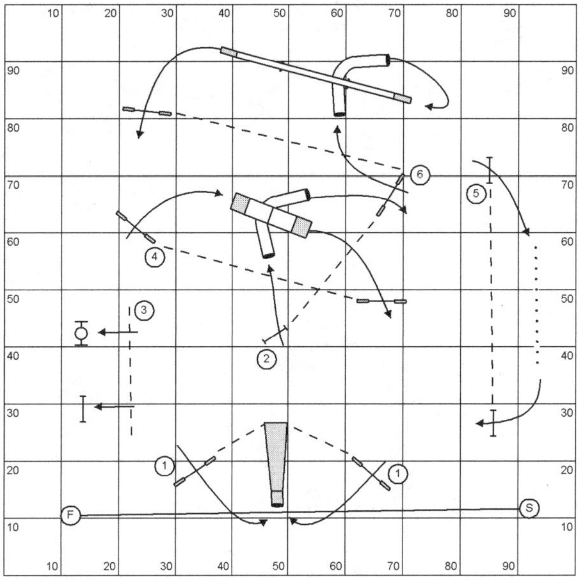

This is a Gamblers Anonymous course run in Dogwood's agility league. The individual jokers were described as follows:

The #1 Joker (10 points) is only two obstacles, the first being either jump, followed by the collapsed tunnel. Either jump may be used to make the approach to the collapsed tunnel. The containment line will be on the side of the jumps away from the entry to the collapsed tunnel.

The #2 Joker (10 points) is jump to the tunnel beneath the A-frame to jump. This joker can be taken in either direction. The containment line is on the side of the jumps away from the tunnel.

The #3 Joker (10 points) is tire-jump, or jump-tire, with this one stipulation: each must be taken in the same direction. The containment line is about 8' away from the two obstacles.

The #4 Joker (15 points) is jump to A-frame to jump. This joker can be taken in either direction. The containment line is on the side of the jumps away from the A-frame.

The #5 Joker (15 points) is jump to weaves to jump and can be taken in either direction. The containment line is on the side of the jumps away from the weaves.

The #6 Joker (15 points) is jump to tunnel to dogwalk and can be taken in either direction. The containment line begins on the inside of the jump. The handler may not step around the jump to the right.

gamblers blessing

Gamblers Blessing is the invention of Lyndal Nichols of the Australian Dog Agility Association (ADAA) and Queensland, Australia. The ADAA recognizes a variety of games for play and for titling. Judges are given some leeway in inventing games as well.

Briefing

This is a four-dog-and-handler relay, requiring the exchange of a baton. The baton must be exchanged before the next dog can run. If the baton is not exchanged before the next dog starts, then that dog is judged as not started yet and has no faults. The dogs and handlers must be behind the line for the baton exchange.

If any dog does not perform all the obstacles in the specified sequence before the baton is exchanged, it is eliminated. Elimination is assessed at 30 faults.

Please note that the rules for faults and scoring change depending on which dog is running.

The first dog runs the first seven obstacles. These have the value of 1 point each. If the handler can send the dog from behind the containment line, the score is doubled (14). Should the handler step over the line at any point in the dog's run, the score will not be doubled.

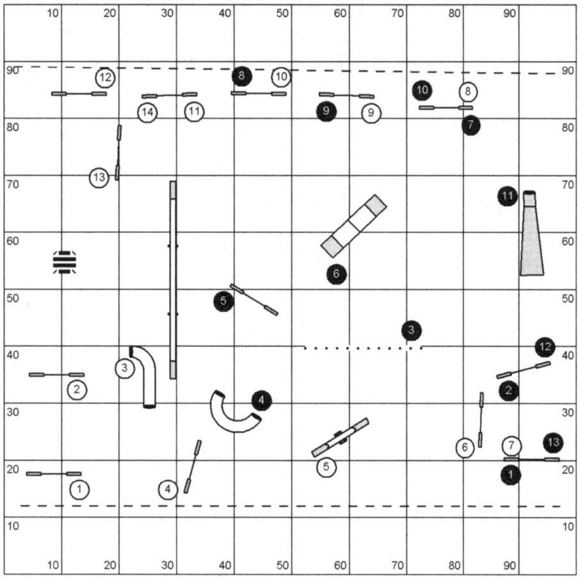

In this course, designed by ADAA judge, Lyndal Nichols, the first dog runs (or is sent over) obstacles numbered white #1 through #7. The second dog works to the opposite side of the field, performing obstacles numbered black #1 through #7. The third dog runs (or is sent over) obstacles numbered white #8 through #14. The fourth, and last, dog will work back to the front of the field, doing obstacles numbered black #8 through #13.

When the dog faults an obstacle by dropping bars or missing contacts, he will earn no score for that obstacle. Refusals are not faulted, but the obstacle must be done correctly before continuing. A wrong course is not penalized.

The second dog runs the next seven obstacles; refusals and faults are counted.

The third dog runs the next seven obstacles under the same rules that govern the first dog's run.

The fourth dog runs home over the last six obstacles; refusals and faults are counted.

Scoring

Gamblers Blessing is scored time plus faults, minus points. The team with the lowest score wins. This may even be a negative score.

The points accumulated by the first and third dog are taken off the final fault score of the four dogs.

Course Design

The Gamblers Blessing course will have start and finish lines at opposite sides of the field. The course should be designed with consideration of the respective tasks of the dogs. For example, the first dog has the option of performing the obstacles while the handler remains behind a containment line. So, the first sequence should be designed so that the handler can work at a comfortable lateral distance.

The second leg should begin on the same side as the first leg, but make its way across to the opposite side of the field.

The third leg again allows a bonus for working the dog at a distance while the handler remains behind a containment line. And so, this segment should be designed so that the handler can work at a comfortable lateral distance.

The fourth and final leg should begin on the same side as the third leg, but make its way across to the opposite side of the field where, typically, the finish line is common with the start line.

Strategies

The send-away sections where there is opportunity to score points should be attempted by the best dogs for the job. The Gamble sections can be used to make up points to cancel any faults accumulated by the other team members. The team might put the dogs with no appreciable distance handling skills on the long, across-the-field sequences.

gamblers choice

A product of U.K. agility, Gamblers Choice was introduced to the U.S. by Kenneth Tatsch. This game is often played as the Gamblers element in the USDAA Dog Agility Masters® tournament. This game is similar to Gamblers in that points are assigned to obstacles—the more difficult the obstacle, the higher the point value. There is also a point-accumulation period and a gamble or joker period. However, this is where the similarity ends.

Briefing

Gamblers Choice demonstrates the handler's willingness to take risks as well as the accuracy of the handler's mental stopwatch. The objective is for the dog-and-handler team to accumulate as many points as possible in a specified time. A good dog-and-handler team will reach the finish point with less than a second to spare.

Gamblers Choice is a two-part game: the point-accumulation period and the joker period.

Point-accumulation period—The judge sets the length of this opening period. Time begins when the dog crosses the start line or leaves the designated starting position. The handler is usually allowed to lead out. The dog earns points for obstacles successfully performed. An obstacle can be performed only two times for points. The judge will typically call out the point value for an obstacle when it's successfully performed. Point accumulation ends when the timekeeper blows a whistle, announcing the beginning of the joker period.

The time allotted for the point-accumulation period usually ranges from 30 to 50 seconds.

Joker period—On the timekeeper's whistle, indicating the end of the point-accumulation period, the handler's slate is wiped clean regarding obstacles performed for points. During the joker period (also referred to as the gamble period), a handler can perform any obstacle up to two times for double the point values.

Gamblers Choice Scoring

Obstacle	1-2-3-5 system	1-3-5-7 system
All jumps	1	1
Tunnels, Tires, Weave poles (6)	2	3
Contacts	3 or 5	5 or 7
Weave poles (12)	3 or 5	5 or 7

The joker period ranges from 10 to 30 seconds. Scoring ceases when the joker time expires or the dog-and-handler team reaches a designated area, line, or obstacle that stops the clock.

To keep points earned, the dog must reach the finish point before time expires. For example, if the judge allots 40 seconds for point-accumulation and 15 seconds for the joker period, the team must be at the finish point by the 55-second mark. If a dog reaches the finish point even a hundredth of a second after the indicated time, the handler loses all points earned during both the point-accumulation and the joker periods.

The judge may assign a sequence of obstacles a bonus value, usually a doubling of the normal point values of the obstacles. If the team successfully performs the on-course gamble, it will receive the bonus points. Generally, if the team fails to complete the sequence, it will still receive the usual point values for the individual obstacles performed correctly while attempting the sequence.

The judge can exercise considerable latitude in how the on-course gamble is conducted:

- A judge can stipulate that if any part of the sequence is flawed, no points will be awarded, or the judge can stipulate that normal point values will be awarded for obstacles successfully performed, using the same system as in the point-accumulation period.
- A judge can stipulate that dogs are allowed to perform the sequence successfully only once or twice.
- A judge can stipulate that on-course gambles can be performed only during the point-accumulation period, or at any time during both the point-accumulation and in the joker periods.

Scoring

Gamblers Choice is scored points then time. The team with the most points wins. Time is a tiebreaker only.

The scribe will record the points earned by a dog in two separate columns, one representing the regular score for an obstacle performance and one representing a score to be doubled by the scorekeeper.

Obstacle performance in the point-accumulation period usually uses one of two systems: 1-2-3-5 or 1-3-5-7. Point values for obstacles are listed in the following table.

The judge may add up to four points to the value of any obstacle in the 1-3-5-7 system or two points in the 1-2-3-5 system if the obstacle is placed in a position of relative difficulty. The value cannot exceed the maximum point value in the system being used.

Typically, only one high-point obstacle is used.

These point values are guidelines. There are no official rules for this game. Consequently, the judge can make all manner of stipulations for performance by the dog and handler. For example, a judge could stipulate that no points would be awarded for the contact obstacles during the double-point joker

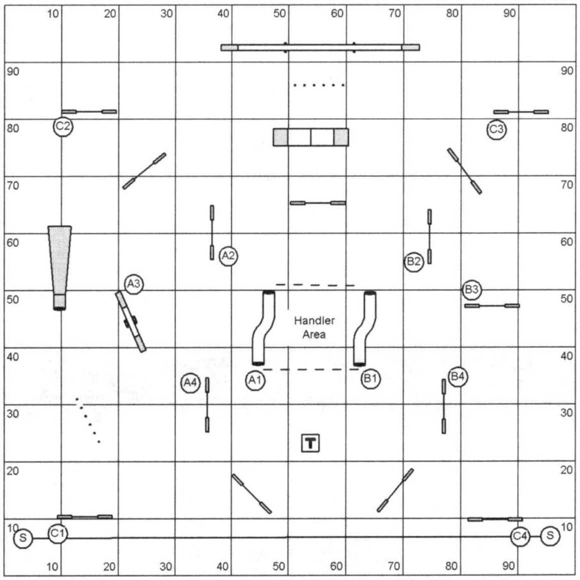

This Gamblers Choice course, designed and judged by David Hanson was played at the USDAA National Tournament in San Diego, California on July 17, 1999.

The judge stipulated a course time of 45 seconds and the following point values for on-course gambles:

Gamble A—15 points

Gamble B—10 points

Gamble C—20 points

Table contact stops the clock. Running over time will cost the team a 20-point deduction.

period. The judge could also specify that the dog earns the joker-period point value for an obstacle that is being performed when the whistle blows to signal the end of the opening period. That means that the dog would be awarded 0 (zero) points if caught, for instance, on the dogwalk when the whistle blows.

Course Design

The design of the Gamblers Choice course is wildly flexible. For example, the judge may stipulate only that obstacles in the closing or "gamble" period are worth double the point values of the opening, and so no special course design criteria is required. On the other hand, the judge may stipulate that certain obstacles or sequences are eligible for double points in the closing. So, the judge must carefully identify these.

The judge may also stipulate a handler containment area.

Strategies

In Gamblers Choice, it is very important to know the speed at which the dog works. It is especially critical in the joker period where being 1/100th of a second over time will result in the loss of all points. It is important not to get greedy and go for more points than the dog can realistically accumulate in the given time.

Similarly, if the dog can get to the table 6 or 8 seconds before time expires, his competition has a lot more time to score more points. Even slower dogs will gain the advantage to accumulate more points.

Qualifying and Titles

Gamblers Choice is a qualifying game for both JFF and TDAA. This game can be nested and leveled. Three or more jokers can be used on the course for different levels of titling, depending on the complexity of the challenge.

The judge should establish a simple requirement for the minimum number of points to be earned in the point-accumulation period in addition to requiring that at least one of the jokers should be performed in the joker period in order to earn a qualifying score.

Variations

- **Laubach variation**—In this variation, a specific sequence of obstacles must be performed in the joker period. However, the obstacles can be performed with the handler running with the dog. For each obstacle the dog performs correctly, the team earns 10 points. The handler (or the dog, for that matter) may choose to perform any number of obstacles in the sequence, from #1 to #5. After performing that number, the dog must retrace the sequence in reverse and cross the finish line to stop the clock. If the dog breaks the sequence coming back or fails to cross the finish line before the final whistle, the dog gets no points.

  The course designer needs to be mindful of an interesting sequence of obstacles to finish the round. For smart ring administration, the final sequence should point abruptly to the finish line to stop the clock.

go for broke

Go For Broke is the invention of Deb Richey for play in the Just For Fun Runners agility league in Chicago, Illinois. This game is a variation of Gamblers that takes it to the next logical dimension. Go For Broke is sometimes called "Survivor Gamble."

Briefing

Go For Broke is played in a manner opposite to the traditional gamblers game. This game starts with a gamble, which, if successfully completed, allows the team to go on to point accumulation.

During point accumulation, the dog must earn exactly 16 points, using a 1-3-5 point system:

- Jumps, tunnels, and tire—1 point
- Contact obstacles and 6 weave poles—3 points
- 12 weave poles—5 points

Once the team has earned 16 points, the handler must either: direct the dog to perform the gamble again, this time from the second gamble line; or send the dog to the table to stop the clock. If the dog is successful with the second gamble, he goes back to point accumulation.

If the team manages to get another 16 points, the handler must either: direct the dog to perform the gamble again, this time from the third gamble line; or send the dog to the table to stop the clock. If the dog is successful with the third gamble, he goes back to point accumulation.

After point accumulation for the third gamble, the handler must direct his dog to the table to stop time.

If the dog fails in any gamble attempt, the team may not proceed to the point-accumulation period. The handler must direct the dog to the table to stop time. If the dog faults a gamble, then all points are lost.

Obstacles may not be performed back-to-back for points and may be taken no more than twice in any one point-accumulation period. If a dog knocks a jump bar during point accumulation, he must go to another jump to get the single point. If the dog faults a contact obstacle, he is required to perform that obstacle again until he completes it successfully.

There is no standard course time in Go For Broke. The handler may continue to work his dog until he has successfully completed the three nested gambles or has faulted out.

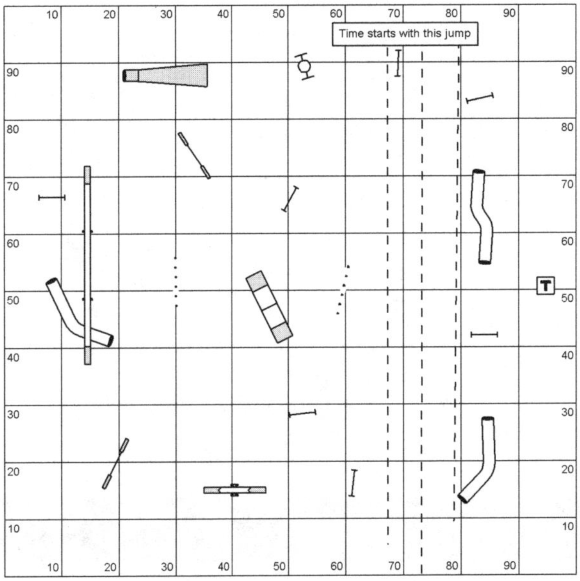

This is the original Go For Broke course designed by Debbie Richey for the JFFun Runners in Joliet, IL. The gambles can be nested, as those shown here, or they can be unique and located in different parts of the course. If unique gambles are used, they should be designed with increasing levels of distance or complexity.

Scoring

Go For Broke is scored points then time. Time is a tiebreaker only.

Points must be earned in blocks of 16. The dog's score will be one of: 16, 32, or 48. If the dog earns more than 16 points in point accumulation, or attempts a gamble with fewer than 16 points, or faults a gamble, then all points are lost.

Course Design

Like all Gamblers courses, the Go For Broke course should be designed with the agility equipment set in a random manner with no discernable and logical flow. The course should be designed with a jump placed so that the dog has some momentum when making the initial approach to the gamble.

The progression of jokers might be the same joker taken from incrementally greater distances. Or, the progression could be a series of different jokers of increasingly greater complexity.

Strategies

The first prerequisite in this game is that the dog's handler understand the point system awarded for obstacles and be able to do the math (either by design or on the run) to score points in blocks of 16.

The handler should understand the limitations of his dog's training. Don't overreach. If the dog does the first gamble and earns his 16 points, it is probably a good idea to go to the table to stop the clock (and earn a Beginner's qualifying score).

In league play, the handler is under pressure to balance doing the right thing for his team, versus going for the gusto and personal glory. There is no right answer in keeping this in mind for the sake of a working strategy.

Qualifying and Titles

Go For Broke is eligible as a titling game under JFF and TDAA rules. Qualifying should reflect the level of the competitor:

- Games I—16 points
- Games II—32 points
- Games III—48 points

go hawaiian

This is a pretty zany game, probably at the top of the silly list. But it is a game that's ideal for a club picnic. Go Hawaiian is the invention of Michelle Vroman.

Briefing

Dogs are required to run a simple numbered course. The object of the game is to score the most points.

Points are earned as follows:

- The handler leaves the dog at the start line in a sit or down, runs to a marked area in the center of the course and dons the following apparel: grass skirt, straw hat and two leis—10 points
- The handler performs a hula dance after dressing up—10 points
- The dog successfully completes an obstacle—10 points

Scoring

Go Hawaiian is scored points then time. The highest score wins. Time is only used to break ties. It is recommended that prizes also be awarded for the best and worst hula dancer.

Faults are assessed using modified USDAA Starters/Novice rules. If an obstacle is faulted, no points are earned for that obstacle unless the handler corrects the fault as follows:

- If the dog knocks a jump bar, the handler must reset the bar and do a hula dance.
- If the dog misses a contact or a weave pole, the handler must do the hula for each occurrence.

Course Design

The course should be a straightforward square of obstacles, suitable for dogs and handlers of all levels.

group choice

Group Choice is the invention of Marq and Rebecca Cheek. Their goal was to have a game that didn't require moving any obstacles. It can be played before or after almost any other agility game without any obstacle movement since it is extremely unlikely that there would be any significant repeated patterns from the previous class.

Briefing

The objective is to perform all obstacles on the course, as quickly and accurately as possible, according to the following groups:

- Jumps, tire, and tunnels group
- Contact obstacles group
- Weave poles only group

The handler must negotiate his dog through all the obstacles in a particular group before continuing to the next group. The order in which each group is completed is up to the handler, but all three groups must be completed.

The handler can start anywhere along the start line that runs from one side of the ring to the other. Obstacles may be taken in any direction with the obvious exceptions (teeter, collapsed tunnel, spread hurdles). Each obstacle may be taken only once. After completing all the groups, the dog will finish on the table.

If all groups and obstacles have been completed, if the dog takes any on the way to the table, he will earn a 20-point deduction.

Time will begin when the dog crosses the start line and will end when the dog's four paws land on the table.

Course time is generally set at 70 seconds for big dogs and 75 seconds for small dogs.

Scoring

Scoring is on a 100-point basis. Time is used as a tiebreaker only. A score of 100 will be given to a dog that finishes the course with no faults under the allotted time.

Faults will result in a deduction of points.

- Knocking bars, missing a contact, failing to do an individual obstacle—5 points
- Performing an obstacle outside the group; repeating an obstacle—20 points

Course Design

In Group Choice, obstacles are laid out randomly on the field. It's a game that can be played with an existing set of obstacles, for example, after a standard course has been run.

The difficulty of Group Choice is for the judge to get in position for all contacts without knowing the handler's strategy and remembering if all the jumps have been taken or if any were duplicated.

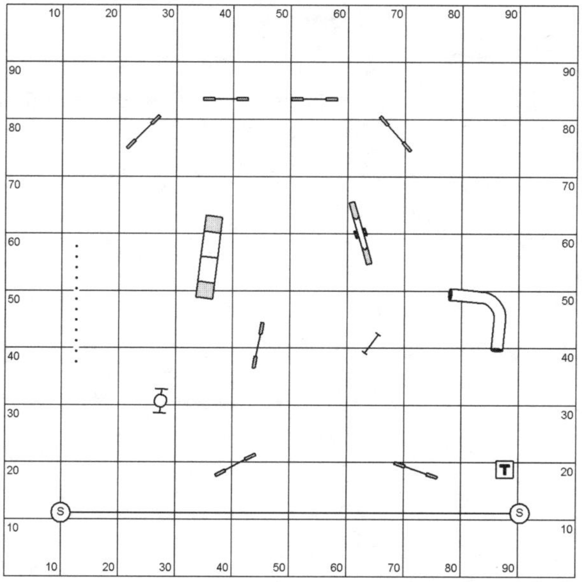

Agility league play at Dogwood in June, 2002, used this Group Choice course, designed by Bud Houston. What do you think was the winning strategy?

Strategies

Group Choice is, after all, a game of strategy. The key to winning is to define the shortest path to perform all the obstacles, one group at a time. The choice of which group to begin can be as important as which obstacles to begin with within the group.

Qualifying and Titles

Group Choice is a qualifying game for titling for both JFF and TDAA. The standard course time should be set at 4 or 5 seconds per obstacle on the course. Obstacle layouts of a more complex nature allow a greater course time than simpler layouts. The qualifying criteria should be:

- Games I—75 points
- Games II—90 points
- Games III—100 points

halloween race

Chris Miele created Halloween Race as a special game to be run annually by her agility classes to commemorate October 31, the eve of All Saints' Day or Halloween. Trick or Treat!

Briefing

The Halloween Race is run as a single elimination knockout. The dog that wins each race will advance to the next round. The dog that loses each race is eliminated.

The course is divided into two sequences. Two dogs and handlers will be on course at the same time to run these sequences. Each dog will begin on a different sequence, then run the other sequence immediately after finishing its own. One dog will run the first sequence and then run the second sequence. The other dog will run the second sequence, then the first sequence. The dogs must switch sides of the course somewhere in the middle of their runs.

Each dog's faults will be added to its time. Therefore, a dog that crosses its finish line before the other dog still may lose when those faults are added to its time as seconds.

If one dog catches up with the other dog, the lagging dog must give right of way.

Scoring

The dog and handler that win every race win the competition.

Two judges are required, one to follow and judge each dog. Two timekeepers and two scribes are also required, so that a timekeeper and scribe are assigned for each dog. At the end of a run, each dog's faults will be added to its time to determine who won and who lost.

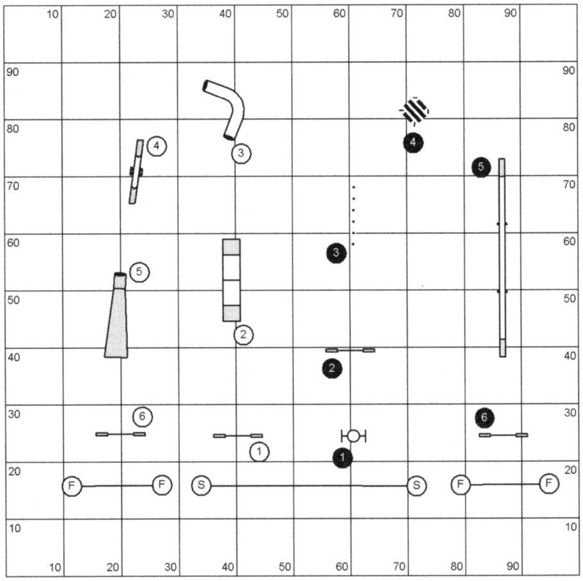

This is an example of a typical Halloween Race course.

To determine third and fourth places, the dogs that are defeated by the two finalists should run against each other.

Any scoring system can be used. USDAA Starters/Novice rules are recommended:

- Knocked pole, missed contact, or off-course—5 points
- Failure to perform—20 points

Course Design

Since both dogs have to perform all the obstacles, the only real design constraint is that the path from the end of one course (white numbers) to the beginning of the other course (black numbers) should be equidistant. That way one team does not have a time/speed advantage over the other on the flat when changing courses.

Obstacles should be arranged so that the contact obstacles are easy to judge by the respective judges.

Even more important than the placement of the obstacles on course is the placement of appropriate Halloween accessories on course. In proper spirit, plastic goblins should be attached to the contact obstacles, witches and ghosts added to jumps, pumpkin heads placed on the tops of the weave poles, and so on. It wouldn't hurt to have a few bats hanging from tree limbs or lighting fixtures. Judges should also dress appropriately.

Strategies

This would seem to be a matter of the fastest dog winning. In fact, a race of this type will often go to the steadier dog. Therefore, the best strategy for Halloween Race is to run fast, but to work hard to run clean. A steady dog will beat a faster dog, particularly if your opponent is recklessly pushing for speed.

Variations

- **Costume rule**—For added fun, require handlers to either wear suitable Halloween attire or receive a two-second time fault before the race even starts just for being boring.

handler go jump

Okay, so this is a perfectly silly game that is more ideal for a club outing than any kind of serious competition. Handler Go Jump is the invention of Karen Gloor. The game is included here mostly for the amusement of those who know her.

Briefing

In Handler Go Jump, the dog is required to run a standard agility course. However, each time the dog performs a tunnel of any type, the handler must jump over a designated hurdle. Handler hurdles will be set at 12".

Standard faults will apply to the dog's performance of the obstacles, notwithstanding the antics of the handler. This means that the dog will be faulted for an off-course if he follows the handler over a handler jump. If he wishes, the handler can place the dog in a sit-stay or a down-stay so that the handler can take the jump.

Scoring

Handler Go Jump is scored time plus faults. The dog with the lowest score wins the game.

Course Design

Any standard course design suitable for the level of competition will work for Handler Go Jump. Handler jumps should be thoughtfully placed to accommodate the handler's natural path.

Variations

- **Alternative handler obstacles**—From the dog's point of view, Handler Go Jump is a standard agility course. What sets this apart from standard agility is that the handler is required to perform an obstacle. Clearly, if you really want the class to be entertaining, it is possible to designate a set of weave poles or a pipe tunnel, rather than a jump, for the handler's performance.

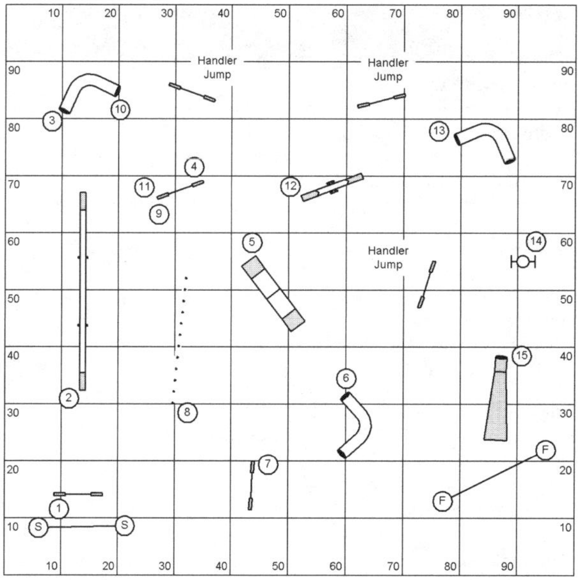

On this sample course, the handler would have to perform five jumps, one for each of the following tunnels: #3, #6, #10, #13, and #15.

handler's choice

Handler's Choice is a game invented by Webb and Leslie Anderson, who noticed that many of their advanced students were handling beautifully in classes but were having trouble making the transition to the show ring. They were not really comfortable using some of the handling skills they had worked on in class. They came up with this game, Handler's Choice. The students loved it! This game originally appeared in the Clean Run *magazine in October 1999.*

Briefing

This game has two purposes: to help students recognize spots on a course where various handling skills could be used and to encourage students to choose the most effective handling movement. Courses should be designed in such a way that many handling skills could be used.

Points are awarded for each handling movement successfully completed. If the dog faults because of a handling movement, the team does not get the points for those moves (for example, a missed weave entry on a rear cross at the weaves). The judge will call out the handling maneuvers as they are performed during each dog's run. A scribe will record these points.

Scoring

Handler's Choice is scored points only. The team that accumulates the most points wins. Points are awarded based on a 1-3-5-7 basis. Harder maneuvers are worth more points.

See the sample score sheet for Handler's Choice on the next page.

Course Design

The Handler's Choice course should be designed with some thoughtful consideration to creating opportunity for specific movements or handling skills. For example, a serpentine sequence nearly always requires the handler to

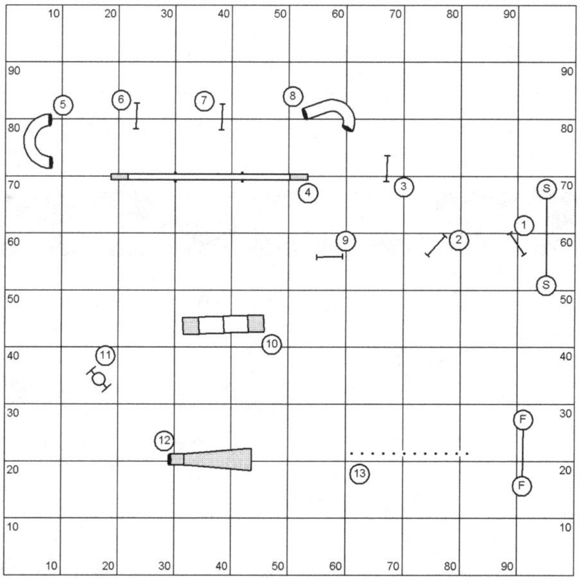

This course is closely based on one originally designed by Leslie and Webb Anderson. What handling movements would you use on this course to earn high points?

Handling Skill	Times performed	Points	Total
Running with dog from start		1	
1 obstacle lead-out from start or table		1	
2 obstacle lead-out from start or table		3	
3+ obstacle lead-out from start or table		5	
Lead-out pivot		5	
Rear cross at jump		1	
Rear cross at tunnel		1	
Rear cross at contact		3	
Rear cross at weaves		7	
Front cross at jump		1	
Front cross at contact		3	
Front cross at weaves		7	
Blind cross (not at tunnel)		7	
Reverse flow pivot		5	
Tandem turn		5	
Counter rotation		3	
Framing		3	
Call-off		1	
Layering		7	
Off-side weaves		5	
Total Score			

A sample score sheet for Handler's Choice

change sides to his dog. A handling movement is required for the handler to make this change of sides. What movement will be used is left largely to the wit and creativity of the handler.

Strategies

The competitor should try difficult movements. Be brave. Go for the points! For example, if the handler wants to switch on the upside of the A-frame and then switch again on the downside, he should go for it! The purpose of the game is not only to help the handler recognize good opportunities for particular handling movements on a course, but more importantly, to help the handler practice those movements so they become second nature.

helter-skelter

In the U.K., there is a dog agility class called Helter-Skelter. The game is named after a children's ride at parks and fairs where a slide spirals down the side of a tower. This game is extremely popular with dogs and handlers alike. The early Helter-Skelter courses tended to start with the dogs on the table at the center of a clockwise spiral course. The dogs had to negotiate the first, closely spaced jumps carefully on sharp turns, but as the course progressed, the dog could speed up as the spiral unwound. Over the years, the class has evolved and nowadays it's often simply a heel-side spiral starting in the center. The courses look deceptively easy, but with the increase in speed that these courses encourage, the traps come up really fast.

Briefing

Helter-Skelter is run on a Jumpers course and may contain tunnels and weave poles. The dog is required to perform each obstacle on the course at the handler's direction in the sequence designated by the judge. The handler may use voice commands and signals but may not touch the dog or any obstacle.

The judge will set a very aggressive standard course time based on a range of 5 to 6 yards per second.

The competition is between dogs at a given jump height and skill level.

Scoring

Helter-Skelter is scored faults then time. The dog with the fewest faults wins. Time is a tiebreaker only.

Faults are assessed as follows:

- Off-course (one paw)—20 faults
- A dropped bar or tipped long jump plank—5 faults
- Failure to perform—Elimination
- Exceeding the standard course time—Faults are assessed on a 1:1 basis for each second over the standard course time.
- Refusals are not faulted.

Course Design

The Helter-Skelter course is typically designed as a spiral, beginning in the middle and sweeping outward in increasingly long loops around the center point. The course should consist of jumps, tunnels, and weave poles only. One or more tables may be used to start or finish the run.

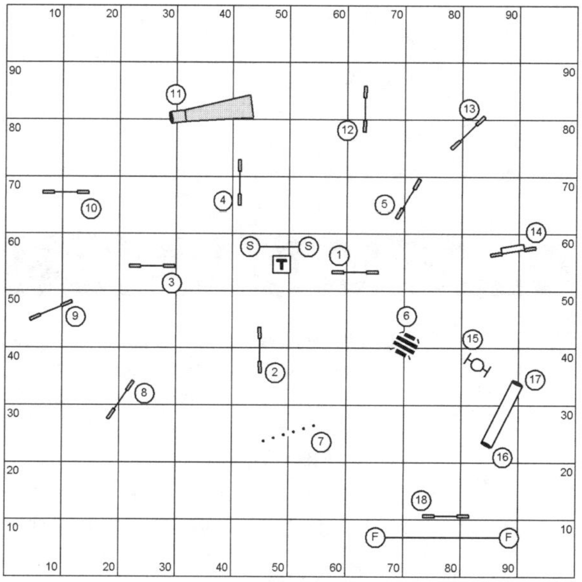

This is a Helter-Skelter course designed by Sally Jones, a British agility competitor and agility judge who writes for the top agility magazine in the U.K., The Agility Eye.

Strategies

In the interior of a Helter-Skelter course, the turns are tighter, the transitional distances between obstacles are shorter, and the potential for dropping bars is higher. Dropping bars on the interior of the course will be minimized if the handler shows the dog turns only after the dog has committed to a jump.

In the Steeplechase variation, technical obstacles (A-frame and weave poles) are allowed in the outer loop of a Helter-Skelter course. The handler should be mindful that the dog is building up tremendous speed as he works. The handler should be prepared to slow down the dog for an approach to the weave poles so that the dog makes a controlled entry.

Qualifying and Titles

Helter-Skelter and its Steeplechase variation are qualifying games for titling for both JFF and TDAA. In a dual-leveled course, (as in the sample Steeplechase variation of Helter-Skelter), qualifying criteria might be:

- Games I—Novice course with no more than 5 faults
- Games II—Novice course with zero faults or Advanced course with no more than 5 faults
- Games III—Advanced course with zero faults

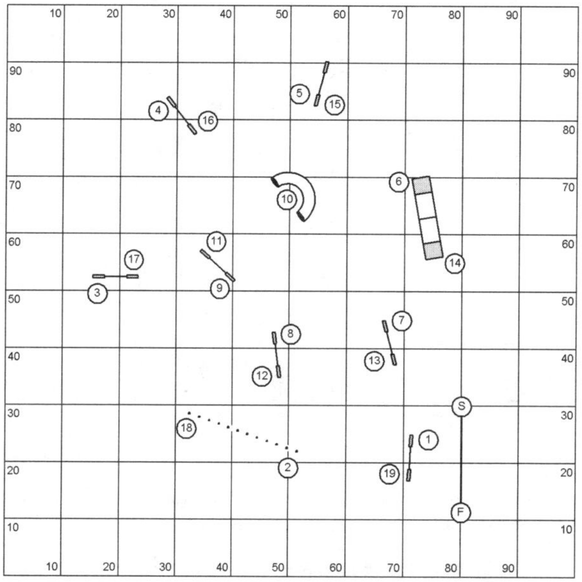

This Steeplechase variation of Helter-Skelter was used in the Dogwood agility league in 2002 and is based on a course originally designed by Sally Jones (who did not include the A-frame). This course layout can be used for both Novice and Advanced competitors. The Novice version begins at jump #3 and ends at jump #17.

Variations

- **Time plus faults**—Alternatively, Helter-Skelter can be scored on a time plus faults basis
- **Steeplechase variation**—In this variation, an A-frame is included in the course and will be judged under JFF rules for obstacle performance.

Impossible tunnel game

The Impossible Tunnel Game is a training game played at Bud Houston's Camp Dogwood in Ostrander, Ohio, and in agility league play. This game teaches the handler to sharpen his movements and make clear presentations to the dog when working with tunnels. It also helps with course-memorization skills. The action is brisk and upbeat. The handler can't miss a trick.

Briefing

Run the sequence as numbered. The dog will be faulted for any off-course. When jumps or contacts are used, the dog will be faulted for dropped bars or missed contacts. At the judge's discretion, refusals may be faulted.

Scoring

The Impossible Tunnel game is scored time plus faults.

- Off-course—5 faults
- Dropped bars (when jumps are used)—5 faults
- Missed contacts (when contact obstacles are used)—5 faults
- Refusals—5 faults (optional)

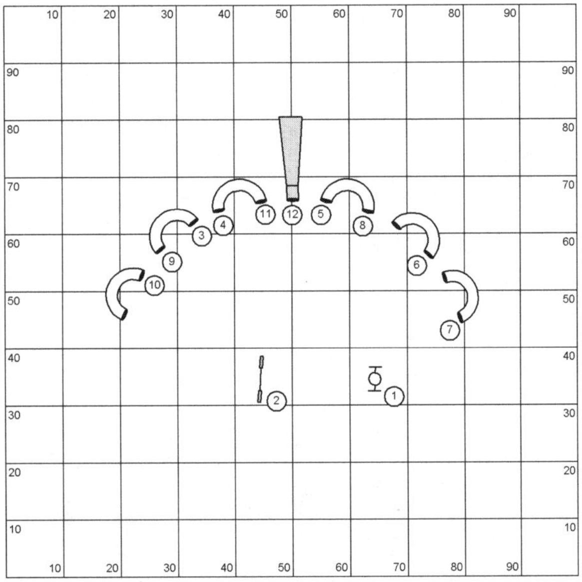

This is the classic Impossible Tunnel Game configuration, with a concave curve to a series of tunnels. However, the tunnels might also be set in a convex curve.

Course Design

The tunnels should be arranged in a semi-circular pattern with an even 3' spacing between the apertures. A couple of hurdles are used to create flow into the arrangement of tunnels, making the first approach one of the most difficult. In a more advanced course, the judge may use a set of weave poles or a teeter in the stem, as these obstacles tend to "trap" the handler at the dog's side.

The collapsed tunnel is typically the exit obstacle.

Strategies

Surviving this game requires the same simple strategies the handler should consider when approaching a tunnel in any competition. For example:

- The handler should position his body on the turning side of a tunnel whenever possible. This is especially useful for Novice dogs that will tend to refuse a tunnel if the handler is away from the turning side.
- When making a transition between tunnels, the handler should keep his body between the dog and off-course tunnels.
- It's worth remembering that the dog turns when the handler turns. The handler should use the rotation of his body to turn the dog and line him up for the correct tunnel entries. If the handler turns when the dog is lined up with an off-course tunnel, the dog will likely take that tunnel.

Qualifying and Titles

The Impossible Tunnel Game is eligible for qualification for both JFF and TDAA Games. The game should be played time plus faults, using a standard course time appropriate to the level at which the dog is competing.

Variations

- **Use fewer tunnels**—If the host club doesn't have so many tunnels, it can surely be played with fewer. It's nearly as challenging with only four pipe tunnels.
- **Tunnel Tangle variation**—In this variation, other obstacles are allowed on course. The Impossible Tunnel game will be central to the course.

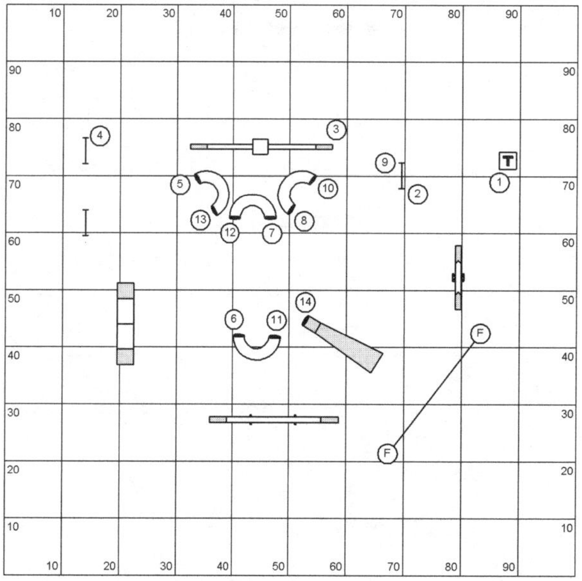

This is an example of the Tunnel Tangle variation of the Impossible Tunnel game, showing other obstacles integrated with the curve of tunnels.

in and out

Sheri Boone created In and Out to encourage handlers to think about motivation and strategy. The game is considered motivating because movement and point accumulation on a course do not stop until time runs out. The game is considered strategic for the sole purpose of accumulating points in several different ways.

Briefing

The course is divided into three different segments. The "inner" loop, the "in-and-out" loop and the "outer" loop. The dog must start with the inner loop, move to the in-and-out loop, and finish with the outer loop.

If a fault occurs during a loop, the dog must immediately restart from the first obstacle in that loop. The loop is repeated until completed without fault. Then the dog must start the next loop. The judge will call out "fault" when a dog has faulted an obstacle.

The game is scored under USDAA Master's rules. The exception is that an off-course is not elimination. The dog is faulted for dropping a jump bar, missing a contact, or going off course. Refusals are not faulted.

The standard course time will be 50 seconds. The timekeeper will blow a whistle at the end of standard course time. If the dog has not completed the course, he must be directed to the finish line to stop time.

Scoring

In and Out is scored points then time. The dog with the most points wins. Time is a tiebreaker only.

Each obstacle has an assigned point value. The system for assigning point values may be arbitrary or fixed for the technical merit of the obstacle. For example, the point system might be:

- Jumps—1 point
- Tunnels and the tire—3 points
- Contact obstacles—5 points

If the dog completes the entire course before time runs out, the difference between the dog's time and the course time becomes bonus points added to the score. All times are rounded up to the next second.

Course Design

The In and Out course is always quite a design challenge for the course designer. Any of the agility obstacles may be used in the course design. Yet, the obstacles should be layered into two essential loops, which are performed by the dog in their entirety, and can be interwoven into a unique loop in the second leg of the dog's performance of the course.

A table is typically used to start the dog.

Strategies

Points never stop accumulating. Every time an obstacle is performed correctly, points are awarded for that obstacle.

The handler should be careful not to let down because a mistake has occurred. Keep running the course until time runs out. Points continue to accumulate.

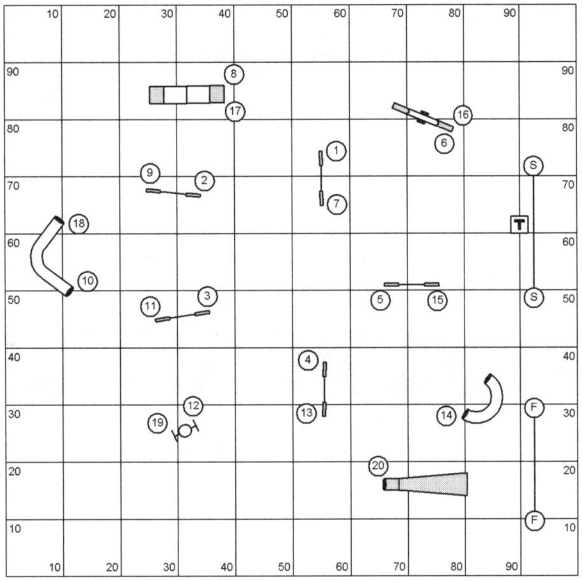

Sheri Boone designed this In and Out course, divided into three different segments: the inner loop (obstacles 1-5), the in-and-out loop (obstacles 6-15), and the outer loop (obstacles 16-20).

This game encourages handlers to push the limit. They must decide if faulting an obstacle will give them more points (because they would have the chance to repeat the same loop) or if they should run clean (bonus points for coming in under time). Note that faulting an obstacle in a loop is not advantageous in the Rukis variation.

Qualifying and Titles

In and Out is a qualifying game for both JFF and TDAA.

For TDAA courses, the standard course time for each different level should be set at a rate consistent with those specified in the TDAA rules and regulations for standard classes.

In JFF, the standard course time should be set at a rate using a rational system, such as that specified in the USDAA rules and regulations.

Variations

- **Rukis variation**—No points are awarded in a faulted loop. Allowing points to be kept within a faulted loop is a flaw of the game and could encourage bad or unsafe execution.
- **Zelinger variation**—The team may go to the table to stop the clock and end the run, thus earning the points accumulated so far. If the handler thinks he can make it around the outer loop a second time and get his dog on the table before the course time lapses, he doubles his points. If he fails, he loses all points.

jackpot

A titling game in CPE, Jackpot is the invention of Linda Eickholdt. Jackpot is intended to test the course-planning strategies of the handler and the dog's ability to work at a distance. Traditional Jackpot in CPE is much like the Gamblers class in USDAA or NADAC (see page 62) with some technical differences, but the core concept is the same. In the opening sequence, the team accumulates points, after which the team attempts a gamble, which must be completed in time, or all goes for naught Q-wise.

Briefing

Jackpot is run as a two-part course. The first part consists of the handler and dog working the course, attempting to accumulate at least the minimum required points for their level, in the stated amount of time. The end of the accumulation time is signified by the timekeeper's whistle, followed by the gamble period.

During the point-accumulation period, back-to-back performances of obstacles are allowed at any time. The following obstacles may be taken back-to-back, provided the dog makes a complete loop and approaches the obstacle in the correct direction safely: teeter, ascending broad jump, ascending double jump, triple jump, and collapsed tunnel. If the judge deems the back-to-back performance unsafe, no points will be awarded for the performance. One obstacle or combination of obstacles that is designated as judge's choice may be executed only once for the higher point value.

The handler then must send the dog to work at a distance through a series of obstacles within a time set by the judge. The handler must stay out of a designated area while the dog works within this area with only commands from the handler. The dog must execute the obstacles in the correct order, without faults, and cross the finish line within the gamble time.

No two gamble obstacles can be performed in a row in the opening sequence, forward or backward, unless the judge declares differently in his briefing. If a gamble jump bar is knocked down in the opening sequence, the gamble is null and void. The bar will not be reset.

If the judge says "Thank you" (or signals with a whistle) at any point, the team must move immediately to the finish line to stop the clock. Any delay in heading for the finish line or attempting to perform any obstacle on the way to the finish line will result in the loss of the last point value earned. The team will not lose the last point value earned if the dog takes an obstacle without handler direction. The judge's decision is final.

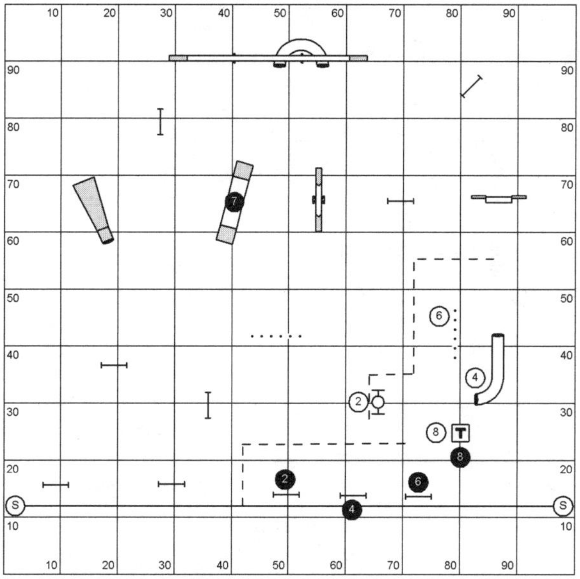

This course was designed by CPE judge Al Ceranko and played on August 18, 2001 at Ravenna, OH. The judge specified that the handler must attempt either one or the other of the two gambles after the point-accumulation period.

Scoring

When the handler and dog have earned the required accumulation points or greater, and they have performed the gamble without faults within the required time, they have earned a qualifying score.

Point Accumulation

- For 8" and 12" dogs, 40 to 45 seconds, as determined by the judge
- For 16", 20", and 24" dogs, 35 to 40 seconds, as determined by the judge

Gamble

- For 8" and 12" dogs, up to 18 seconds, as determined by the judge
- For 16", 20", and 24" dogs, up to 16 seconds, as determined by the judge

  Fractions of time are dropped for scoring purposes. The timekeeper will report time in 1/100th of a second for placement purposes.

For the purposes of point accumulation, the point values of obstacles are listed below.

- Jumps—1 point
- Tire or window jump, pipe tunnel, collapsed tunnel, weave poles (5 to 8)—3 points
- Weave poles (10 - 12, in higher levels of play), contacts—5 points
- Judge's choice, only one of the choices listed below—7 points

One or more obstacles are designated as judge's choice due to difficult placement or distance from the start line.

- Jump combo—2 to 3 jumps, single bar only
- Contact or long set of weaves
- Tire, pipe or collapsed tunnel, triple spread: If the triple is designated the judge's choice, it can only be performed once during the point accumulation for 7 points. The second time will be for the normally assigned points.

Jackpot Gamble Setup

L1 and 2	Beginning at 5', graduating to 7'-10'
L3	Beginning at 10', graduating up to 15'
L4, L5, and "C"	Beginning at 15', graduating up to 20'

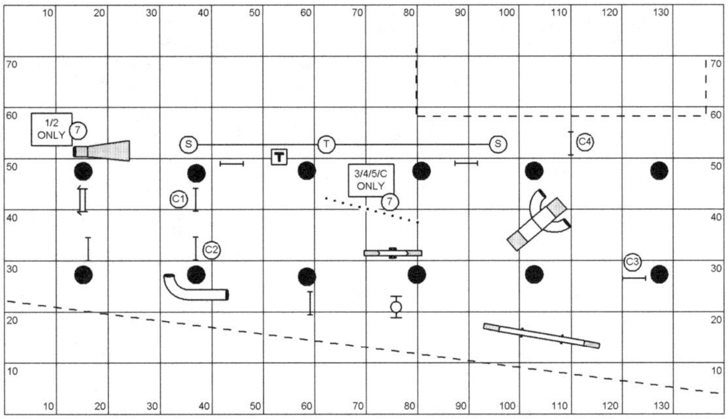

This course, designed by Al Ceranko and played at Gem City on April 7, 2001, is the 4-Corners variation of Jackpot. The judge specified that, to qualify, the dog must complete all 4 "C" jumps (gamble), earn the required points, and get his paw on the table to stop the clock before the whistle.

Obstacles in the gamble are numbered 2-4-6-8. The corresponding number of the obstacle is the value of the obstacle performed successfully by the dog.

Course Design

In CPE, one obstacle may begin the gamble at the handler restriction line. The remaining gamble obstacles must be no closer than the distances stated on the chart.

The gamble must consist of four obstacles at L4, L5, and "C" levels and include up to two dummy obstacles. The dogwalk, broad jump, or double jump, and the triple spread cannot be used as gamble obstacles.

The last obstacle of a traditional gamble must be a bar jump, a tunnel (open or closed), or the table. If the table is used as the last obstacle, the dog must place at least one paw on the table to stop the clock (this is considered the finish line). Otherwise, the finish line must be at the end of the last obstacle. If the last obstacle is a tunnel of any type, the timer stops the clock when the dog's nose exits the tunnel. If the last obstacle is a bar jump, the timer stops the clock when the dog's nose is over the bar, whether or not the bar is knocked down.

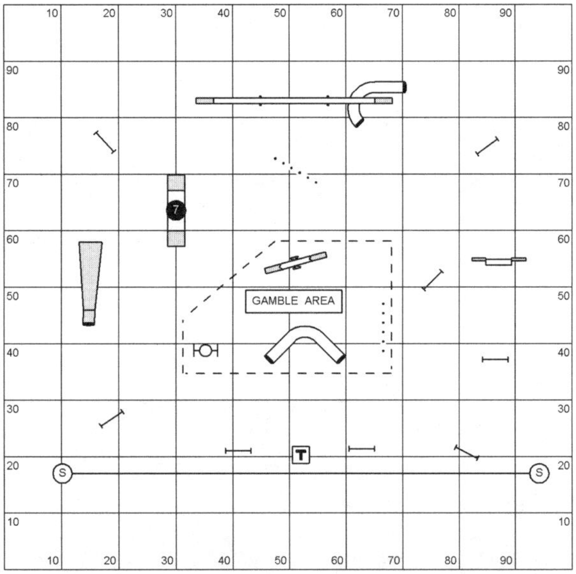

CPE judge, Al Ceranko presented this example of the Create Your Own variation of Jackpot at Tinley Park, IL on September 8, 2001. The judge stipulated that levels 4, 5, and C must complete the weave poles and one more gamble obstacle; Level 3 must complete the teeter and one more gamble obstacle; and Levels 1 and 2 must complete either the tire or the tunnel, plus one more gamble obstacle that's different from the first obstacle.

Qualifying and Titles

In CPE, each level requires successful completion of the entire gamble and a specific number of points during point accumulation for the team to qualify:

- Level 1—16 points
- Level 2—20 points
- Level 3—24 points

Variations

The CPE Jackpot game is rich with variations. Al Ceranko, a judge and course reviewer for CPE, explains the evolution of Jackpot: "Observation and experience pointed up that some exhibitors had a fear of the game, simply because it looked too difficult. Others had become disheartened because they had been unsuccessful with Gamblers in other registries so often. It seemed logical that there should be a bridge to help build or restore handler confidence and a way to teach at a trial."

In CPE, a judge may use a gamble variation in lieu of the traditional gamble. The judge will be responsible for adequately explaining the variation to the exhibitors.

- **Four-Corners variation**—No distance is involved in the gamble. Four obstacles are stipulated in "four corners" of the course, which the dog must complete at some point during point accumulation, without faulting any. The dog must get the required points in the time allotted.

  This game has a point-accumulation period, a judge's choice (in this case, different between the levels), and a gamble period, following the rules of the basic version of the game. Obstacles may be taken twice in the point-accumulation period and back-to-back if done safely, as determined by the judge. Scoring is the 1-3-5 point system with 7 points for the judge's choice.
- **Create Your Own variation**—This variation is traditional in the sense that there is a defined opening and gamble. But in the gamble, the handler must stay outside the gamble obstacle box. The judge will designate an obstacle sequence that the dog must perform and get to the table before time expires to earn the gamble points.

This game has a point-accumulation, a judge's choice, and a gamble period, following the rules of the basic version of the game. Obstacles may be taken twice in point-accumulation period and back-to-back if done safely, as determined by the judge. The four obstacles in the gamble area may be performed twice each during point accumulation, with no restrictions on sequence or order.

- **Gamblers Choice variation**—In this variation, multiple gambles will be defined on the course and there will be no traditional gamble period. The handler may direct the dog to perform any gamble at any time during point accumulation. The handler will be allowed to attempt each gamble only once. The gambles may be nested or exist in entirely different parts of the course. The dog must complete at least one of the gambles to qualify.

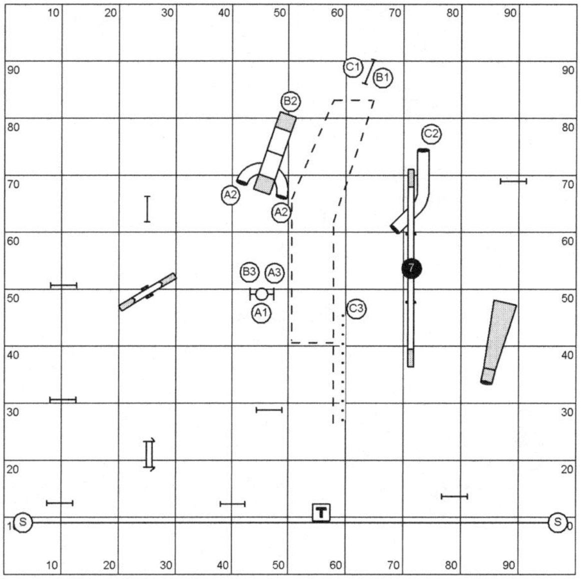

CPE judge, Mary Beam designed this Gambler's Choice variation of Jackpot, which was played on October 13, 2001. The judge stipulated that any of the gambles could be attempted at any time. If the gamble was unsuccessful, the normal points would be awarded for successfully completed obstacles. Each gamble could be attempted once and only once. Gamble obstacles could be performed back-to-back only after that gamble had been attempted. A dog had to complete at least one successful gamble to qualify.

j.c. & hazel's stand in the middle

This game is named with great affection for J.C. and Hazel Thompson who thrilled agility spectators in the early 1990s as they traveled all over the country to show their dogs, Robby and Rick Rack. J.C. would walk out into the middle of the ring, stand there, and direct his dog from a nonchalant post, remaining in the middle of the ring. The response around the ring was electric. Was this the future of agility? That hasn't turned out to be the case (dang, it's best to actually run with your dog). But for all who remember J.C. and Hazel in the early and great days of dog agility, this is a fun and playful game of verve and training, not to mention a fair dose of showing off.

Briefing

This course must be run in the order and direction specified by the judge.

The handler will confine himself to one of two containment areas. If the handler remains in the larger containment area, the dog will earn a bonus of 30 seconds. If the handler remains in the smaller containment area, the dog will earn a bonus of 60 seconds.

Scoring

This game can be scored either faults then time minus bonus, or it can be scored time plus faults minus bonus. The latter is essentially the same format as Jumplers.

Faults are assigned as follows:

- Knocked bar—5 faults
- Wrong course—5 faults
- Missed contacts—5 faults
- Failure to perform—20 faults
- Refusals are not faulted.

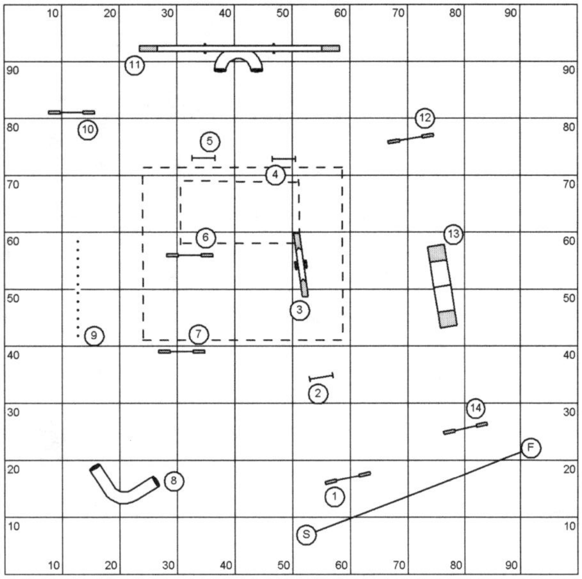

This sample is a NADAC course (author unknown).

Course Design

The course should be of simple design, something at the Open or Starters/ Novice level. It's too much to ask a dog to run the upper level courses of the AKC and the USDAA while his handler maintains a stationary post in the middle of the field.

Strategies

Buy yourself a copy of *Go the Distance* from Clean Run (www.cleanrun.com). You have to train your dog to work at a distance if you have any expectation of playing a game like this.

Qualifying and Titles

This game is eligible for qualifying games scores under both JFF and TDAA rules. The judge should try to ensure that the level of challenge is appropriate for the level of dogs in competition. Please note that a JFF qualifying run can be earned by showing under any judge, in any venue. If using the Gorilla variation, be sure to get the judge of record to sign your JFF dance card. To obtain a JFF dance card, email Bud Houston at info@dogwoodagility.com.

The Katie Duke variation is not eligible for a qualifying games score.

The Monkey in the Middle variation uses qualifying criteria that are based upon point accumulation. The number of points required really depends on the amount of time given to accumulate points as well as the number and values of obstacles on the field. In the sample course shown above, the qualifying rates were set as follows:

- Games I—18 points
- Games II—36 points
- Games III—72 points

Variations

- **Gorilla variation**—Okay, do you want to leave a NADAC or a USDAA judge confused and nonplussed? Then, try the Gorilla variation of Stand in the Middle. When you get a Novice or Open course and you don't need the leg, take up a position in the middle of the course and have yourself a game of J.C. and Hazel's Stand in the Middle. You'll either thrill the natives or have them sniggering about your lack of movement. It all depends on whether you get away with it.

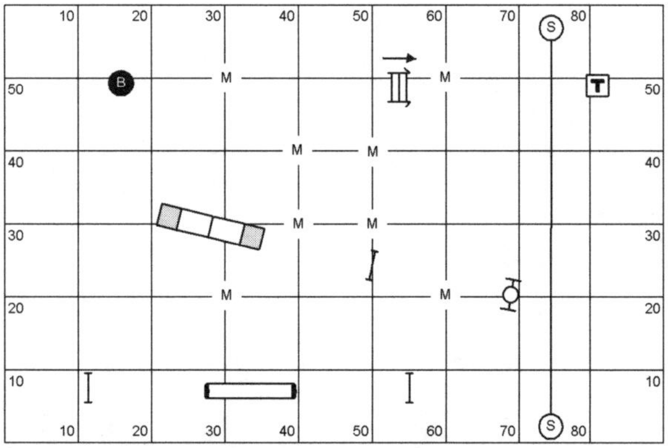

This sample Monkey in the Middle variation was played in Just For Fun League Play at Bud Houston's Dogwood Training Center. This course includes a "Barrel" obstacle. Three points were awarded for sending the dog around the barrel, in either direction. Of course, these points were doubled if the handler stayed inside the smaller containment area.

- **Katie Duke variation**—In this variation, the dog might not actually do all the obstacles on the course, or necessarily in the direction the handler is hoping. Nonetheless, the dog will earn points for each obstacle performed, whether or not the order and direction of performance coincides with what the judge intended. There are no qualifying and titling implications to this variation. The only thing the handler might win is the respect and admiration of his peers.
- **Monkey in the Middle**—In this variation, the dog will have 30 seconds to perform any of the obstacles on the field as in the point-accumulation period of a gamblers class. The dog can earn no points unless the handler is standing inside one of the two containment areas designated by the four markers on the course. If the handler is standing inside the larger containment area, the point values for obstacles shall be: jumps, 1 point; tunnel and tire, 3 points; contact obstacles and weave poles, 5 points. If the handler is standing inside of the smaller containment area, the point values are doubled. Obstacles can be taken as often as the handler (or dog, as the case might be) desires. However, back-to-back performances

are not permitted. A faulted obstacle can earn no points for the dog. If a bar drops on a jump, the jump is out of play for the duration of the dog's performance. At the end of point accumulation, the handler is required to direct his dog to the table to stop time. If the handler remains inside of the larger containment area, all points the dog has earned will be doubled. If the handler remains inside of the smaller containment area, all points will be quadrupled. The table is not active until the end of point accumulation is sounded.

jokers wild

Jokers Wild is the invention of Ken Tatsch. This version of the Gamblers game is intended for dog agility enthusiasts who have mastered the basic elements of distance work. This game has been significantly abridged from the original and simpler version and is used in agility league play.

Briefing

While Time Gamble tends to cater to newer agility handlers, Jokers Wild is exactly the opposite. Most dogs and handlers who do well in this game have mastered all the elements of standard Gamblers to a high degree.

Jokers Wild is a series of gambles that contain one or more of the four elements (distance, direction, obstacle performance, and discrimination) described in the Gamblers section of this book. Each gamble is slightly harder than the previous one.

All dogs will run under a maximum performance time of 60 seconds. Fifteen seconds should be allotted for each gamble. A simple point value is assigned to each gamble when completed in its entirety.

- A gamble—10 points in 15 seconds or less
- B gamble—20 points in 30 seconds or less
- C gamble—30 points in 45 seconds or less
- D gamble—40 points in 60 seconds or less

A dog must successfully complete a gamble within the set time to go on to the next higher (and more difficult) gamble. Dogs that do not complete the gamble are eliminated, and the handler must direct the dog to the table or finish line to stop time. Faulting any obstacle in the gamble (knocked bars and missed contacts) will be counted a failure.

A handler and dog continue on the course, going from gamble to gamble, until they either complete the entire course successfully or fail a gamble attempt and are eliminated.

Since Jokers Wild requires distance and obstacle control, most new handlers can be eliminated quickly. Thus, this particular game should be reserved for more advanced dogs and handlers.

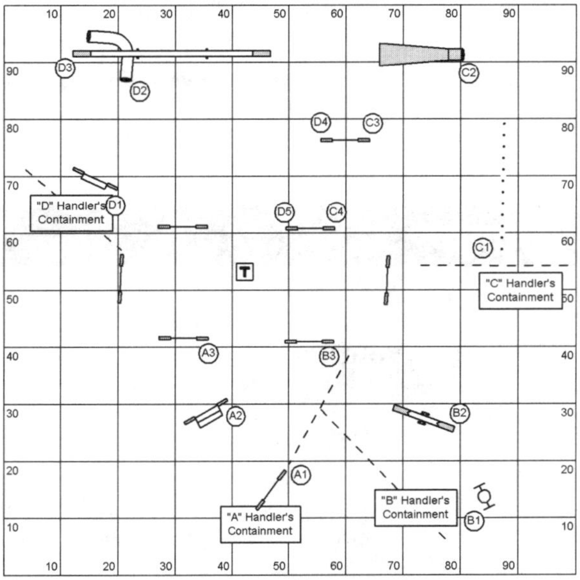

This advanced Jokers Wild course is for competition at the Masters level only. Each of the four distance challenges here keeps the handler back in a flat-footed position with little to direct the dog other than verbal commands.

Scoring

The winner of Jokers Wild is the dog that completes the most advanced gamble in its entirety in the fastest time.

Course Design

The Jokers Wild course should be designed with a progressively more difficult series of distance challenges. The handlers' containment line for each should be clearly marked. The table should be positioned somewhat centrally to all the distance challenges on course, since it will be used to stop time if the dog fails in any one of the jokers.

Strategies

It might be true that a good distance-training program is the only reasonable means to prepare for a game like this, particularly if the handler is required to stand flat-footed at a predetermined handling point and send the dog away to work.

However, if the course and the judge allow it, the distance challenges should be approached wherever possible with the handler working in a smooth, flowing path. At all costs, avoid standing, pointing, and sending. Dogs react much better to movements than to voice commands.

Qualifying and Titles

Jokers Wild is a qualifying game for both JFF and TDAA. For each, the qualifying requirements are:

- Games I—A gamble
- Games II—B gamble
- Games III—C or D gamble

The judge should be careful to design Gamblers challenges appropriate to the experience and competition level of the class.

Variations

- **Progressive Gamblers**—This variation of Jokers Wild can be used in training. Initially, a very simple gamble is attempted. With successful completion of the first gamble, a second gamble is attempted. The second gamble uses the first gamble as a basis, adding another obstacle. Beginning dogs tend to have more success at this form of Jokers Wild since the dog will key partly on a previously performed gamble. In essence, part of the gamble can be pattern-trained.
- **League Play variation**—Each distance challenge on the course is assigned a point value based on its complexity. Unlike the standard Jokers Wild game, the dog's turn does not end if the handler fails an early distance challenge; he gets the opportunity to try the next one. The dog and handler with the most distance challenge points win.

jump

The game JUMP is like the old version of HORSE in basketball, an elimination game in which failures earn the player a letter beginning with "H". Any player who earns all five letters is "out." JUMP may be a game of distance, of style, or of sequencing. JUMP is the invention of Terri Everline who trains in northwest Illinois with two agility schools, BC Dog Training and Meyer's Kennel

Briefing

A running order is created by random draw. The first "shooter" must declare the sequence or challenge then run it with his dog. If successful, each competitor in turn takes a shot at the sequence. The shooter may incorporate a specific handling movement or some other challenge.

Scoring

If the shooter fails when demonstrating the sequence, the dog-and-handler team earns a letter in JUMP. Failure is when the dog goes off course, faults an obstacle, or fails to meet some other stipulation of the original shooter. Another team is designated as shooter to declare a new challenge and must attempt the declared challenge.

If any team fails in attempting the shooter's challenge, the team earns a letter in JUMP.

If each team is successful at the sequence, then the next player in the original random draw gets to be the shooter and set the next challenge for the players. The game continues until only one player is left who has not spelled the word JUMP and is declared the winner.

Course Design

Almost any set of equipment can be used for JUMP, since it is a freestyle game limited only by the imagination of the participants.

Participants may rearrange obstacles to state their challenge for the group.

Strategies

The handler should be very aware of his dog's capabilities. The key to winning the game might be to make the most effective use of your turn and do something you know you can't fail at, yet is challenging enough to cause others in the field to earn letters.

Variations

- **Game length**—The game can be adapted in several ways to lengthen the play or shorten it. For example, if a team is the only team to complete the sequence, then they'll get to take off a letter. This would possibly lengthen the game. The game could be played with all distance challenges, which would surely shorten the game.
- **Who gets the penalty**—If the shooter cannot demonstrate the sequence correctly, then everyone else gets to take off a letter. This would also lengthen the game.
- **Large groups**—When the field of competitors is quite large, it probably should be broken down into smaller groups of five or six. The importance of breaking up the group is to keep handlers from failing before they've even had an opportunity to make up a challenge for the group. After the first round, when each group has had a winner, the winners of each group would be combined into a single group to determine the ultimate winner.

jumpers

The Jumpers class measures a dog's ability to jump and turn, and the handler's ability to exert control and timing in this fast-paced version of the agility game. Though the dog only needs to learn to jump to begin competing, Jumpers is one of the most difficult games to perfect, since dogs move at a much greater speed than in other classes.

Briefing

Jumpers courses consist only of hurdles and tunnels, with some limitations between the different venues. The dog is required to run the course in the sequence indicated by the judge.

Off-courses and knocked bars are always faulted.

Scoring

Jumpers is usually scored faults then time, the winner being the dog with the fewest faults. If two dogs have the same number of faults, then time breaks the tie.

Jumpers can be scored time plus faults (in USDAA Starters and Novice and in the USDAA DAM tournament). The winner would be the dog with the lowest score.

Faults are assessed for several performance errors. Time faults are assessed on a 1:1 basis. The table opposite summarizes performance faults for Jumpers.

Jumpers Faults Chart

Performance Faults	NADAC	USDAA Starters and Novice	USDAA Advanced	USDAA Masters
Displaced bar	5	5	5	5
Refusal	N/F	N/F	N/F	5
Off-course	10	5	20	E
Failure to perform	20	20	E	E
Touching the dog or obstacle	N/F to E	5 to E	5 to E	5 to E
Collar on the dog	E	E	E	E
Banking†	N/A	5	5	5
Touching the long jump	N/A	5	5	5

† *Banking occurs when the dog pushes off on wall jumps or the wishing well. Touching the aperture of the tire is not faulted.*

E = elimination

N/F = not faulted

Course Design

Only tunnels and hurdles may be used on the course.

As the level of competition rises, so does the complexity of the course, but the standard course time decreases.

USDAA requires a triple spread-hurdle and two performances of the double spread-hurdle (which may be the same obstacle performed twice).

NADAC does not allow double or triple jumps and does not have a broad jump. In NADAC, tunnels may be used two times in Novice, one time in Open, and not at all in Elite, although they may be set as dummy obstacles for handling challenges.

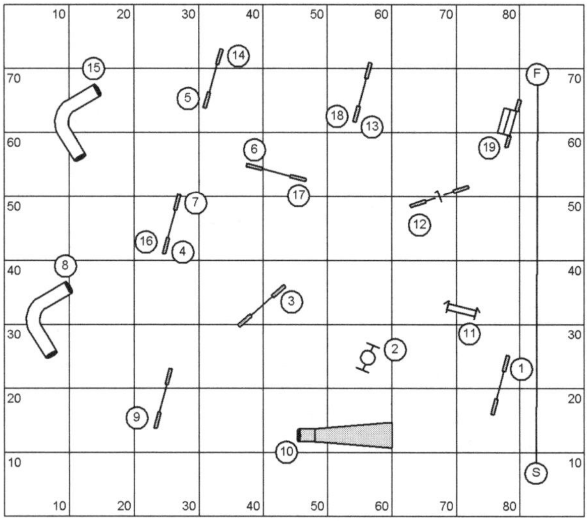

This is an example of a USDAA Masters course.

Strategies

Since only jumps and tunnels (where allowed) are used, Jumpers courses tend to be more difficult for handlers to memorize than other types of courses. To be successful in Jumpers, it is more important than ever to remember course flow and sequences rather than individual obstacles.

Also, body positioning and body language become even more important in controlling the dog on Jumpers courses. After all, a command to jump may mean any one of several jumps that the dog is looking at. Thus, handlers should make attempts to tidy up movement and body language.

The most common faults in Jumpers are wrong courses and (in USDAA Masters) refusals. Thus, the handlers should consider carefully approaches, angles, and distances to obstacles during the course walk-through. Jumpers courses tend to be tighter and more closely spaced than standard courses, requiring quicker reactions by the handler and the dog.

The key strategy for Jumpers is to train the dog to jump and to be responsive to handling in fast, flowing situations.

Qualifying and Titles

Both USDAA and NADAC offer titles for Jumpers. NADAC offers Jumpers titles at each level from Novice to Elite. The USDAA offers a Jumpers title only at the Masters level.

USDAA Jumpers YPS*

	Advanced	Masters
Mini	3.00-3.75 yps	3.00-4.00 yps
Open	3.50-4.00 yps	3.50-4.25 yps

USDAA

At present, Starters/Novice Jumpers is for experience and fun and does not count toward qualifying for titles. In Advanced Jumpers, however, a dog-and-handler team can earn the right to move up to the Masters Jumpers class by achieving two qualifying scores at the Advanced level. In Masters Jumpers, the team can begin earning the five qualifying scores required for the Jumpers Master title. As we go to press, the USDAA is in the process of revamping its titling process in both the Championship and the Performance Programs, making it possible for dogs to earn games titles at all levels, not just Masters. Please consult www.usdaa.com for updates.

To earn a qualifying score, a dog must be under the standard course time and without course faults. The chart at left presents course rates for a dog to qualify in Advanced or Masters.

NADAC Jumpers YPS*

	Large 20" and 20"+	Medium 16"	Small 8" and 12"
Elite	5.00	4.75	4.5
Open	4.5	4.25	4.00
Novice	4.00	3.75	3.50

**YPS = yards per second*

NADAC

To qualify in Jumpers, the dog is required to run under the standard course time specified by the judge with no course faults. The chart at left lists course rates for qualifying at each level.

For small dogs, courses less than 160 yards have 5 seconds added to the time, and 8 seconds are added for distances over 160 yards.

JFF and TDAA

Jumpers is a qualifying game for titling for both JFF and TDAA. In determining a TDAA qualifying score, the judge should measure the dog's path and base the score for each level of games on the yards per second specified in the TDAA rules and regulations.

In JFF, the game would be judged faults and then time. No standard course time would be used, and placement would be based on faults then time.

Variations

- **USDAA Dog Agility Masters® (DAM) tournament Jumpers**—The format for DAM Jumpers is different from the Jumpers played in USDAA titling classes: 1) weave poles are often included; 2) a refusal is penalized 2 points; and 3) the scoring system is time plus faults.

- **Land Rover Drive**—This game, also known as Jump and Drive, is perhaps a historical footnote. The Land Rover Drive and Jumping contest grew out of the sponsorship by Land Rover for agility trials in the U.K. The handler loads his dog into a Land Rover, drives a designated course, parks the vehicle in a garage, and then jumps out to run his dog over a Jumpers course. The judge will designate the starting point for the Land Rover, the path of the vehicle, and the garage where the vehicle must be parked. Dog and handler (and the course clock) start on foot across a starting line designated by the judge.
- **Black and Whites**—This British variation is Jumpers for black and white border collies only (or black and white dogs with any hint of border collie in them).
- **USDAA Starters/Novice**—At this level, Jumpers is usually scored on a time-plus-faults basis and, currently does not count toward qualifying for titles, but this is in the process of being changed. Please consult www.usdaa.com for updates.

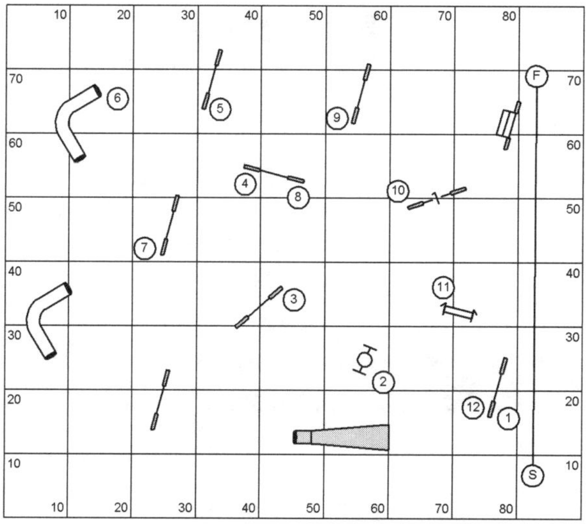

This Beginners course nests perfectly with the Masters course on the opposite page. In NADAC and JFF, competitors of all different levels often compete on the same course—only the numbers change. This setup tends to allow more "dummy" obstacles on a course than one would usually find but also enables a certain course-building economy.

jumpers cds (call, direct, send)

Jumpers CDS is a curious combination of a Jumpers course and a Gamblers course. This unique AKC game is the invention of Will Koukkari and Sharon Anderson. It tests the dog and handler in several distance challenges. Jumpers CDS was once considered by the AKC as a "distance" game that might have become a part of the suite of titling games required by the AKC, but this game was abandoned. The AKC might have wondered that, if a USDAA judge can skunk a field of exhibitors with one distance challenge, what could an AKC judge do with three?

Briefing

In Jumpers CDS, a handler must call, direct, and send his dog to perform three series of obstacles. The three separate distance challenges in this game include: a call over one to three obstacles, a direct or mid-course distance challenge of two to five obstacles, and a send portion over two to three obstacles to close out the game. The complexity of each distance challenge depends on the level at which the dog is competing.

In Jumpers CDS, boundaries are drawn to indicate an area into which the handler may not advance while the dog performs obstacles at a distance. If the handler steps on or over any containment line while the dog is performing the indicated obstacles, the dog will earn a failure to perform.

Call—The Call is a lead-out at the start line, requiring the handler to call the dog over the opening obstacles. During this portion of the course, the dog is placed on a wait at the beginning of the course while the handler leads out to a point on the course designated by the judge. The handler must then call the dog over the initial obstacles and continue on course.

Direct—The Direct is a mid-course gamble sequence of two to four obstacles that the dog must perform at a distance, usually parallel to the handler. The handler must direct the dog over the sequence of obstacles without crossing a containment line indicated by the judge. Once the dog has finished the Direct portion of the course, the dog and handler can continue.

Send—The final sequence for the course is the Send. In this challenge, the objective is to see if the dog will go away or send over a series of obstacles at the end of the course. The handler must not cross the containment line indicated by the judge.

Scoring

Jumpers CDS is scored points then time. The team with the highest score wins.

Scoring is based upon a 100-point system, 100 being perfect. Faults are subtracted from the 100 points. 85 points are required to qualify. Time is used as a tiebreaker.

Faults will be scored as follows:

- Each refusal is faulted 5 points. In the Novice class, three refusals will be scored elimination. In the Open class, two refusals will be scored elimination. In the Excellent class, one refusal will be scored elimination. (Note: An improper entry or missed weave pole in AKC is scored a refusal).
- Each off-course is faulted 5 points. Three off-courses in any class will be scored elimination.
- A knocked bar is scored elimination.
- Failure to perform any obstacle is scored elimination.
- Failure to perform any of the three distance elements (Call, Direct, or Send) will be scored elimination. This includes stepping on or crossing the containment line.

Scoring for all other areas is consistent with the basic agility classes.

Standard course times are set according to the yards-per-second requirements at left.

Jumpers CDS YPS

Class	Small Dogs	Large Dogs
Novice	2.00	2.00
Open	2.50	3.00
Excellent	2.75	3.50

Course Design

The basic Jumpers CDS course includes jumps, tunnels, and except for the Novice agility class, one set of weave poles. The contact obstacles are not used. The course must have a well-defined start line, a finish line, and three boundary lines from which a handler works apart from his dog to perform the specific sequences of obstacles. The broad jump is not allowed in any class. Weave poles and the triple bar jump are not allowed in the Novice class. Besides single bar jumps, each course should include the tire, double bar jump, collapsed tunnel, and one to three pipe tunnels.

Both Open and Excellent level courses include 17 to 20 obstacles. Weave poles should not be used for the last obstacle. A Novice course has 13 to 16 obstacles.

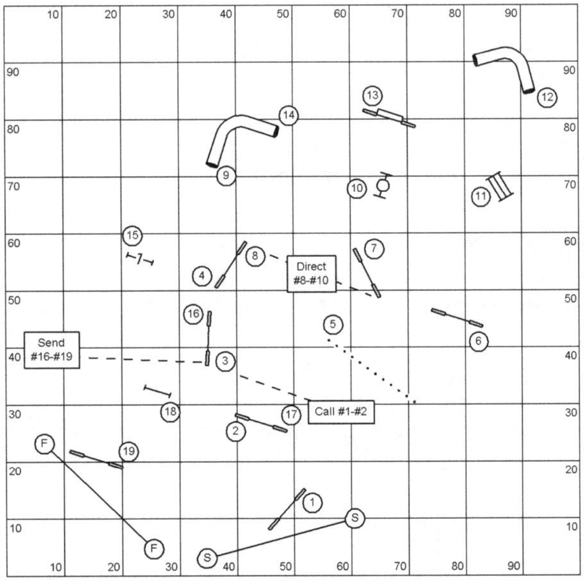

This sample Jumpers CDS course is based on an Excellent JWW course designed by AKC judge Melinda Harvey at Oriole DTC on April 18, 1999.

The CDS sequences are progressively more difficult from Novice to Open to Excellent.

- **Call**—The distance between dog and handler at the start depends on the level of the course. In Novice, the call portion might be only one jump, whereas an Excellent course may have up to a four-jump call.
- **Direct**—A Novice course might include a jump to a tunnel and then a recall over a jump, whereas in an Excellent course, the dog might have to perform a three-jump pinwheel or serpentine before coming back to the handler.
- **Send**—As with the call and direct portions of the course, the distance and difficulty depends on the level of the course. Excellent sequences are longer than Novice ones.

Qualifying and Titles

Jumpers CDS is a qualifying game for titling for both JFF and TDAA. For each, the qualifying requirements should be based upon completion of the course in a reasonable standard course time for a Jumpers class.

In JFF, there will be no stipulation that a dog be eliminated for failing any one of the three distance challenges. Instead, the dog will earn a bonus for each completed distance challenge, which affects placements only. The game should be scored time plus faults, minus bonuses earned. The dog qualifies so long as the total score is less than the stipulated standard course time. The judge can stipulate either AKC or USDAA rates of travel to determine the standard course times to be used for the game. However, faults will be assessed according to the JFF schedule of faults.

In TDAA competition, there will be no stipulation that a dog is eliminated for failing any one of the three distance challenges. Instead, the dog will earn a bonus for each element it completes successfully, which affects placement only. The game should be scored time plus faults, minus bonuses earned. The dog qualifies so long as the total score is less than the stipulated standard course time, using rates of travel defined in the TDAA rules and regulations. Faults will be assessed according to the TDAA schedule of faults.

Variations

- **CDS Technical Obstacles variation**—Call, Direct, and Send can be run on a standard course using the technical obstacles (contact obstacles and weave poles).

jumpers with weaves

Jumpers with Weaves (JWW) was conceived as a result of the AKC's participation in international agility during the Agility World Championships. AKC adopted the game as a competitive forum for the international style of agility that prepares handlers for competition anywhere in the world. This game provides the AKC with the means to select future teams for the Agility World Championships.

This game differs from the USDAA's Jumpers class only by use of weave poles in a Jumpers course, hence the unwieldy name. The use of weave poles in Jumpers is widely accepted in international-style agility but is resisted in the USDAA.

Briefing

This class is intended to be an enjoyable yet competitive way to demonstrate a working relationship between dog and handler. In this class, dogs are not slowed down by the careful performance of contact obstacles and can race through a course composed primarily of jumps as fast as economy of handling and movement will allow.

The dog is required to run the course at the handler's direction in the sequence indicated by the judge. A standard course time will be observed.

Scoring

Jumpers with Weaves is scored faults then time. The maximum possible score is 100 points. To earn a qualifying score, a dog must achieve the minimum allowable score required for each level with no non-qualifying deductions (chiefly refusals, see chart at right). Course time deductions are calculated after rounding down any fractions of a second. A dog that reaches 1.5 times the course time cannot qualify and will be excused. The standard yards-per-second rates for AKC are summarized at right.

Scoring is similar to international-style jumpers:

- Refusals—5 faults each
- Wrong course—Elimination
- Knocked bar—Elimination
- Intentional or beneficial handler contact—Elimination

JWW Course Faults

Level	Time Deductions	Refusals Allowed
Novice	1 pt/second	2, 5 faults each*
Open	2 pts/second	1, 5 faults
Excellent A	3 pts/second**	0

* *In the Novice class, refusals will not be faulted regarding the approach and the performance of the weave poles; however, the dog must successfully complete the obstacle.*

** *Excellent B does not allow time faults.*

JWW YPS

YPS	Novice	Open	Excellent
8" - 12" (maximum)	2.50	3.00	3.25 (52 sec)
16" (maximum)	2.75	3.25	3.50 (50 sec)
20" - 24" (maximum)	3.00	3.50	3.75 (48 sec)

Course Design

The course setup for Jumpers with Weaves is similar in every respect to regular Jumpers with the addition of the weave poles.

The course should be designed to test a dog's ability to run, jump, weave, and maneuver at a fast pace under the direction of the handler. The complexity of the course should match the level of competition.

JWW Obstacles

	Novice	Open	Excel.
Weaves, 1 set, performed once	R(1)6	R (1)6-12	R (1)9-12
Open Tunnel	A(3)	A(3)	A(3)
Closed Tunnel	A(2)	A(2)	A(2)
Bar Jump	R	R	R
Double Bar jump	R(1)	R(1)	R(1)
Panel Jump	A	A	A
Tire/Window	A	A	A
Broad Jump	A(1)	A(1) *	A(1)
Triple Bar	N	A(1)*	R(1)
One-Bar Jump	N	A	R
# OBSTACLES	13 - 15	16 - 18	18 - 20
Approach angles	90° 135° (2)	135° 180° (2)	180° 270° (2)

R = required A = allowed N = not allowed
** A minimum of 2 different and a maximum of 3 spreads must be used.*
In all Open classes, either the broad jump or the triple jump must be used.

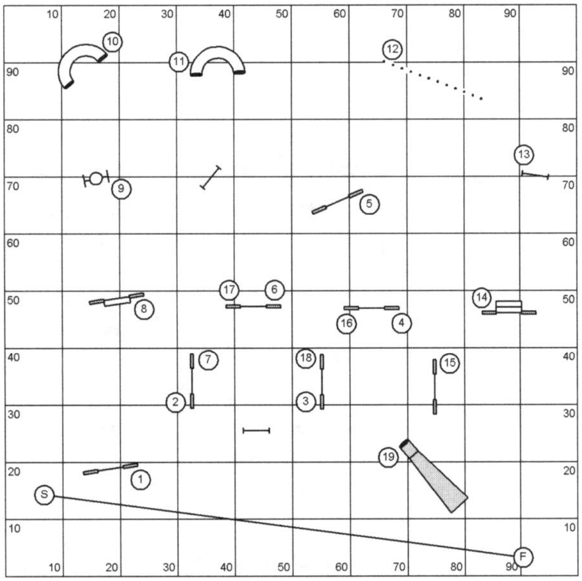

This is an Excellent JWW course designed by AKC judge Denise Thomas for play at the Sheltie Club of Baltimore on July 25, 1998.

Obstacle spacing may be varied to provide challenges and interest, although the normal spacing between obstacles should be 18' to 21'

Qualifying and Titles

AKC

The AKC awards the following titles for Jumpers with Weaves:

- Novice A or B .... NAJ .... 3 legs, each with score of 85 or better
- Open .... OAJ .... 3 legs, each with score of 85 or better
- Excellent A .... AXJ .... 3 legs, each with score of 85 or better
- Excellent B .... MXJ .... 10 legs, each with score of 100

At least two of the qualifying scores must be under two different judges.

TDAA

Both JWW and JWW Plus (see variations, below) are eligible as qualifying games under TDAA rules. The game should be scored time plus faults as stipulated in the TDAA rules and regulations. When using this game as a TDAA qualifier, a baseline for the standard course time should be established by the judge that reflects the yards per second in the respective standard level classes of the competing dogs.

- Games I—score of 90 or better
- Games II—score of 95 or better
- Games III—score of 100

JFF

Both JWW and JWW Plus (see variations, below) are eligible as qualifying games under JFF rules. No standard course time is set, and the game is played faults then time. Faults will be assessed according to the JFF schedule of faults. Courses typically will be leveled and nested so those competitors at different levels can compete on the same course.

Variations

- **JWW Plus Variation** is the invention of Ilze Rukis who designed the game in 2003 for a Teacup Dogs Agility Association trial in Decatur, Illinois, where it was played for the first time. In this variation, the course may consist of tunnels, jumps, and two to three sets of 6-pole and 12-pole weaves. Unlike the AKC's JWW, where the weaves are taken only once, in this variation, the weaves may be presented to the dog two to four times.

  In the JWW Plus Variation, exhibitors start with 100 points. A 5-point fault deduction occurs upon any of these events: dropped bar on a jump, missed or "popped" weave poles, or wrong course. One-point time faults will be assessed for each second over standard course time. No penalty is assessed for multiple tries at a correct entry into the weave poles and scoring of the weaves will begin only after the dog has made a correct entry. All weaves must be completed in order to earn a qualifying score.

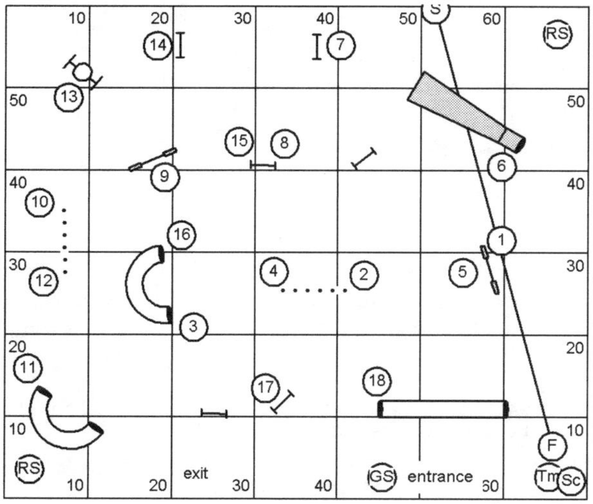

The sample course is a Jumpers with Weaves Plus Superior course designed for play at Decatur Dog Training Club April 12, 2003 by Ilze Rukis, Judge.

jumplers

Take a little bit of Jumpers, add a little bit of Gamblers… shake it up, and you've got Jumplers. Always guaranteed fun at a trial, this game marries speed and jumping to distance work

Briefing

A Jumplers course must be run in the sequence specified by the judge. The dog will earn bonuses for successfully performing distance challenges. These bonuses will be deducted from the dog's total score.

The judge will specify a containment area. The handler will have the option of remaining inside the containment area throughout the dog's run or remaining outside. The course will be balanced so that either option is equally challenging. Should the handler leave containment at any time during the dog's run, the bonus subtraction of points from the total score will be lost.

There is no penalty for not attempting the distance challenges. The handler may opt to run portions of the course, or the entire course, as a straightforward Jumpers round.

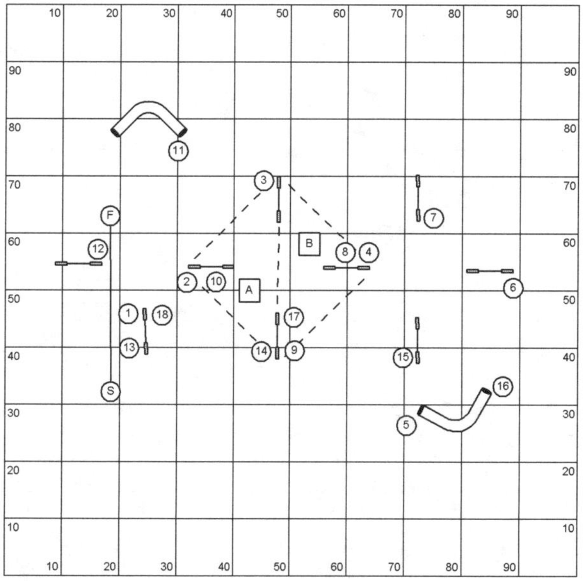

The course consists only of jumps and tunnels. As the level of competition rises, so does the complexity of the course and the difficulty of the distance challenges presented.

Scoring

Jumplers is scored time plus faults, minus bonus. The team with the lowest score wins. In an Advanced class, faults are based on USDAA Advanced rules. In a Novice class, faults are based on USDAA Starters/Novice rules. This is significant particularly for off-courses. Under Starters/Novice rules, an off-course is only 5 faults while under Advanced rules an off-course is 20 faults.

Each failure to perform should be faulted 20 points, with no stipulation that the dog be eliminated.

Course Design

The Jumplers course will include only those obstacles typically found in a Jumpers course or a Jumpers with Weaves course, though there is no list of required obstacles. The handlers' containment area should be fairly large and

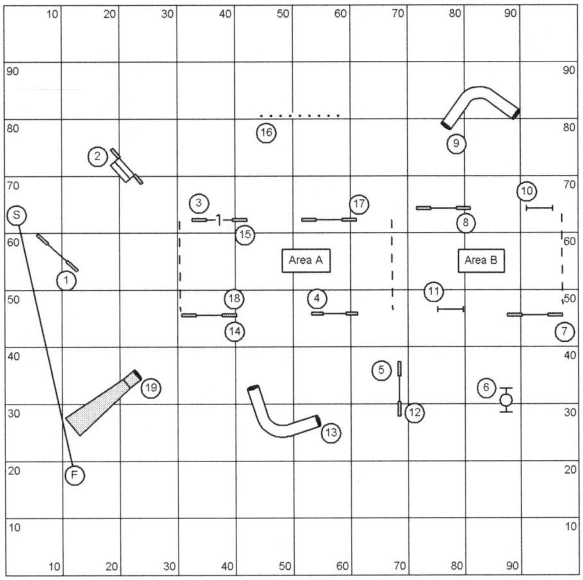

This advanced course was based on an original Jumplers course by USDAA judge, Dan Dege, and was run in league play at Dogwood Training Center in Ostrander, Ohio, on June 17, 2002. A 30-point deduction was specified if a handler stayed either completely outside or completely inside the containment area at the center. A 60-point deduction was specified if the handler stayed inside one of the two smaller areas, "A" or "B" that make up the big containment area. Staying inside a smaller box significantly increases the difficulty of the distance challenge.

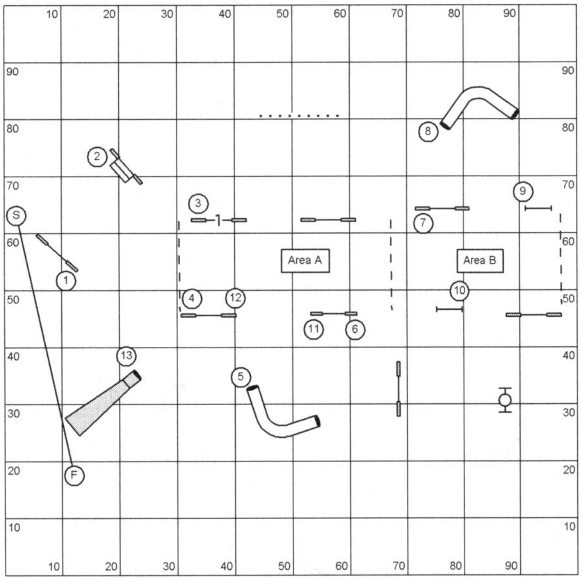

Based on the more advanced course shown in the previous example, this nested, simpler Jumplers course is more appropriate to the Novice skill level. The distance bonus is completely challenging at either level.

defined by an arrangement of jumps. This box should be easily divisible into two separate, clearly marked containment areas.

Note: The finish line is placed so that the dog must cross the line on the completion of the final obstacle. It is not fair to dogs to be sent away to an "imaginary" line that is not shaped by the invitation of an obstacle to be performed.

Strategies

When running in a league play format, the Jumplers course is a real dilemma for the competitor. If the handler doesn't think his dog will do the work at a distance, it's probably a better idea to just run the Jumpers course without even attempting the distance challenges. If the distance work goes wrong, the dog is unlikely to be able to place.

It is likely that the dog that completes the course while the handler stands in a containment area will be the one that actually wins. If more than a few dogs manage to work the course at a distance and win a bonus, then the strategy for not running the course at a distance has backfired.

The handler must also consider whether he should do the right thing by his team. Conservatively running the course as a Jumpers course will be respectable. Crashing and burning on the distance send may cause the entire team to fail. On the other hand, working at a distance and earning the bonus will likely put the team in a winning position.

Qualifying and Titles

Jumplers is a qualifying game for titling for both JFF and TDAA. For each, the qualifying requirements should be based upon a reasonable standard course time for a Jumpers class. There shouldn't be any stipulation that the handler will have to work the entire course from the containment area. This is an option for the intrepid (or crazy) individual, who will gamble everything for the elusive win.

In JFF, a course of 140 yards might establish qualifying criteria like this:

- Games I = Novice course—score of 50 or lower
- Games II = Advanced course—score of 40 or lower
- Games III = Advanced course—score of 35 or lower

Note that this is based on nested Novice and Advanced competition courses.

Variations

- **High-Stakes Jumplers**— a variation on standard Jumplers invented by Tara Choate from Portland, Oregon. The dog will have 60 seconds to accumulate as many points as possible. Points are distributed according to the numbers on the course. Points will be doubled for sequences completed while the handler is behind the line. Each sequence can be handled behind/inside the box or "with" your dog.

  High-Stakes Jumpers is scored points, then time. Qualifying score is 210 points (that is the total for completing the entire course outside the box plus 20 points). If you knock a bar, your points for that obstacle are removed from the score, but you can still get double for the obstacles your dog successfully completed while you were in the box.

The High-Stakes Variation of Jumplers is consistent with the traditional Jumplers game. A central area on course should be set aside as a contiguous containment area from which the handler can manage the movement of his dog throughout the course.

High Stakes Jumplers Score Sheet

Sequence	Doubled?		Points
1-2	Yes	No	___ 3 6
3-4-5-6	Yes	No	___ 18 36
7-8-9-10-11-12	Yes	No	___ 57 114
13-14-15-16	Yes	No	___ 58 116
17	Yes	No	___ 17 34
18-19	Yes	No	___ 37 74
		Total	

Please note: The scribe would circle the number the dog scores and "Yes" or "Doubled?" as the judge calls it. If an obstacle were faulted, the judge would not award the points.

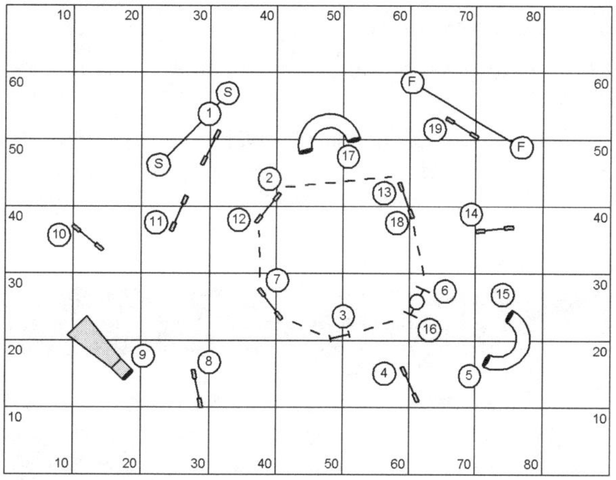

This is an example of a course designed for the High-Stakes Variation of Jumplers for play in the TDAA. Note that obstacles are placed considerably closer together for the teacup dogs. In other venues, the spacing between obstacles should be more generous.

junnel

The invention of Adra McCleskey, a founding member of Phoenix, Arizona's Jumping Cholla, Junnel is a simple game suited for a training night exercise or a club picnic.

Briefing

The dog is required to perform a jumping sequence and a tunnel.

If the dog knocks down a bar at any point, the handler must put the dog on the table and replace the bar. The dog may then continue on course at the faulted jump. The judge may require a specific performance on the table (down or sit).

If a dog goes off course, the handler will be instructed to start the entire course from the beginning.

The course must be performed in the following manner:

- Jump #1
- Backjump #1
- Jump #1 then #2
- Backjump #2, then #1
- Jump #1, #2, then #3
- Backjump #3, #2, then #1
- Jump #1, #2, #3, tunnel, #3, #2, #1

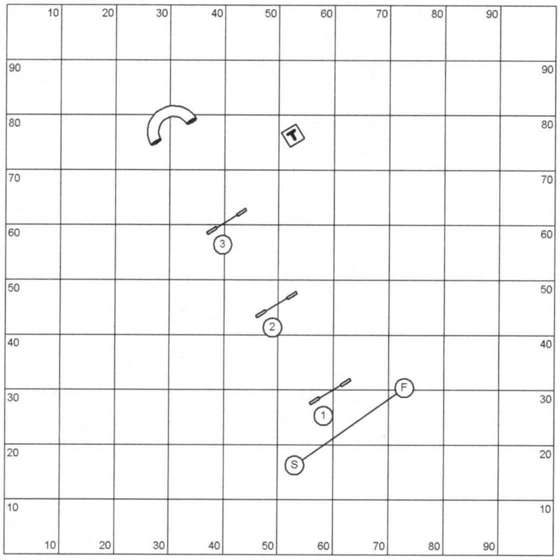

This is a simple representation of a Junnel course, showing all obstacles within easy reach of the table.

Scoring

Junnel is scored time only, since the time required to fix faults and complete the course correctly is penalty enough. The dog with the lowest time wins.

Since an off-course results in the handler restarting the course, a maximum course time should be observed.

Course Design

Three jumps, a tunnel, and a table are required. The course design should be compact with all obstacles within easy reach of the table.

Aside from the arduous course flow, Junnel isn't much different from standard Jumpers. What makes the game different is the correction that the handler must make if a jump bar is knocked down. With that in mind, it probably wouldn't be much of a stretch to designate almost any equally arduous jump and tunnel sequence, so long as the table is featured central to the obstacles used.

just in time

Just in Time is the invention of Bud and Marsha Houston as a training game for Gamblers, a popular game in USDAA and NADAC. The idea for the game came from a student who asked for training help with strategies for Gamblers. This game is intended to teach students an important Gamblers skill, making the approach to the start of a gamble in a timely fashion. This game was first played at Dogwood in March 2002.

Briefing

The objective of this game is to arrive at the table as quickly as possible after the point-accumulation period expires.

Just in Time is identical to the point-accumulation period of USDAA Gamblers. The dog has precisely 30 seconds to score points before the whistle blows. This is a "dog's choice" game. The dog can perform obstacles in the order and direction of his choosing (one would hope, with some collaboration from the handler).

If the dog arrives at the table before the 30-second whistle, time stops and no time bonus can be earned.

Obstacles can be performed only twice for points. Back-to-back performances are permitted.

Scoring

Just in Time is scored points then time.

The points system is 1-3-5.

- Jumps—1 point
- Tunnels and the short set of weave poles—3 points
- The dogwalk and teeter—5 points

Unproductive loitering near the table is not permitted and will result in loss of time bonus points.

The dog will earn a time bonus for getting to the table or the finish line after the end of the 30-second point-accumulation period.

- Less than 2 seconds—30 bonus points
- Less than 4 seconds—20 bonus points
- Less than 6 seconds—10 bonus points

Course Design

As with the typical Gamblers course, the Just in Time course should be designed with the obstacles set with no discernable flow. The table is the designated time-stopper and may be placed anywhere on course, but probably should be placed in a manner that allows a timely departure from the course by each competitor.

Strategies

The idea of "strategy" in a game can be unnerving to some competitors. Since this game is intended to introduce students to an essential strategy for Gamblers, it's worth mentioning that strategy here. In a Gamblers class, with limited time allotted for completing the gamble, it pays for the handler to be near the start of the joker rather than entirely across the field when the whistle blows.

The more *intrepid* strategy will be the "no guts, no glory" strategy: Don't wait for the whistle. The handler must time the send of the dog to the table, considering the time to travel to the table, such that the dog arrives just after the 30-second whistle to earn the maximum possible points.

On the other hand, in this game the handler loses all if the dog actually gets to the table before the whistle blows to end the point-accumulation period. In a league play scenario, the competitor should consider what's best for the team before embarking on the no guts, no glory strategy. The rest of Bud's team also attempted this strategy and all failed. Therefore, Bud's team went down the tubes in the competition, though Bud's dog Bogie did earn high MVP (most valuable puppy) honors for the week.

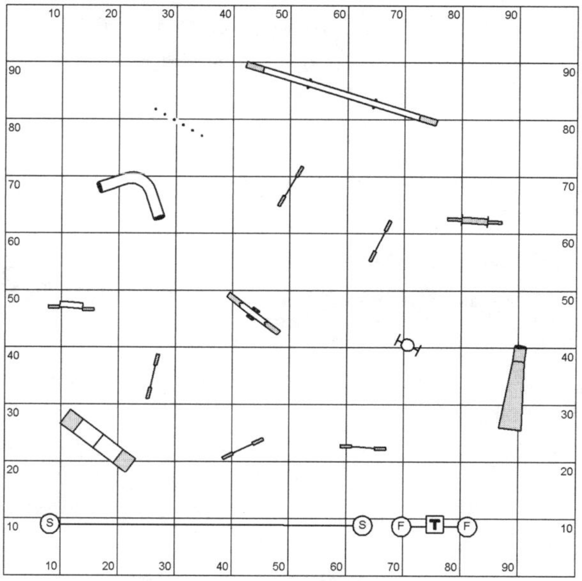

In this Just In Time Course, the judge has designated the table the "time-stopper." Just In Time lends itself to nearly any setting of obstacles with only minor movement of equipment.

Qualifying and Titles

Just in Time is an eligible game for titling in both JFF and TDAA.

The dog must earn 21 points in the opening and earn a time bonus to qualify.

- Games I = 21 points in opening; time 34.01–36.00 (10 point bonus)
- Games II = 21 points in opening; time 32.01–34.00 (20 point bonus)
- Games III = 21 points in opening; time 30.00–32.00 (30 point bonus)

Variations

- **Tatsch's Gamble variation**—This variation was reported by Kenneth Tatsch and is played like standard Gamblers, with a sequence of obstacles to be performed after the whistle sounds marking the end of point accumulation. The final sequence is *not* a distance challenge and must be run with the handler alongside the dog. The intention of the game is identical to the standard variation of Just In Time, to teach handler to make a timely approach to the gamble at the end of the point-accumulation period.
- **Wicked variation**—This variation, first played at Dogwood Training Center, is much like a standard Gamblers game, in which a 35-second point-accumulation period is followed by a distance challenge. However, there will be no whistle marking the end of point accumulation. In this version, the dog will not lose points from the point-accumulation period for arriving early at the gamble line. Based on the timeliness of the dog's arrival at the line, he will earn a multiplier on his earned gamble points.. There are four bonus scenarios, based on time and performance: 1) If the dog arrives at the first jump of the joker before 35 seconds, then he is not eligible for any joker points; 2) If the dog arrives at the first jump of the joker within two seconds after 35 seconds have expired, all joker obstacles performed before the 50-second whistle will be tripled in value; 3) If the dog arrives at the first jump of the joker within four seconds (and more than two) after 35 seconds have expired, all joker obstacles performed before the 50-second whistle will be doubled in value; 4) If the dog arrives at the table more than four seconds after the 35 seconds have expired, all joker obstacles performed will be awarded at their regular values.

kentucky derby day

Here's a game that's for the handlers. Even spectators can get involved. Kentucky Derby Day is a fun, fundraising idea invented by Bud Houston. Participants in the show place bets, using play money, on the outcome of each agility class. At the end of the day, prizes are auctioned to the highest bidder.

Briefing

Each exhibitor has a certain amount of Kentucky Derby Bucks (or Dog Dollars) in his exhibitor package. This money is used to place bets prior to the beginning of each game. Each jump height in each of the classes is considered a separate game.

At the end of the day, a series of prizes will be auctioned off that can be paid for only in Kentucky Derby Bucks.

Running the Games

To maximize the betting activity, the field of competitors in any game should be limited to seven or eight. If you are running a standard agility course and have 20 dogs participating, this field should be split up into three individual competitions of seven dogs, seven dogs, and six dogs.

Nearly any agility game can be used in a Kentucky Derby Day fundraiser so long as winners and placements can be clearly defined.

KY Derby Prize Chart

Cost	Item
$500	Dogwalk
$250	Tire jump
$125	3 jumps
$60	Dog crate
$30	Dog bed
$15	Dog lead
$7	Tug toy
$3	Chew toy
0	Donated items
0	Cash pot

Running the Betting Cage

The betting cage is not intended to make a profit. All the Kentucky Derby Bucks that come in must go out. The only exception is if no one bets on the dog that actually wins a game. All the money that comes in for a specific game will be distributed evenly to the bettors that picked the winning dog. This is done by determining the payout on a percentage, for instance:

- If $3,200 Kentucky Derby Bucks are bet on a game and $550 were bet on the winner, then the winner pays out at 5.8 to 1 ($3,200 divided by $550). A bettor placing $120 Dog Dollars on the winning dog would receive $700 in winnings, rounded to the nearest hundred dollars ($120 times 5.8).
- If $3,200 Kentucky Derby Bucks are bet on a game and $2,550 were bet on the winner, then the winner pays out at 1.25 to 1. A bettor placing $120 Dog Dollars on the winner would receive $150 in winnings.

Betting is open to all games until the first dog is called to the line for that game. The betting will close for that game only. Payouts for each game are made as soon as the results of a game are posted from the scoring table.

Exhibitors who have been wiped out by imprudent bets can purchase new Kentucky Derby Bucks at a rate equivalent to 100 Dog Dollars for every U.S. Dollar. Half of the real money should go into the cash pot, which will be auctioned off with all other prizes.

Conducting the Auction

The auction should take place when there are no other distractions. Start by auctioning the lowest value prize and then work up the list.

Exhibitors may pool their money to have enough money to win the auction. For example, an entire club might pool their Dog Dollars to purchase the dogwalk prize.

Planning a Derby Day

Aside from being a lot of fun, running a Kentucky Derby Day is a way of returning some of the entry money to the exhibitors. At the same time, the game will generate additional income for the host club.

Use a certain percentage of the entry income as seed money. For instance, 20 percent would be designated as a fund that goes to prizes. Consequently, if the show generates an entry income of $5,000, $1,000 of that would be spent on prizes for this game.

You should purchase prizes that have a scaling value. The table above shows a series of prizes that diminish in value by roughly half.

The quantity of Kentucky Derby Bucks you initially give to each exhibitor will depend on the amount of money that the exhibitor paid to enter the event. For instance, a handler with one dog who only spent $31 to enter the show would get $3,100 in Kentucky Derby Bucks (the real value of those Doggie Dollars is only $6.20 or $31 times the 20 percent designated for the fund). Round up the money so that the exhibitor is working exclusively with $100 bills and $500 bills.

The quantity of Kentucky Derby Bucks the exhibitor ends up with at the end of the day is another matter. That depends entirely on the exhibitor's ability and luck as a bettor.

King of the Hill is a truly mixed-pairs agility format. It's a wonderful idea for a club outing or mixer. Mixing is what it does best. King of the Hill is the invention of Bud Houston and is adapted from a popular game of dice.

Briefing

King of the Hill must be played in multiples of four. For the purposes of this discussion, there are 16 dog-and-handler teams divided into four groups with four dog-and-handler teams in each. The groups are seeded at first by size of the dogs, the larger dogs being put into Group 1 (Bottom of the Hill) and the smallest dogs into Group 4 (Top of the Hill).

Each dog-and-handler team initially must be partnered randomly with another dog-and-handler team in the group. In the end, it won't matter too much.

The game will have exactly six rounds, an intermission, and six additional rounds. This is a fixed format and not a reflection of the number of teams.

Scoring

King of the Hill is scored simply. The dog with the most wins on individual rounds wins the competition. A tiebreaker might be determined for the end of play in case teams have the same overall score. On the other hand, you could just accept the draw and break out the beer.

Wins are accumulated over the 12 rounds of the competition. After each round, dog-and-handler teams will change groups and switch partners. Movement from group to group is described below.

After the first round, the groups will be reseeded.

- The two dog-and-handler teams that won in groups 1, 2, or 3 will go up to the next group.
- The two dog-and-handler teams that lost in groups 2, 3, or 4 will go down to the previous group.
- When moved to the next group, the team must split up and partner with the other two dogs and handlers in that group.

Obviously, the losers in Group 1 (Bottom of the Hill) cannot go down and the winners in Group 4 (Top of the Hill) cannot go up.

- At the Bottom of the Hill, the losers will stay in that group. After the round, they must split up and partner with the two dogs and handlers moved down from Group 2.
- At the Top of the Hill, the winners will stay in that group. After the round, they must split up and partner with the two dogs and handlers moved up from Group 3.

Course Design

King of the Hill can be played in any pairs or foursome agility format. For example, it is ideal for Pairs Pursuit, which is designed specifically for a two-pair competition.

The format might also be like knockout, making it a race between two dogs on side-by-side, identical courses, with a baton exchange between partners.

Given that King of the Hill is designed to go 12 rounds, the number of obstacles should be kept to a reasonable maximum to avoid exhausting the dogs. If an A-frame is used, it should be lowered at the apex to minimize wear and tear on the dogs.

Games that might serve as a basis for King of the Hill that are described in this book include:

- Baseball taking the combined scores of the two players.
- Blackjack using a strategic baton exchange in the accumulation of the 21 points.
- Bomber (a knockout variation) using four identical courses. In a Bomber format, the dogs wouldn't be teamed. Two dogs go up and two dogs go down.
- Boxed Pairs

- Knockout
- Pairs Pursuit
- Relay
- Strategic Pairs
- Tag 10 alternating between the two dogs. The point-accumulation time should be reduced to 30 or 40 seconds instead of 60.
- Three-Tunnel Barrel Race using a baton exchanged in a timed format.
- Tunnelers using a baton exchange in a timed format.
- What's My Line? using a baton exchange in a timed format.

knockout

Knockout is a game of fast-paced excitement where the winner takes all. Like the NCAA basketball tournament, the field continues to reduce in size by half, as the loser sits down and the winner advances to the next round. This is intense competition, not for the timid.

Briefing

Knockout usually follows a games format, typically in the form of a race between two dogs on side-by-side, identical courses. Dogs are started on a whistle. The goal is simple: Finish the course before your opponent. The winning dog goes on to the next round; the losing dog is eliminated. Competition continues until only one dog remains.

In training, Knockout is useful for stimulating increased excitement. Dogs that are sluggish with routine exercises will often perk up in the excitement of the competition. Knockout also provides a way to place some competitive stress on the handlers to better prepare them for the show stress everyone experiences.

Scoring

The dog-and-handler team that wins every race wins the competition.

Two judges are required, one for each dog. Time faults are usually assigned on a 1:1 basis. For example, if a dog runs the course in 15 seconds but drops a bar (5 faults), his score would be 20. If the other dog runs clean in 18.56 seconds, the slower dog advances.

To determine third and fourth places, the dogs that were defeated by the two finalists should run against each other.

Course Design

There are many variations of Knockout; some using tunnels and jumps, some using contacts and weave poles. However, two identical courses are always set side by side, usually in an up-and-back configuration.

Variations

- **Jag Race 4-H**—Lorraine Brown invented this variation for the 4-H Junior Agility Group in Massachusetts. Dogs run legs of equal complexity but not of identical obstacles.
- **Racers**—This variation by Tara Choate uses two identical courses of 8 to 12 obstacles. The judge sets a standard course time so that time faults are assessed. Two dog-and-handler teams run the courses at the same time. The team with the best score (time plus faults) moves on. However, no dog may accumulate more than 20 faults and still move on (this would give the next dog in the knockout bracket an automatic advancement).

  In round one only, a dog that is knocked out, but finishes under course time with fewer than 20 faults, may reenter competition.
- **Texas Shootout**—This variation, reported by Kenneth Tatsch, requires handlers to stop in the middle of side-by-side courses to shoot an aluminum can off the top of a tire jump frame with water guns. They cannot proceed on course until successful. Since handlers are on either side of the same tire frame, someone is likely to get wet!

- **Watered-Down Knockout**—This variation by Stephen Lewis is played on two side-by-side, straight-line sequences. Two 50' sprinkler hoses are run down the center of each sequence, spurting up 6' to 8' streams of water. Instead of the winner advancing, the loser advances to the next round. The more a handler loses, the more he runs the course, and the wetter he gets!
- **Bomber**—This is a variation played in the U.K. where four identical courses are run. The winner gets to run against the next three dogs.
- **Team Knockout**—Teams (multiple dogs and handlers) who advance together to the next round can also play Knockout.

Knockout Ladder Grid

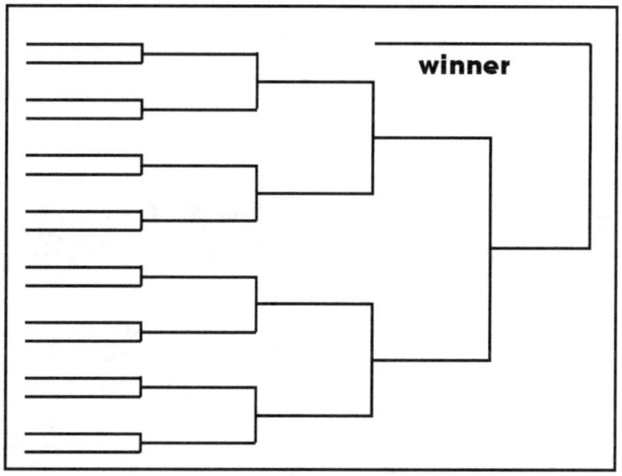

The Knockout Ladder

Before running a Knockout, create a Knockout Ladder or elimination brackets so that your competition comes out evenly.

The key to making the numbers right in a Knockout is that the brackets for advancement must be powers of two: 2, 4, 8, 16, 32, 64, 128, and so forth. It's no coincidence that the NCAA basketball championships have a field of 64 teams—64 is one of the magic numbers for a Knockout.

It is likely that the number of dogs entered in the competition will not be one of the magic numbers. To remedy this, some dogs will get an automatic bye in the first bracket of the Knockout Ladder. A bye means that the dog will advance to the next round without having to compete. This might not be entirely fair, but this is the way that it's done.

Here's the formula to determine the number of dogs that must compete in the first bracket: (N–B) x 2

N = Number of competitors

B = Bracket number

To see how the formula works, suppose there are 23 dogs entered in the Knockout competition.

1. Find the magic power-of-two number that is equal to or just less than the number of competitors entered in the Knockout. This is the bracket number (B in the formula). In the example, the bracket number is 16 because it is the power-of-two number that is equal to or lower than 23.
2. Subtract the bracket number from the number of competitors entered in the Knockout (N in the formula). In the example, the formula would be: 23–16=7.
3. Multiply the result of the subtraction by 2. In the example, it would be 7x2, and the answer would be 14.
4. Take the result and enter that many handler/dog teams in the first bracket of the ladder. Enter the remaining names in the next bracket. In the example, 14 dogs and handlers would run against one another in the first bracket. The remaining 9 dogs have a bye in the first round so they are automatically advanced to the second bracket.

Making the choice of which dogs get the bye and which compete in the first round is a problem for each club or organizer. Names could be drawn from a hat. Whatever the selection method, try to be as fair as possible.

last of the mohicans

In the years before the American Revolution, certain frontiersmen were greatly feared and respected by hostile Indians because they had learned to load their muskets with powder and shot, and even fire them, while on the run without stopping or even slowing down. This agility game was devised as a means of teaching the very Novice handler to stay in motion when running an agility course (and to avoid stopping alongside every jump on the way). Last of the Mohicans is the invention of Bud Houston.

Briefing

The purpose of this game is to stay in motion through a small course. The dog will earn one point for each obstacle performed, so the dog with the most points wins. Time is a tie-breaker only.

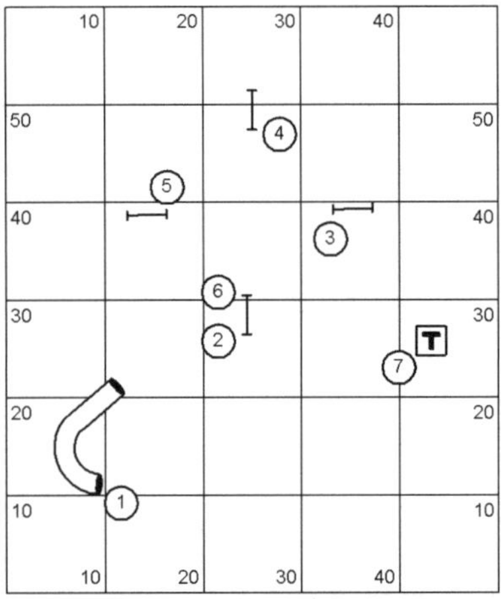

A typical Last of the Mohicans course is a short flowing sequence that encourages novice handlers to stay in motion.

There's one important catch to the game. The handler is not allowed to stop or correct any obstacle the dog misses. If the handler stops, he is dead. He earns no points, and the game is over. Along the way, the handler will have to do his best to clearly present each obstacle to the dog.

Scoring

Last of the Mohicans is scored points, then time. Time is a tie-breaker only. The dog earns 1 point for each obstacle performed correctly.

If the handler stops or attempts to go back to correct any obstacle, he is deemed *dead* by the judge. At that point the game ends, and the team earns zero points.

Strategies

It's worthwhile to acknowledge the *Laws of a Dog in Motion*. The dog tends to move in a path parallel to the handler's path, and the dog turns when the handler turns. So the handler should press ahead of the dog, if at all possible, and use his lead hand to show the dog the way. The handler would be well advised not to turn on the course until the dog has actually committed to the obstacle before the turn.

The handler should measure his pace so that he is working on the same obstacle that the dog is working on, at the same time that the dog is working on it.

las vegas

Las Vegas is the invention of Ilze Rukis. Ilze teaches for Northwoods Agility Group (NAGs) in Northern Wisconsin. Quirky (agility) minds are always at work.

Briefing

The object of Las Vegas is to accumulate as many points as possible in 60 seconds by running sequences of varying point value. Time starts when the team crosses the starting line to any chosen sequence. To get points for a sequence, the dog must complete the sequence without fault.

For Novice: knocked bars, missed contacts, and off-courses are faulted. For Advanced: all the novice faults, plus refusals and missed weave poles are faulted. If a dog faults an obstacle, then the entire sequence has been lost. The team must restart any sequence eligible for point accumulation from behind the containment line.

If a dog drops a bar on a sequence, the bar is not reset and the sequence is deemed ineligible for point accumulation.

Point accumulation stops at 60 seconds. No points are given for partially completed sequences.

Teams must run across the start/finish line to stop time.

Las Vegas Scoring

	Sequence 1 10 points	Sequence 2 5 points	Sequence 3 15 points
Two of a Kind face value times 2	20 x 2 = 40	10 x 2 = 20	30 x 2 = 60
Three of a Kind face value times 3	30 x 3 = 90	15 x 3 = 45	45 x 3 = 135
Flush (all 3 sequences once) face value times 5	<---------- 30 x 5 = 150 ---------->		
Straight Flush (3 sequences twice) Face value times 10	<---------- 30 x 10 = 300 ---------->		

Scoring

Las Vegas is scored points then time. Time is a tiebreaker only.

When any single sequence is completed without fault (there and back), the team is awarded the face value of that sequence: 5, 10, or 15 points. When a sequence is performed multiple times, point values are awarded as shown in the table.

If the team earned both a Two of a Kind, Three of a Kind, or each of the three sequences, then the scores will be added together.

Course Design

Traditionally, the elements of the Las Vegas course are designed in straightaway sequences that double back on themselves. The point values for the three separate legs of the course should be based on the complexity of the sequence or difficulty of the obstacles in each sequence.

For the Dogwood High-Roller Bonus variation, the sequences might be designed so that the obstacles are distributed more at a lateral distance from the handler, giving the exhibitors a more modest chance for success in doubling the earned performance when sending their dogs from behind a containment line.

Strategies

The handler should do the sequence on which his dog is least likely to receive a fault. If a dog has problems with contact obstacles, stay away from the contact sequence. If the dog is likely to have weave pole faults, stay away from the weave poles. If the dog drops bars, stay away from the sequence made up predominantly of jumps.

Taking advantage of the dog's strengths will maximize point accumulation. For example, a team that completes Three of a Kind twice will have 270 points versus a team that risks going for it all and attempts all three sequences twice for 300 points.

Qualifying and Titles

Las Vegas is eligible as a titling game for both JFF and TDAA. Qualifying criteria will be:

- Games I—60 points
- Games II—90 points
- Games III—150 points

Variations

- **Dogwood High-Roller Bonus variation**—In this variation, invented by Bud Houston, the dog can be sent to complete any sequence from behind a containment line. If the handler sends his dog through the entire performance of any single sequence (while staying behind the containment line) the dog will score twice (as though the dog had just run the sequence twice). Consequently, sending the dog is equivalent to a Twosome.

  In the Dogwood High-Roller Bonus variation, if the handler is confident of sending his dog ahead for the performance of one of the sequences, it is actually not a good idea to send the dog twice on the same sequence. Remember that Four of a Kind is actually worth less than a Full House in this game. The handler would be smarter to run with the dog once on the sequence to pattern the dog before attempting the distance send.

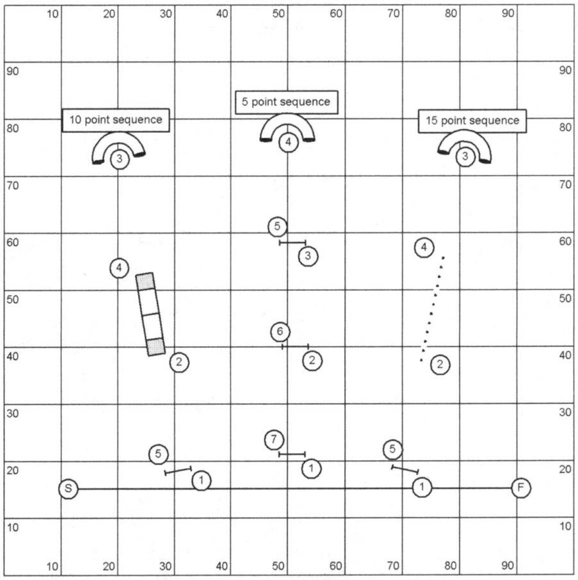

This is the classic Las Vegas course design), with straightaway sequences and the 10-point and 15-point sequences on opposite sides of the course, making it harder to rack up points.

Agility league play is rather like being in a bowling league, except that the participants don't bowl, they do agility. League play is intended as an inexpensive recreational form of the sport that focuses on playing a variety of agility games. Bud Houston at Dogwood Training Center in Ostrander, Ohio, inaugurated league play in this country. League play developed from Just For Fun Agility but can be played under the rules and regulations of any agility organization.

Forward

It is so difficult these days to encourage and support agility as an inexpensive recreational sport. More often, it's about a title chase, national championships, individual breed rankings, and getting on the USDAA Top 10 List.

Agility league play is a format that not only encourages but also demands the game be played recreationally and for fun.

At Dogwood Training Center in Ostrander, Ohio, the league costs $8 for eight weeks. That amounts to $1.00 a week. Obviously, this isn't something done for money. League fees are used to pay basic expenses of running the league. The winning team gets a Dogwood polo shirt or sweatshirt. The MVP (Most Valuable Puppy) each week wins a nice toy for the dog. Dogwood also provides a free class for the two top-scoring Advanced MVP dogs, and the top-scoring Novice MVP dog.

Organization of the League

1. The league will run eight weeks with a separate competition held each week, beginning on a specific date and ending on a specific date.
2. The league should be named and the location (including whether games will be held indoors or outdoors) should be specified.
3. The agility league may operate under the sanction of the United States Dog Agility Association or Just For Fun Agility or operate as a local "for-fun" league, without sanction.
4. The league fee should be specified. It is highly encouraged that this be a nominal fee, just enough to cover expenses. The fees should be consistent, whether the dog is on an active team, is a designated alternate, or is participating for exhibition only.
5. Teams may be organized in several different formats. For example: run-four/score-three, run-two/score-two, run-five/score-three. The format is completely up to the host club and should be static for the duration of league play. Additional stipulations may be made that each team include one dog from the novice list or have one assigned by random draw.
6. Individual dogs may be on one team only.
7. A handler may have more than one dog entered in the league so long as each dog is on a separate team.
8. Teams may use alternates as temporary substitutions. A designated league secretary will maintain a roster of alternates.

Competition and Placements

1. Dogs may compete at the jump height of the handler's choosing.
2. The league secretary will publish a complete schedule of games in advance. A games briefing and course map will be posted prior to each competition.
3. The league secretary will be responsible for maintaining a roster of teams and for posting results of league competitions and accumulated scores in a timely fashion. The league secretary will be eligible to participate in competition with one or more dogs.
4. Games will be scored according to any rules basis stipulated by the designer of the game. Any game can be used so long as placements are clearly defined, and all participants can play the game in a timely fashion.
5. A team is allowed a single absentee in a given week. When a member of the team is absent, the league secretary will assign an alternate by random draw.
6. If a team has two absentees in a single competition, that team will forfeit that competition.

Determining Team and Most Valuable Puppy (MVP) Scores

1. Team scores will be based on the aggregate score of individuals that make up the team after the worst score is discarded. Points are awarded each week determined by overall placement. Teams will accumulate points in the following manner:
   - 10 points—1st place team
   - 7 points—2nd place team
   - 5 points—3rd place team
   - 3 points—4th place team
   - 1 point—5th place team
2. Top dog (MVP) scores will be determined by placement. MVP placements will accumulate points in the following manner:
   - 10 points—1st place dog
   - 7 points—2nd place dog
   - 5 points—3rd place dog
   - 3 points—4th place dog
   - 1 point—5th place dog
3. At the end of the league play schedule, the team with the highest accumulated points will be the team winner. Ties between two or more teams will be resolved by a runoff between individual members of both teams.
4. At the end of the league play schedule, the dog with the highest accumulated points will be the MVP winner. Ties between two or more dogs will be resolved by a runoff between those dogs.
5. Each member of the first-place team and the handler of the MVP dog will receive a trophy or prize at the discretion of the host club.

League Reporting

Team and individual (MVP) results will be tracked by the league secretary and reported to the participants on a weekly basis.

Conduct

1. Exhibitor conduct will be consistent with the conduct expected of the major agility organizations. Training in the ring and harsh treatment of a dog will result in immediate elimination and excusal from the ring.
2. Harsh treatment of a dog will be considered a conduct excusal. A second excusal for this reason in the same league season will result in the handler being banned from league competition for one month, whether or not that extends into the next league season. This sanction includes all dogs worked by that handler.
3. Use of food or toy lures is deemed training in the ring and will result in elimination and excusal from the ring. (Note: this rule is entirely at the discretion of the league rules, and occasionally, the judge. Some games may specifically allow the use of food or toy lures).

Qualification and Titling

Under Just For Fun rules, any game played in league with clearly defined qualification requirements is eligible for qualification toward Just For Fun titles.

meet in the middle

Meet in the Middle is the invention of Sherry Bryant, Barbara Atkinson, and Claire Schwartz.

Briefing

Meet in the Middle is a pairs relay, requiring one dog and handler to run a short course and then exchange a baton with a second dog and handler, who will run a second short course.

Each dog and handler will run the whole course, but only half of the course at a time, exchanging the baton each time the two teams meet in the middle.

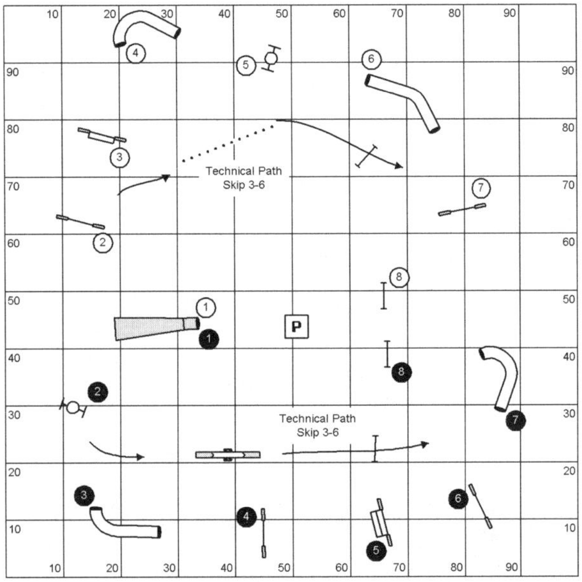

This is an example of a Meet in the Middle course for novice dogs that gives the advantage to a dog that can negotiate the teeter or the weave poles.

Each of the two short courses is big and round. Sequences are built for speed. However, each includes a shortcut if the handler thinks he'll do better with the technical obstacles on the shortcut than on the regular path of the course.

Scoring

Meet in the Middle is scored time plus faults. The lowest score wins.

Course Design

The course is laid out in a figure eight, with half the course going clockwise and the other half going counterclockwise. Each half of the course will consist of ten obstacles, eight on the outside circle, representing the speed course, and two in the middle, representing the technical shortcut.

Strategies

The handler should take into account not only whether his dog can gain some advantage by taking the technical shortcut but also whether his dog is more likely to fault one side or the other. If there's some likelihood that the dog will fault the technical obstacles, the shortcut probably should be avoided. On the other hand, if the dog has a propensity to drop the bar of a spread hurdle or tends to flatten out and drop bars when moving fast, it could be that the technical shortcut is the better course.

miniature golf

Stuart Mah invented Miniature Golf (a.k.a. Bye-Bye Birdie), which first appeared in Clean Run *magazine. This is one of those games in which almost anything can happen and generally does. A team can win either by demonstrating great directional discrimination or a great aptitude for improvisation.*

Briefing

Miniature Golf is usually played as a team game with four dogs and four handlers to a team.

There are three courses on the field. Each course begins with a different tunnel. The dog will run whichever course is selected based on which tunnel the dog goes through first. All sequences have the same course time, regardless of the disparity of difficulty.

Each dog must start with its handler in the area designated as the tee. No lead-outs are allowed. The handler must send his dog into the tunnel of choice and then run the course indicated by whichever tunnel the dog actually chooses. If all four of the dog's paws go into a tunnel, the dog has committed to that tunnel, and it must be completed along with its associated course. The handler may call a dog back out of a tunnel, however, if three or fewer paws are committed.

The handler may not stand in or walk through the area designated as the handler exclusion box.

Scoring

Miniature Golf is scored as a golf score. The team with the lowest score wins.

The golf score is based upon time plus faults. Displaced bars and missed contacts are scored as 5 seconds added to the running time. Off-courses are scored as 10 seconds added for being out of bounds. Each instance of the handler moving or stepping into the exclusion box will result in a 5-second penalty.

The judge will set a course time or par for the course. Measuring all three courses, applying a yards-per-second rate of 2.5 to 3.5 yards per second, and dividing that by 3 will establish the course time. Generally with a course consisting of 9 to 11 obstacles, par would be in the 25- to 40-second range.

Based on the dog's course time plus its faults, the dog is awarded a golf score as follows:

- Eagle, 15 seconds under or more, is scored as -2.
- Birdie, 5.01 seconds to 14.99 seconds under, is scored as -1.
- Par, 5 seconds over or under, is scored as 0.
- Bogie, 5.01 seconds to 15 seconds over, is scored as +1.
- Double Bogie, 15.01 to 25 seconds over, is scored as +2.
- Triple Bogie, More than 25 seconds over, is scored as +3.

Ties are broken by a sudden-death playoff. One dog, and only one dog, is selected to run the same course from each team. The winner is the fastest dog on course, including faults. This is a quick way to determine a winner in a manner that appeals to spectators.

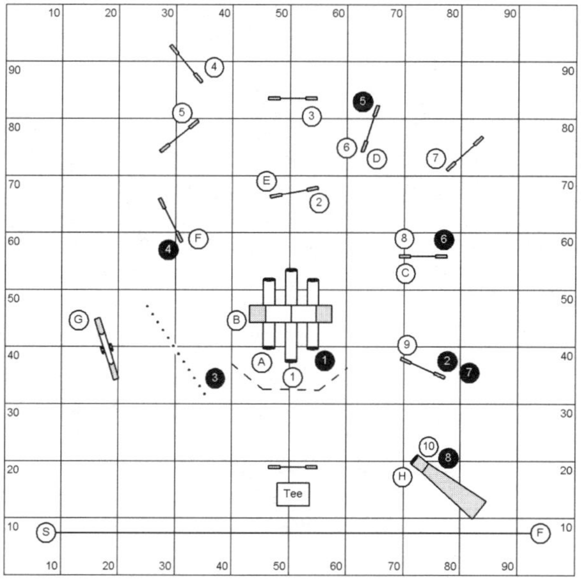

Stuart Mah designed this example of a Miniature Golf course.

Course Design

The design of the Miniature Golf course requires three straight pipe tunnels to be set side-by-side under the A-frame. The middle tunnel extends 3' beyond the tunnel on either side. A semicircular handler exclusion box is marked 4' from the tunnels. The center tunnel leads to the Jumpers course, the left tunnel leads to the contact course, and the right tunnel leads to the weave pole course.

The setup can be of various designs, but the initial sequence for each of the three courses is always a jump to a tunnel under the A-frame.

Each course has a dominant obstacle:

- The jumpers course, consisting of jumps and tunnels
- The contact course, containing the A-frame and teeter (optional)
- The weave pole course, containing a set of weave poles

The jumpers course will consist of at least eight obstacles but may contain more. The average is 10. It should be longer in yardage and go further beyond the A-frame than the other two courses. The weave-pole and contact courses will run one or two obstacles shorter than the Jumpers course.

Variations

- **Singles Miniature Golf variation**—The game can be played as singles rather than as foursomes.

minuet

Minuet was invented by Bud Houston at Dogwood Training Center in Ostrander, Ohio, as a physical conditioning exercise for his dogs and a training game for his students. The game was first played in 2001 in Dogwood's ongoing agility league. On the surface, Minuet is a simple game with a simple sequence repeated over and over again. In fact, the game will expose every flaw in movement the handler might have, since the handler must also repeat his movement over and over again. There will be dropped bars, refusals, and even off-courses. This game demonstrates a simple principle: Most performance errors are the fault of the handler and not of the dog. Just a note about the "physical conditioning" exercise: Bud reports that it is so strenuous that he never actually uses it for that purpose.

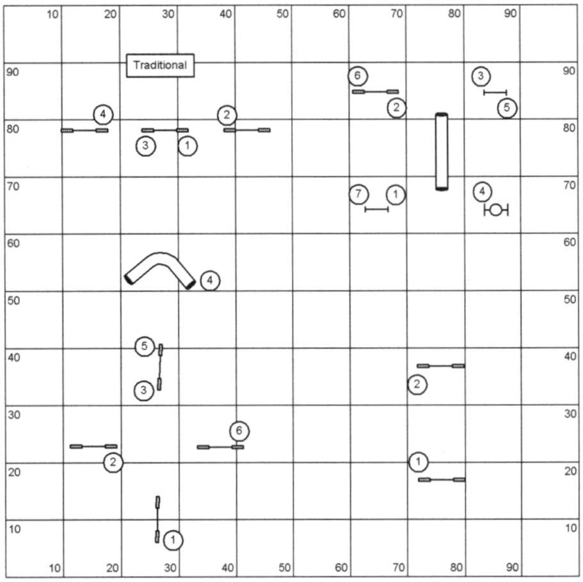

Of four possible designs of the Minuet, the original design, shown in the upper left, requires the performance of three jumps in a figure of eight. A design like this will ultimately expose every error in movement on the part of the handler. Other designs might be used, but the pattern should be consequential in terms of the handling required.

Briefing

The dog and handler have 50 seconds. Repeat the sequence as a continuous loop until time expires.

The judge may specify that the dog has to cross a finish line or go to a table to stop time after the whistle blows to end scoring.

Scoring

One point is earned for each completion of the loop. One decimal point is earned for each jump in an uncompleted loop when time expires. For example: In 50 seconds, the dog does 7 complete loops and the first two jumps in the sequence. The dog's score will be 7.2.

If the dog drops a bar, the handler must stop and reset the bar.

If the dog goes off course, one point is lost. Counting of the loop will not continue until the dog returns to the next on-course jump.

Course Design

The design principle for Minuet is simplicity. The sequence should be designed in such a way that it can easily be restarted from the last obstacle back to the first.

Strategies

The handler should work in clean lines through the jumps and show turns only after the dog has committed to each jump. These are simple disciplines that keep the bars up and help prevent refusals. If the handler's movement gets lazy, something bad is bound to happen.

Qualification and Titling

Minuet is a qualifying game for both JFF and TDAA. In the traditional course, qualifying would be set at:

- Games I—3 points
- Games II—5 points
- Games III—7 points

Qualifying rates for other course designs would depend on several factors:

- The complexity in arrangement and the number of obstacles
- The transitional distances between obstacles

In determining a TDAA qualifying score, the judge should measure the dog's path and base the score for each level of games on the yards per second specified in the TDAA rules and regulations.

In JFF, the qualifying score might be based on a rational yards per second system, such as that used by the USDAA.

Variations

- **Gamblers variation**—In this variation, the handler directs the dog to do as many jumps as possible in 50 seconds. Three "send" lines are indicated on the course; 1 pt (5'-send), 2 pts (10'-send), 3 pts (15'-send). The only restriction in this game is that the dog is required to do all three jumps at some point during the 50 seconds.

  If the dog drops a bar, that jump is out of play for the duration of the game, and no more points can be scored on it.

  The game starts and stops on the table. Time starts when the dog leaves the table. At 50 seconds a whistle will sound to indicate end of scoring. The dog should be directed to the table to stop time. Time is a tie-breaker only.

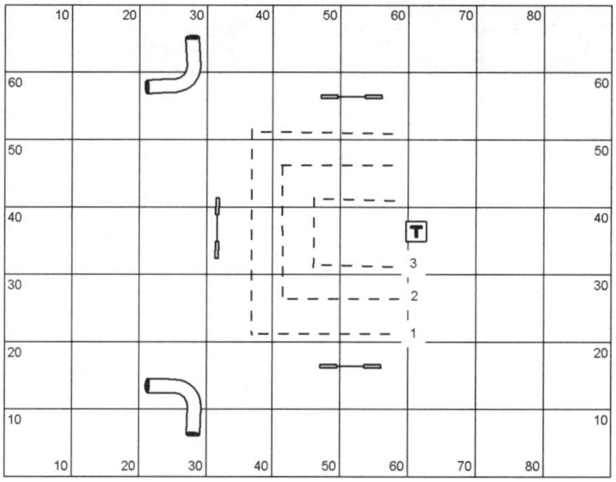

The example of the Minuet, Gamblers Variation shown here was played at Dogwood Training Center in February of 2003. The JFF requirements for qualification were: Games I: 10 points or better; Games II: 20 points or better; Games III: 30 points or better.

musical chairs

Musical Chairs won third place in the 1995 Clean Run *magazine Games Contest. Sue Tovino and Betty McArthur submitted it. Like the popular children's game, Musical Chairs features a diminishing number of seats when the music stops.*

Briefing

Musical Chairs is played like the children's game of the same name. Four dog-and-handler teams begin the course when the music starts. When the music stops, the handler must put his dog into a stay in one of the designated pause boxes. When the handler has his dog in the box, the handler must find any available chair and sit in it. If his dog gets up or out of the box before the handler sits in a chair, he must vacate the chair and get his dog into a box again.

The dog and handler failing to find a box and chair are eliminated. After the first round, one chair and one box are removed and the process is repeated. The winner is the dog/handler team not standing in the final round.

Performance faults are not assessed. However, unsafe performance results in elimination. Dogs that catch up to another dog must wait their turn for the obstacle. Overtaking a dog while it is performing an obstacle is not permitted.

The judge chooses the course direction of the round. The direction may be reversed in subsequent rounds.

Musical Chairs is played as a Knockout. Each successive round will be comprised of the pool of teams that advanced from the previous round, until eventually arriving at the final four. The final four compete until only the winner remains.

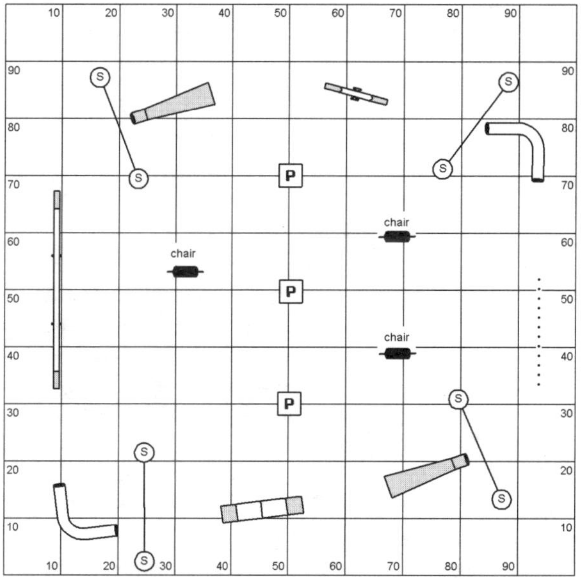

In this typical Musical Chairs course, batches of four contestants line up, one team per start line, to run a course with no jumps.

Scoring

The winner is the dog-and-handler team not standing in the final round.

Course Design

There are four starting lines for four teams. There are also three chairs and three pause boxes. The pause boxes are located in the center of the course with the chairs placed randomly.

In Musical Chairs, any obstacle except jumps can be used.

Musical Pairs is the invention of Heidi Fuge and Fran Seibert as a game for a JAZZ Club meeting. Fran reports that it was hysterical. For music, they considered "The William Tell Overture" and "Flight of the Bumblebee" but settled on two Glenn Miller selections, "In the Mood" and "Pennsylvania 6-5000." Dogs ran and spectators danced. Someone suggested 5 "style" points be deducted if the handler in the pause box did a credible dance number.

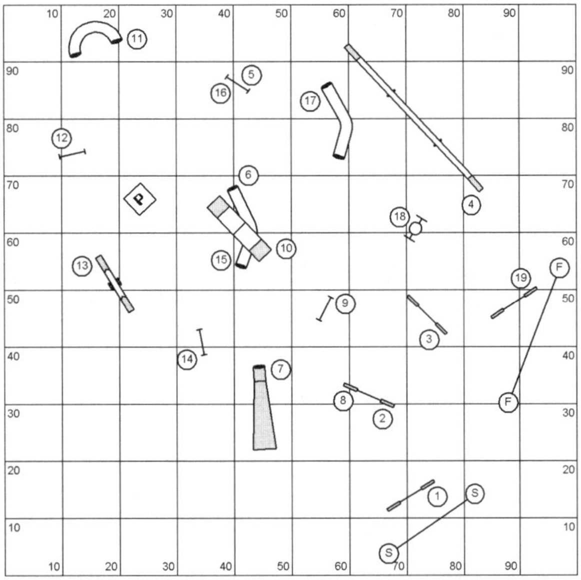

This Musical Pairs course presents challenges at nearly every turn.

Briefing

Musical Pairs is a relay with two dog-and-handler teams on the course at the same time. It is run on any standard agility course. Both dogs must jump the same height; if they normally jump different heights, all jumps will be at the lower height.

At the start of the game, one dog-and-handler team will wait at the start line with the handler holding a baton while the other goes to the pause box or a low table. When both are in place, the music will start and the starting team begins the course, continuing until the music stops. When the music stops, the running team may finish any obstacle they are caught on or in and then proceed immediately to the pause box or table to replace the waiting team. The first handler passes the baton to the second handler and positions his dog in the pause area. The music resumes as soon as the second handler receives the baton. He then proceeds to the point where the first handler was when the music stopped (which is not necessarily where the first handler stopped doing obstacles) and continues to run the course from that point until the music stops again. When the music stops again, the exchange is made as before, and the game continues in this fashion until one dog completes the course and crosses the finish line.

Dogs may wear collars, and the handler may hold the collar of the dog while it is in the pause area.

If any bar is dropped, either by dog or handler, the handler must reset it before continuing.

Scoring

Scoring will be faults only with time as a tiebreaker. Five faults each will be assessed for dropped bars, refusals, off-courses that occur while the dog is running its part of the course, and leaving the pause area without the baton in hand. Ten faults will be assessed for missed contacts. If a dog refuses an obstacle, the handler should reattempt it until the music stops. If that team fails to complete the obstacle, the other team should start at that point. Fault scores can be kept separately for each dog then added for a team score. Failure to complete an obstacle will result in elimination. There is no off-course penalty for repeating an obstacle at the beginning of a turn or for taking obstacles on the way to starting a turn.

Notes on the Conduct of the Game

All dogs should get precisely the same amount of music. The person will have a specific schedule. For example, give team #1 twelve seconds, then team #2 twelve seconds; then team #1 five seconds and team #2 five seconds; then each ten seconds and so on. The music restarts to continue the game as soon as the baton is passed. The timekeeper times the run from the moment the music starts until one of the dogs has completed the last obstacle.

Course Design

The course should be fairly complex, include traps, and provide plenty of opportunities for refusals and off-courses. Weave poles are optional, depending on the skill level of the participants. The pause box or table should be out of the direct running line. The person controlling the music should give equal time to both teams: perhaps starting with two 15-second turns, then going to 5 seconds, and then to 10, and so on randomly. Lively music is desirable.

Strategies

When deciding who should be the first runner, teams should try to estimate how far they may get on the course. For instance, if one is weak on the teeter and that is the second obstacle, chances are that the first runner will be required to do it. It is imperative that the handler in the pause area pay attention to where the other team is when the music stops, even though many dedicated dogs and handlers might do several obstacles after the music stops. If in doubt, the handler may repeat an obstacle previous to where he suspects he should start to avoid being eliminated for a failure to complete. Handlers may tell each other where they were when the music stopped and may offer verbal assistance to the one running the course.

The "paused" team is supposed to restart at the point where the running dog was when the music stopped to end his turn, unless he was in the middle of a dogwalk or something similar, in which case the paused dog must pick it up at the next obstacle.

mute agility

As a training exercise or for a real competition, Mute Agility is a wonderful test of the dog and handler relationship and often a lot of fun for spectators. This game is frequently used to show how the handler's body position and movements influence the dog's performance of the course. This game is sometimes called Silent Snake.

Briefing

Mute Agility can be run on any standard agility course. The dog must perform each obstacle on the course in the sequence designated by the judge.

Unlike on a standard agility course, however, the handler must run the entire course silently. No verbal cues are allowed; that means no verbal commands, no clapping, no stomping the ground, no whistling, and so on. Body language must speak for itself.

There is no standard course time, only a maximum course time.

Scoring

Scoring is on a time plus faults basis.

The system used for judging faults should be consistent with the game that is being played.

Mute Agility adds a fault restriction for speaking. Usually, the judge will assess the handler 5 faults for each word spoken on course.

Course Design

The design of the course should include appropriate challenges for the level of competition.

Variations

- **Silent Snake variation**—In this variation of the game, created by Sue Tovino and Betty McArthur, the course consists of constant changes of side or a snaking motion. The first time a handler breaks the silence, 15 faults are assessed. The second occurrence results in elimination.
- **Single command**—In this variation, the handler can give one command, which must be declared to the judge before the dog's run. Thus, for example, a handler may choose *tunnel* or *weave*. Ideally, a handler should choose the command that is most necessary to control the dog. A *come* command might be a good choice.
- **Mute Agility games**—Almost any agility game can be played in the Mute Agility format. However, this format might not lend itself too well to games like Gamblers, which often rely on the handler's voice commands to achieve the joker.
- **Monetary penalty**—This variation of the game is a good club fundraiser. The handler is penalized $1–$5 for speaking (or whispering!).

near and far

Trisha Stall from Latham, New York, designed Near and Far in fulfillment of a test to become a judge for the Teacup Dogs Agility Association.

Briefing

The objective of this game is to negotiate a course as numbered. At two specified places on course, the dog will go ahead to perform obstacles (the "far" section) while the handler stays behind a specified line.

Crossing the containment line to help the dog will result in a fault. At the Beginner level, one crossing of the line is permitted. The fault will not disqualify the team. At the Intermediate and Superior levels, any crossing of the handler line will result in a non-qualifying score.

Other qualifying rules at each level are the same as for the standard course.

Scoring

Near and Far is scored faults, then time. The lowest score wins. Time is a tiebreaker only.

The TDAA schedule of faults should be used. In addition, a 10-point penalty will be assessed for the handler crossing a containment line.

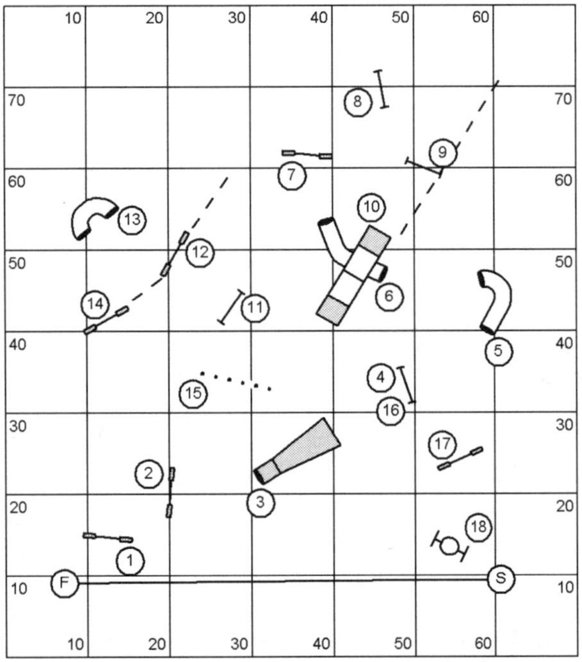

In this sample of a Near and Far course, the handler must perform gambles at #6–#9 and #12–#14.

A standard course time will be established according to the rates of play designated in the TDAA Rules and Regulations. Each second over course time, or a fraction thereof, will result in a 1-point penalty or fault.

Course Design

Near and Far is a game that can be run on a modified Standard course, minus the table, and using only one or two contacts.

The maximum "far" distance between dog and handler will be 6' at the Beginner level, 8' at the Intermediate level, and 10' at the Superior level. The "far" sections will consist of one to two obstacles at the Beginner and Intermediate levels. Any combination of send-away distance and lateral distance can be used.

Qualifying and Titles

TDAA

Near and Far is eligible as a qualifying game under TDAA rules.

- Games I—score of 10 faults or fewer
- Games II—score of 5 faults or fewer
- Games III—zero faults

JFF

Near and Far is eligible as a qualifying game under JFF rules using the same qualifying criteria as for TDAA qualifying except that no standard course time will be set.

Never a Dull Moment is the invention of Bud Houston. Usually, agility is a matter of whatever works is right. They don't give style points in agility. Oops! Never a Dull Moment is the style-points game, rewarding the handler for technical (however gratuitous) handling movements.

Briefing

In a standard sequence, the handler will earn points for the conduct of specific movements but only if the dog doesn't fail in his task.

Scoring

Never a Dull Moment is scored points then time. Simple movements are awarded only 1 point. Compound movements are awarded 3 points. Thus, the schedule of points might be:

- Front cross—1 point
- Blind cross—1 point
- Post turn—1 point
- Tandem turn—1 point
- Back cross—1 point
- Unchecked movement in the lead out—3 points
- RFP (a combination turn, crossing turn to crossing turn) —3 points
- Flip (a combination turn, crossing turn to blind cross) —3 points
- BLT (a combination turn, blind cross to tandem) —3 points
- Post and tandem (a combination turn, post turn to tandem turn) —3 points

The intention of Never a Dull Moment is to provide the handler an opportunity to demonstrate technical prowess. The schedule of points doesn't have to be limited to the specific handling movements shown here. For example, the judge may allow performance points for working the dog at a distance, layering, employing a V-solution, and so forth. This game is limited only by the imagination.

Note: If you make up your own movement or should you have a movement named after you, make it something pretty.

Course Design

The game can be played on any standard course. The technical merit of one handler's run will be compared to the entire field on precisely the same course. The course will have a designated starting line and finish line. It will not be run under a standard course time. Time is a tiebreaker only.

Strategies

The keys to success in agility are threefold: 1) having the right plan, 2) executing that plan, and 3) luck. Finding the right movement for the right moment is more difficult than learning and practicing the movements themselves.

The handler should take note that combination movements are worth three times the value of simple movements. Why use a simple movement when a gratuitously fancy movement will do just as well?

The handler should know his dog and understand how his dog responds to movement. Using those movements that are well practiced, the handler increases his chances for success.

Variations

- **Freestyle**—Rather than basing the game on a standard course that everyone must run, exhibitors are given a random arrangement of obstacles that can be taken in the order and direction of the handler's choosing. The freestyle course should have a defined start and finish line. However, the handler is allowed to find his own line on course. The handler's routine may be limited either by time or by the number of obstacles.

octagon game

The Octagon Game was invented by Chris Miele, who writes: "We tend to get too serious about our training at times. We clench our teeth, set our jaws, and go about teaching, determined that our dogs will learn! It often helps us to lighten up and get back to the sense of play that brought us to agility in the first place. As a result we find that our dogs learn, through the game, the very skill we had been trying to teach for months." This game originally appeared in Clean Run *magazine in May 1999.*

Briefing

Starting with the 12 o'clock jump, dog and handler must perform all jumps in a serpentine fashion in the direction designated by the judge (either clockwise or counterclockwise). If the dog knocks a bar, crosses the line of poles in the center of the octagon, or refuses a jump, the dog must do the weave poles. The correct weave pole entry is the entry closest to the point of the mistake.

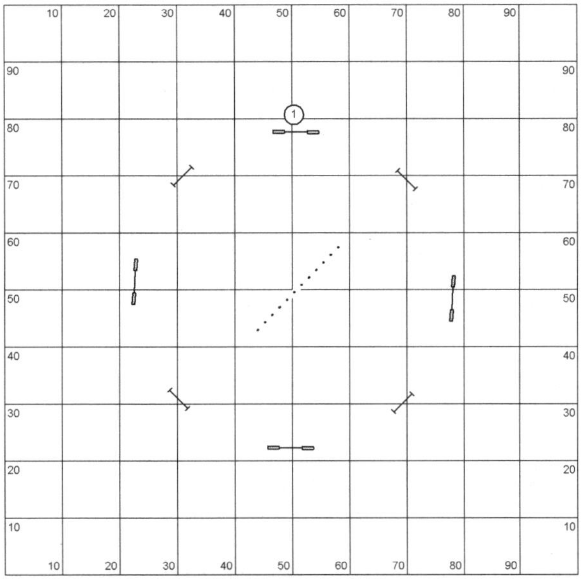

This is the essential design of the Octagon game.

Scoring

The Octagon Game is scored time only. The judge will whistle for any fault to indicate that the dog must go to the center of the octagon to perform the weave poles. Weave poles are judged using USDAA Starters/Novice rules. That is, there is no fault for an improper entry or a missed pole. But the handler must redirect the dog to fix a missed entry or a missed pole.

Course Design

The essential design of the Octagon game is a series of eight jumps arranged in the shape of an octagon. The course designer can use tire, panel, winged, and non winged jumps. For novice dogs and handlers, use only six weave poles. Increase the number of poles with the skill level.

Variations

- **Threadle variation**—The Octagon Game can be run as a series of *threadles*. That is, all jumps are taken in the same direction, such as from the outside of the octagon to the inside, or from the inside of the octagon out, as directed by the judge. The dog must be threaded between the jumps between each performance.

odd dog

As a training exercise or a game for competition, Odd Dog is a guaranteed hoot that delivers absolutely unpredictable results. Is it the dog or is it the handler? Odd dog is also a good mixer game, getting people and dogs introduced who otherwise might not have met on such an intimate basis.

Briefing

Odd Dog is usually played on a standard agility course. However, this game requires a handler to work with another person's dog.

Odd Dog demonstrates a handler's ability to adapt to a strange dog, and further challenges the handler to bond with the dog and establish a working relationship in a short time.

Some dogs will not work for anyone except their owners. This is unfortunate but also is a matter of the luck of the draw in Odd Dog. Some handlers will draw dogs that are excellent agility partners. By the same token, some dogs will draw experienced handlers, and some will draw novice handlers. These dogs may stretch their prowess as handlers.

Ideally, partners will be drawn early in the morning for a game to be played at the end of the day. This gives handlers and dogs time to bond and prepare. A handler who draws his dog or a dog with which he is very familiar will be required to redraw.

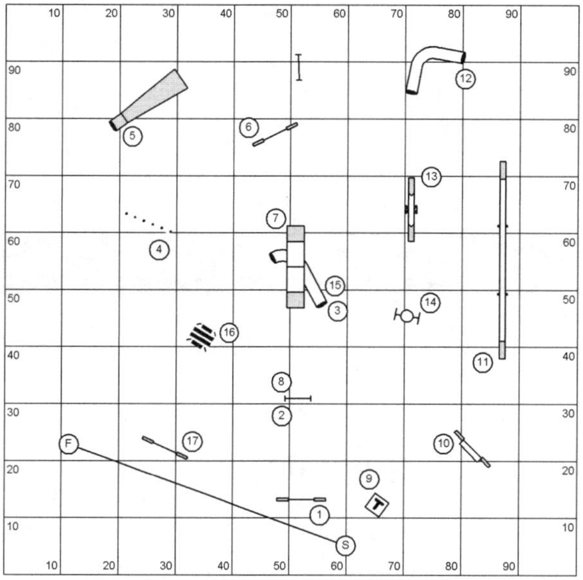

This Odd Dog course designed by Bud Houston is a relatively fast and flowing course, which is better suited to running a strange dog than might be a choppy, challenging course. While there are certainly challenges, they are at an intermediate level and might be surmounted by some good handling.

Scoring

Typically, Odd Dog will be played on a standard agility course. However, any agility game will be equally entertaining and interesting when a handler runs another person's dog.

The system used for judging faults and scoring should be consistent with the game that is being played. A standard agility course is recommended, using USDAA Starters/Novice rules on an advanced course.

Course Design

The Odd Dog course should be technically challenging but not so oppressive that only handlers and dogs with a finely tuned relationship could possibly survive. However, you don't want to make it a simple down and back course either. The test is for both dog and handler, and it should be amusing for spectators.

Strategies

- The handler of an unfamiliar dog should spend a lot of time socializing and playing with the dog before taking the dog into the ring. If no real connection is cemented between dog and handler, it is likely that the dog will run out of the ring to mama or papa on the first opportunity—if the dog can be enticed into the ring at all! Do a lot of attention heeling and play tug-of-war. Provide the dog with tidbits of wonderful food for paying attention and for responding to the play. Getting the dog's attention will pay off in the ring.
- While competing, the handler must be very upbeat and playful to keep the dog's attention. Handlers must remember that the dog is not familiar with their working style or hand signals. Handlers must be very specific in their commands, body movements, and hand signals.
- Handlers should review what commands the dog's handler uses. One may say *dogwalk*, while the owner may say *walk up*. Speak the language the dog understands whenever possible.

Variations

- **Draw pool**—Create a pool of dogs that will run for anyone and draw from that pool. This would mean that some dogs would run more than once.

pairs eggstravaganza

The invention of Susan Morse, Pairs Eggstravaganza debuted as an Easter game for the Brevard Kennel Club in Florida. This game is a relay with a twist. The format provides a good way to introduce novice agility enthusiasts to "the regulars," to competition, and to the spirit of sportsmanship in dog agility today.

Briefing

A team will be composed of two dogs and two handlers. Novice handlers should be paired with more experienced handlers so that the field is well-balanced. For instance, pair a Starters dog and handler with a Masters dog and handler.

The teams are required to run a standard relay course with an exchange roughly in the middle of the sequence. Rather than exchanging a baton, however, the handlers will exchange an Easter basket that is overfilled with cooked Easter eggs.

There is no fault for dropping an egg so long as the handler picks up the egg and replaces it in the basket before continuing on course. The handler will be faulted for leaving behind a dropped egg.

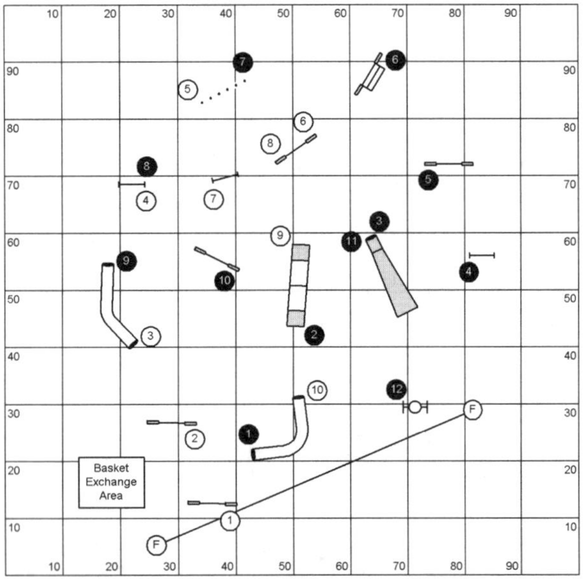

In this sample Pairs Eggstravaganza course, the only contact obstacle is the A-frame, which could be set at a reduced height if there are a large number of exceptionally novice dogs and handlers.

Scoring

Pairs Eggstravaganza is scored time plus faults.

USDAA Starters/Novice rules will be used for judging with one addition: 10 faults will be assessed for leaving behind a dropped egg.

Course Design

Keeping in mind that novice handlers will be making up a large part of the field, the Pairs Eggstravaganza course should either be quite simple, be a jumpers course, or be of mixed levels—half technically challenging and half very basic.

Strategies

In the sample course, the course numbered in black is considerably more technical than the first half of the course. This course might be most suitable for teams of mixed levels, with the novice dogs and handlers running the first half and the more advanced dogs and handlers running the second half.

Pairs Pursuit is a strategic relay played in knockout fashion. The format is unique in agility, but the play is so straightforward that everyone immediately will understand. This one will get those competitive juices flowing and give spectators quite a thrill at the same time.

Briefing

Players are assigned to opposing teams. The knockout proceeds in rounds, with two dogs and two handlers from opposing teams competing against each other on the same course at a time. For each round of the knockout, a dog and handler from one team will be designated for scoring, and a dog and handler from the opposing team will be designated for timing.

Pairs Pursuit Running Order

	Team A	Team B
Run 1	Timing dog runs	Scoring dog runs
Run 2	Scoring dog runs	Timing dog runs

The field will consist of two courses, arranged concentrically. The outer course will be designated the timing side and the inside course the scoring side.

The timing dog and handler will perform the timing side while the scoring dog and handler of the opposing team simultaneously perform the scoring side. In the time it takes the timing dog to complete its side, the scoring dog may repeat its side as often as possible, accumulating points for obstacles completed successfully.

A second running pits another pair of dogs and handlers from opposing teams against one another. This time, the timing and scoring roles are reversed.

The judge may stipulate that the team is required to switch sides from round to round.

Scoring

The winner of each round is the team that accumulates the most points. The team that wins every race they run will win the overall competition.

Faults earned by the timing dog are deducted from a team's score. USDAA Starters/Novice rules are typically used to assess faults. The scoring dog does not earn faults. If the scoring dog faults an obstacle, no points are awarded for the obstacle.

A 1-2-3 system is used to assign point values to obstacles:

- Jumps—1 point
- Tunnels—2 points
- Weave poles and contacts—3 points

However, any point value system can be used since all dogs have an equal chance of scoring.

Pairs Pursuit requires two judges, one for the timing course and one for the scoring course.

Course Design

The inner course is the scoring course and is made up of obstacles whose value is dependent upon the difficulty of the obstacle. The scoring course may contain any type of obstacle but is usually a very short sequence that may be repeated several times.

The outer course is the timing course. It consists of jumps and tunnels, and occasionally, weave poles or contacts.

The course designer has wide latitude in his ability to adjust the speed of the round and the potential for scoring. For example, if the outside or timing course contains contact obstacles, weave poles, or complex handling challenges, more time is given to the inside, or scoring dog, to rack up points. On

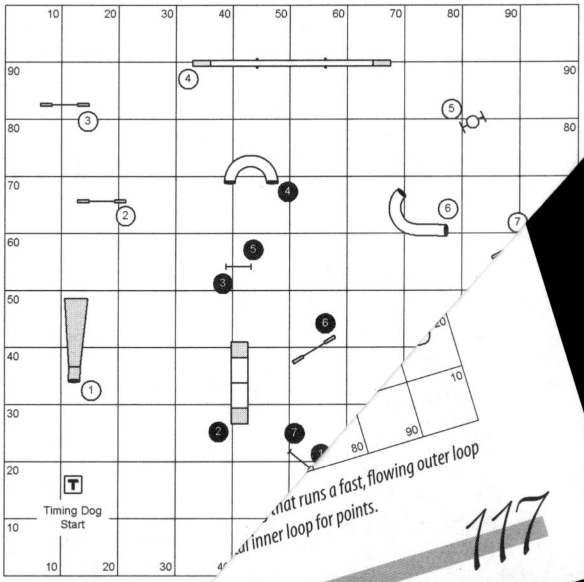

This typical example of a Pairs ... for time against a dog that ... hat runs a fast, flowing outer loop ... inner loop for points.

the other hand, a fast outside course will limit the amount of time the inside dog can accumulate points. In a format that requires dogs to run multiple rounds, it is sometimes better to shorten the scoring time so that dogs don't become exhausted.

Strategies

Strategy for Pairs Pursuit consists of matching each dog on a team against the opponent's dogs so that a team's strengths can be maximized.

It is important in this game that the handler doesn't fall apart if things start to go wrong. A contest can be won despite making errors. The handler should be prepared to regroup and get on with his sequence as briskly and calmly as possible.

Variations

- **Individual competition**—In this variation, individual dogs run against each other. Each dog runs both courses. Scoring is the same.

pass the secret

Do you remember the grade-school game you played where the teacher whispered something in your ear and you whispered it to the person standing next to you. They did the same, and the secret went down the line. The last person wrote on the board what he heard. It was completely different from what the teacher said. Apply that concept to agility, and you've got a game to play with your class or at your agility seminar. Pass the Secret is the invention of Donna Dombourian.

Briefing

The first player will be shown a numbered course map corresponding to the layout of equipment. That player will have precisely two minutes to look at (even walk the course) before getting under way with his dog. Participants are only allowed to watch the person who runs in front of them. After they run, they can watch everyone else run.

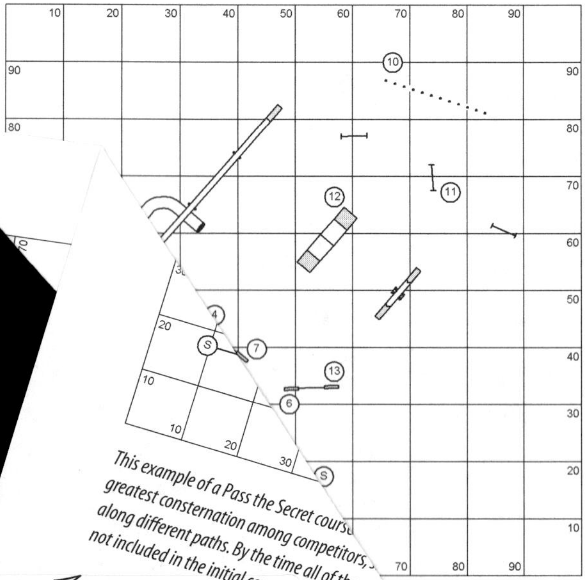

This example of a Pass the Secret cours… guaranteed to cause the greatest consternation among competitors, … ust weave in and out of it along different paths. By the time all of the exhib… ame, the teeter, while not included in the initial course design, may have bee… o the course.

After the first run, the second person runs, trying to duplicate the path the first dog took. This continues until the last dog runs. Then all participants can watch the first dog recreate the initial run. Everyone can laugh at how different the last run was from the first run.

The game can continue with a different handler starting the game each time. This game is good for developing a handler's ability to think and memorize sequences quickly.

Scoring

Any schedule of faults may be observed in the running of this game. A suggested schedule follows. Please note that an off-course for a player is incurred only when that player deviates from the course as run by the previous player, since there is no way for a player to know what was really the course once the game is underway.

- Missed contacts—5 faults
- Knocked bars—5 faults
- Off-course—10 faults

Course Design

The Pass the Secret course should be set up with many options. No numbers are allowed on the course itself, though the initial course map (which only the first competitor gets to see) will be numbered. Obstacles that aren't included in the numbering of the initial course may be included on the field.

Strategies

This is clearly a test of a handler's ability to learn a course with only a scant introduction to it. It's not practical to try to memorize a course as a series of discrete numbers. It would be better for the handler to develop the ability to visualize the course as a series of "flows" or larger shapes that form the dog's path.

Variations

- **First Runner Up variation**—The initial course may also be determined by whoever runs. The first player makes up a course before running it. If the player's dog goes off course, he should just continue as if it were planned.
- **Judge Goes First variation**—The judge may run the course with his dog while the first exhibitor watches.

pillow dash

Pillow Dash is the invention of Sue Tovino and Betty McArthur and was designed to promote skills that will be useful to both the dog and handler in other games.

Briefing

Pillow Dash is run on a course that consists of several obstacles arranged in a line. Each obstacle in the line must be performed in a successively greater number of repetitions. The first obstacle is performed once, the second twice, and so on up to the final obstacle. The final obstacle is performed only once.

Dogs must complete each obstacle the required number of times before going on to the next obstacle in line. Faults will be assessed for incorrect performance on any of the repetitions.

All obstacles must be taken in the direction designated by the judge. Taking an obstacle in the wrong direction will be faulted as an off-course.

After the last obstacle, the handler must cross the finish line and lie down with his head on the pillow. Once the handler's head hits the pillow, he must get the dog to perform a sit-stay in the pause box. Although the dog can be placed in the pause box before the handler assumes his position on the pillow, the dog cannot begin the sit until the handler's head is actually on the pillow. The handler must get the dog to sit within 15 seconds after crossing the finish line. Failure to do so will result in a penalty.

The judge will establish a standard course time. The judge should pad the course time with approximately 15 seconds to be used for putting the dog in a sit-stay.

Scoring

Pillow Dash is scored time plus faults. The lowest score wins.

Faults are assessed as follows:

- Missed contacts—5 faults
- Knocked bars—5 faults
- Off-course—10 faults
- Failing to sit the dog within 15 seconds—15 faults

In addition, time faults will be assessed for exceeding standard course time.

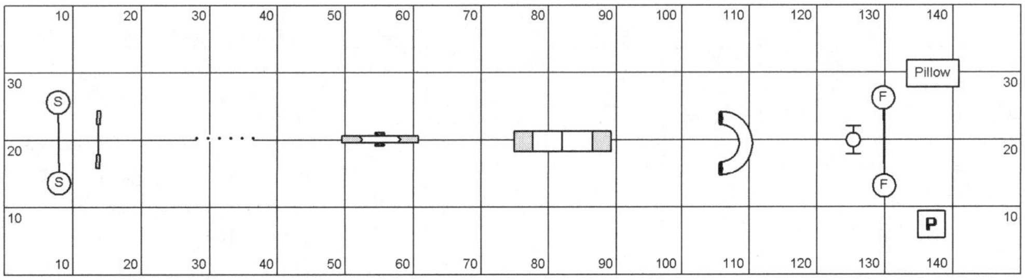

This is the original Pillow Dash course designed by Sue Tovino and Betty McArthur.

Course Design

The Pillow Dash course is long and narrow. All obstacles are arranged in a straight line.

poison

Poison is a training game invented by Cheryl Varney of Youngstown All-Breed Training Center in Youngstown, Ohio. Cheryl reports that her students really like the game. Its unpredictable nature helps them think on their feet.

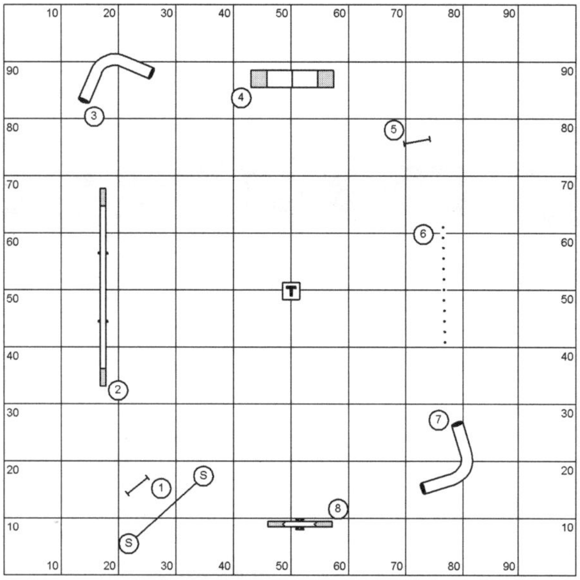

On this simple, novice Poison course, designed by Cheryl Varney, technical challenges are not the point. The handler will have his hands full just trying to keep up with the caller's

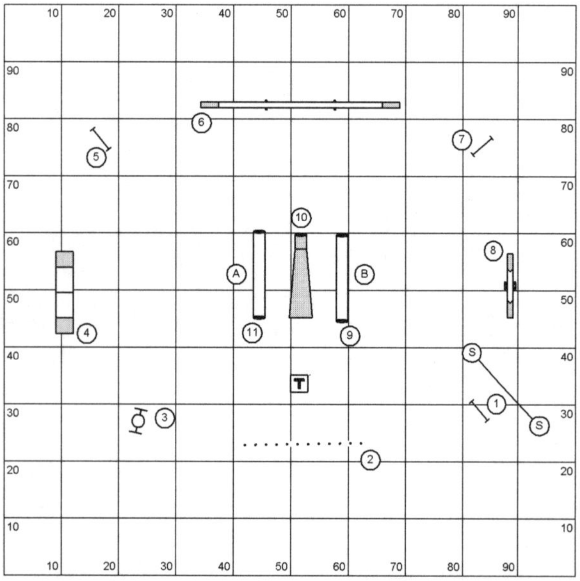

For an advanced game of Poison, Cheryl Varney designed a course that is essentially a circle of obstacles using all the contacts, 12 weave poles, and some jumps and tunnels. At the circle's center is the table, which is "Poison."

Briefing

All dogs will run a sequence in the order and direction specified by the judge while following the directions of a "caller." The caller will call out instructions with which the handler must immediately comply before the dog commits to another obstacle. The calls that may be used are:

- Reverse (immediately change direction and go in the opposite direction)
- Pass (pass the next correct obstacle)
- Down your dog
- Or a specific obstacle name (such as "blue tunnel")

If at any time the dog puts a paw on the table, he is poisoned. The team has to sit down.

The standard course time will be set in a range from 60 to 80 seconds.

If the dog fails to respond to a call within reasonable limits, the team is done and must sit down.

Scoring

This game is most suitable as a training night exercise or a club social function. It would be impossible to level the game for competition so that all things are equal to all teams.

The most rational system, if you must score and place dogs, would be to use a simple faults then time system. Dogs would earn simple faults for performance errors (including an off-course). The dog with the fewest faults wins. Time would be a tiebreaker. It's the time that will be the most difficult element of the game to apply fairly to all players.

Notes for the Caller

The caller should be very careful with timing of calls to make it possible for the dog to safely play the game. Handlers should be advised in the briefing not to push too hard. Safety is the first priority. The caller should be careful when to call "reverse" around unidirectional obstacles, if present (such as the teeter, collapsed chute, and the triple bar hurdle).

The caller's instructions should vary from team to team so that the handler has no real expectation of when to expect a given call. The same calls should be made for all teams. But the order of the calls, and where they are given, will vary from team to team.

An even number of reverses should be given to the team so that the dog ultimately completes the course in the correct direction.

Course Design

Only eight or nine obstacles are typically used in the Beginners course. The caller will usually allow the competitor to get through four or five obstacles before beginning to make calls.

In an Advanced Poison course, 13 obstacles are typically used. The caller will usually allow the competitor to get through 8 to 10 obstacles before beginning to make calls.

poker

Poker is a game invented by John Ostrowski as a just-for-the-fun-of-it activity. The game is designed to measure speed, control, timing, and strategy. As a side benefit, it also teaches competitors to play the card game poker.

Briefing

Besides an agility course, a dog, and a handler, you need a deck of 52 playing cards for this game.

The object of the game is for the handler to collect at least five playing cards (the minimum number required for a hand of poker) in the standard course time specified by the judge.

The player earns the right to collect a playing card by successfully performing obstacles on the course. Only tunnels, tires, spread hurdles, contact obstacles, and the weave poles earn poker cards. However, a bar jump (any bar jump) must be successfully completed prior to performing an obstacle that earns a card. For example, to earn the right to collect a card, the handler might direct the dog to perform jump-dogwalk or jump-weaves.

After successfully completing the card-earning obstacle, the handler must go to the dealer's table to collect his card. The dealer will deal out one card face-up. The handler may then go back on course to earn another card. Dealt cards remain on the table.

It is inconsequential (at least in terms of these rules) what the dog is doing while the handler goes to the dealer's table to collect his card. However, the handler will obviously waste time if he has to recall his dog after collecting a card!

No obstacle can be performed more than once for cards. However, an obstacle may be performed for no cards without penalty. The handler is just using up time.

If the dog faults an obstacle he is performing for a card, the judge will call "Fault," and the handler may at his option repeat the obstacle until the dog is successful or move on to another obstacle.

When the standard course time expires, the timer will blow a whistle. The handler then has 10 seconds to return to the dealer's table and construct the best possible poker hand from the cards dealt during the run.

Five cards are necessary for a poker hand. If the dog earned more than five cards, the handler can choose which five cards to keep and then discard the rest. If, however, fewer than five cards were drawn during the dog's run, the handler must make the best poker hand out of what cards were actually dealt.

Scoring

The dog with the best poker hand wins. In case of a tie (very unlikely), the dogs must play a new hand to determine the winner.

If the dealer runs out of cards, he should reshuffle the deck.

For those who have never played poker before (for shame) or just need a refresher course, here's a description of poker hands in order of their value:

- Royal Flush—10, J, Q, K and Ace all the same suit
- Straight Flush—Five cards in sequence (like 5, 6, 7, 8, 9) and all the same suit
- Four of a Kind—All four cards of any denomination

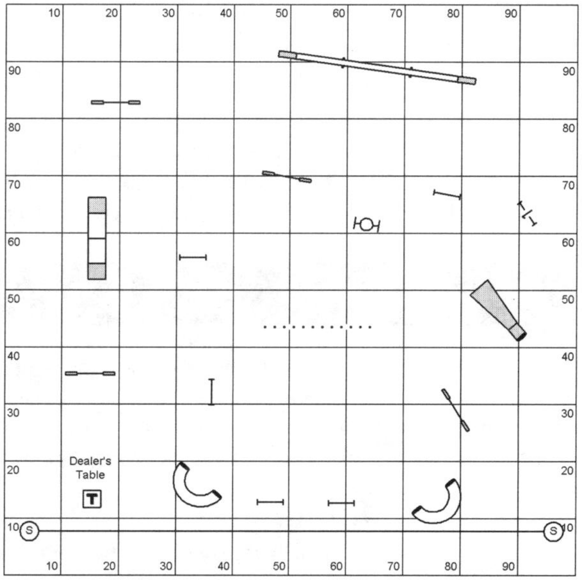

This typical Poker course offers only seven obstacles for the handler and dog to use to earn cards. Jumps do not earn cards, but the team must take a jump before attempting any card-scoring obstacle. With these rules in mind, what kind of flow might be expected in 50 seconds on this course to earn your five or more cards?

- Full House—Three cards of one denomination and two of another denomination (like A, A, A, 8, 8)
- Flush—Any five cards of the same suit regardless of their values
- Straight—A five card sequence of cards (like 2, 3, 4, 5, 6)
- Three of a Kind—Three cards of the same denomination and two unmatched cards
- Two Pair—Two cards of one denomination and two of another with a fifth unmatched card
- Pair—Two cards of the same denomination with three other unmatched cards
- Garbage—Any hand that is so terrible the only thing to do is trade in the whole thing for a new one

Course Design

Obstacles are arranged on the field in a random fashion without any discernible flow.

Course time should range 50 to 60 seconds, plus 10 seconds for assembling the hand. This is more than adequate time to assemble a poker hand given these rules. The time favors novice dogs that might need more time to negotiate a freestyle course successfully and safely.

The size of the course should also be considered when setting the course time. Obviously, the more spread out the obstacles, the more time that should be allowed. Likewise, if playing the game in a very small area, less time is required.

Strategies

Obviously, the more obstacles performed during the run and the more cards collected, the better the chance of assembling a good poker hand.

Variations

- **Seven-card limit**—Instead of allowing handlers to collect an unlimited number of cards, the run can be ended when seven cards have been dealt not exceeding the standard course time.
- **Dealer coaching**—Rather than having the handler construct his poker hand at the end of his run, the dealer can provide coaching to make sure the handler uses the highest possible poker hand.
- **Other types of Poker**—The attraction of poker, the card game, is that there are many interesting variations already. This game could be played as Jacks or Better, High-Low Split, Deuces Wild, Tens or Better, Suicide Kings Wild, Dr. Pepper, or anything that would be interesting and entertaining.
- **Wild cards**—The judge could designate a particularly difficult combination of obstacles on course that allows the handler to collect a wild card if successfully performed.
- **Using a joker**—Another variation on this game is the designation of an obstacle as a joker. If the dog successfully performs the joker obstacle, then the card that is dealt to the handler, along with any like cards, will be wild. For instance, if the card dealt to the handler is a 7, then any other 7 dealt to that handler will also be wild.

pole jacks

This game is an invention of Brenna Fender (credit erroneously claimed by Bud Houston for several years). It is intended as a game of strategy, comparable to Snooker. Pole Jacks creates an atmosphere for intensive work on the weave poles. The game requires consistent performance and pits the dog against the poles with a variety of entries and velocity of approach. Use this game in sharpening everyone's weave-pole work. Pole Jacks has been called Weave Pole Snooker.

Briefing

Pole Jacks is played like the children's game of jacks. The performance of a short set of weave poles is the bounce of the ball. All other obstacles on the course are jacks and have specific point values.

After the "bounce" (doing the weave poles), the team must "pick up" the appropriate number of jacks by scoring an equivalent number of points. The handler and dog team will bounce "onesies," bounce "twosies," bounce "threesies," and so forth until either they reach bounce "sevensies" or time expires.

The dog's time begins when he first makes a "legal" entry into the weave poles, entering between pole #1 and pole #2 from right to left. The judge will establish a reasonable course time, usually 60 seconds, for scoring. The end-of-time whistle ends scoring only; the clock continues to run until the dog crosses the finish line or goes to the table. After the time whistle, there will be no faults and no points for the dog taking additional obstacles on the way to the table or finish line to stop time.

The dog must pick up points equaling the number for which the team is shooting after the bounce. For instance, if the team is shooting for six, they could do a jump and the teeter or they could do a tunnel and the tire.

Obstacles valued at three or more points may be taken only once for points during the run. One-point obstacles may be taken as many times as the handler or dog chooses. No obstacle may be taken twice on the same pick up.

More than one set of weave poles may be used. Either can be used to start time and either can be used for a "bounce."

Scoring

Pole Jacks is scored points then time. The dog's score will be the level of his last complete pick-up, not the accumulation of points gathered during pick-ups. The winner is the dog with the highest points (level) and with the shortest time in case of a tie. The maximum points that can be earned are seven.

The following point values are assigned to obstacles:

- Jumps—1 point
- Tunnels and tire—3 points
- Teeter and A-frame—5 points
- Dogwalk—7 points

If a dog faults during a pick-up, the dog must again bounce (perform the poles) and retry that same number. Faults include the following:

- Any of the usual performance faults (missed contact and so on)
- Picking up more or less than the number of points for which the team is shooting
- Crossing the line of weave poles with incomplete points in the pick up
- Performing a 3+ valued obstacle more than once (an optional rule, rarely used)
- Repeating an obstacle in the same pick up

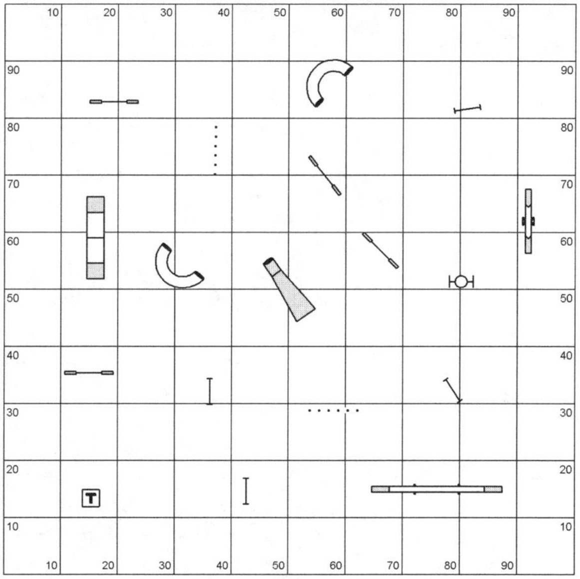

This sample Pole Jacks course employs two sets of weave poles. The dog can begin at either end of either set and can freely alternate between the two during play.

Course Design

Pole Jacks is played with a full set of agility equipment placed randomly in the ring. The weave poles (usually a short set of 5 or 6 poles) should be centrally positioned on the course.

When two sets of weave poles are used, they should be placed in separate areas of the course but near enough to each other that the handler might occasionally make transitions between the two.

Strategies

This is a game of strategy. The handler must plot a path, which will yield seven points in the shortest amount of time. All is not lost should the dog volunteer for an obstacle that was not on the handler's agenda for points, but that challenges the handler to plot a new course to arrive at the number of points for which the team is shooting.

The dog is faulted for picking up more points than he is entitled to in a pick-up. That actually puts the dog that has earned seven points before the time whistle blows somewhat at risk. If the dog takes additional obstacles before time has expired, the judge will call "fault" and the dog will lose his seven-point score. It might be better to actually stop the dog and wait for the final whistle to blow when seven points have been earned. Better yet, devise a strategy that collects seven points on the way to the table with little chance of an off-course.

When handlers have more than one set of weave poles to use for the "bounce," the handler should carefully make use of the flow between the two sets of poles if at all possible. The better the flow the handler can create for the dog, the greater the dog's speed.

Qualifying and Titles

Pole Jacks is a qualifying game for both JFF and TDAA. For each, the qualifying requirements are:

- Games I—Score of 5
- Games II—Score of 6
- Games III—Score of 7

Variations

- **Different bounce obstacle**—Use an obstacle other than the weave poles for the bounce of the ball. This allows handlers to focus on performance of that particular obstacle.
- **Two (or more) sets of weave poles**—The layout of the equipment may include two or more sets of weave poles, any of which are eligible for the "bounce," or at the judge's discretion, for scoring purposes only. When a short set of weave poles is used for scoring purposes, it should be valued at three points.

potluck

Here is a game invented by Natalie Kirkwood in Queensland, Australia, for ADAA agility and for training at the Agility Dog Club of Queensland. Potluck may be run as a training game to work on skills of course-walking and memory.

Briefing

This is a team game for three or more dogs and handlers and requires a pot (bucket), which needs to have a lid with a hole cut in it just big enough for a hand to fit through. In the pot are four colored balls (or similarly marked items) to correlate to the four sequences. If there are more than four handlers in the team, then a second set of four balls needs to be added to the pot. The obstacle layout includes four simple sequences. Colored flags match the balls, and numbers mark the four courses.

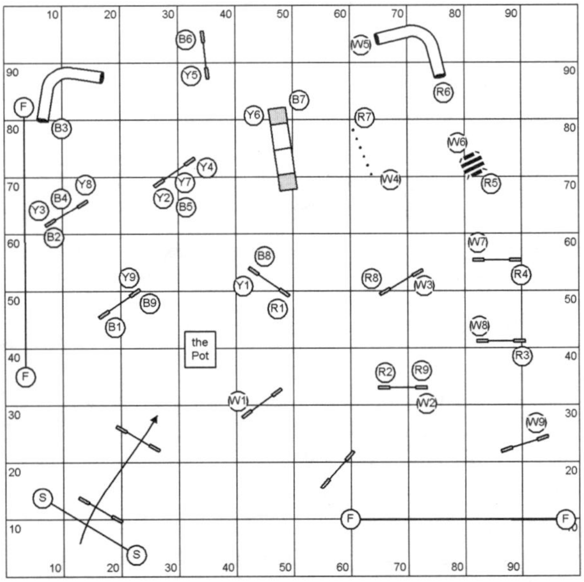

This sample Potluck course is based on an original course by Natalie Kirkwood. One can readily see why guidance from one's teammates often is gratefully accepted.

All members of the team need to learn each course. Potluck is run like a relay. Each dog starts behind a start line. At its turn, each dog goes over a couple of hurdles to the pot sitting on the ground. The handler puts a hand in the pot, pulls out a ball, then directs the dog to do the sequence that matches the ball he pulled. Usually there are plenty of laughs as handlers panic and get confused when they head off to do the wrong sequence or forget the sequence.

Scoring

Potluck is scored faults then time. The team with the fewest faults wins. Use a rate of travel appropriate for the level of competitors. At ADAA competitions, a team qualifies if all dogs in the team earn five or fewer faults and the whole team finishes within the standard course time. The clock starts when the first dog starts and finishes when the last dog crosses the finish line.

Course Design

In Potluck, each course is limited to only nine obstacles to make memorization of the various sequences a bit simpler for the handlers. The beginning of each of the three segments should stem from the area near the pot.

The traditional Potluck course design is rather like a Steeplechase in which the only technical obstacle used is the A-frame.

Strategies

Teammates are encouraged to sing out to help the confused and panicked handler. Sequences may either finish back in the start box or somewhere nearby, and handlers may call out when the next member may go. Balls are kept by the handlers until the completion of their team's run and then returned to the pot for the next team's fun to begin. For more advanced dog-and-handler teams, the sequences may be more complex and wind through each other, or they could be four gamble-style sequences.

power and speed

Power and Speed, a British import game, is the Iron Dog competition of dog agility games. The game demonstrates the ability of the handler to exercise tight control (power) through a part of the course and then show loose control (speed) over another part of the course.

Briefing

Each handler and dog runs a course that is split into two sections: Power and Speed.

- **Power**—The power course will contain no more than 7 obstacles, including 3 contact obstacles, 12 weave poles, and a maximum of 3 spread hurdles. In the Power section, the obstacles should be laid out in a difficult sequence. For example, the distance between certain obstacles might be set at a minimum. Spreads can be set at maximum depth. Approaches to obstacles could be oppressively acute.

  The Power section of the course must be performed without faults and within a maximum course time of 40 seconds. The dog must cross the line dividing the two parts of the course to stop the watch for the amount of time used on the power course. If the time is getting close to the course time, the timer is instructed to watch the dog. If the dog's time exceeds the course time, the dog will still be allowed to continue on the speed course, but there will be no score awarded.

  A dog will earn a 5-second time fault for any mistake. For example, if a dog misses a contact on the A-frame, his score would be 5 for the Power section. Obviously, the ideal score for the Power section is 0.

- **Speed**—The Speed section contains a straightforward sequence of jumps only. The goal is for the dog to run the course as fast as possible, preferably with no faults.

  The Speed section of the course is timed, with faults added to the time.

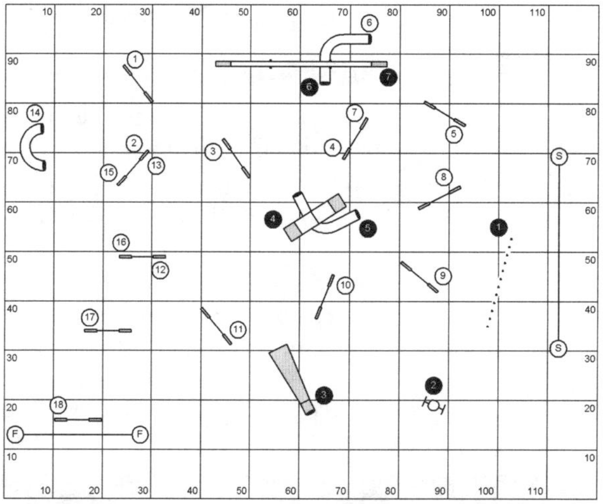

This Power and Speed course was designed by USDAA judge Karen Gloor and played at the USDAA Nationals on July 10, 1998.

Maximum course time is 2 minutes. If both sections of the course are not completed within maximum time, the dog and handler are eliminated.

Scoring

Scoring for Power and Speed is time plus faults: faults from the Power section, plus time from the Speed section, plus faults from the Speed section. The dog with the lowest score wins.

For example, suppose a dog misses the A-frame contact in the Power section and then runs the Speed section in 7.2 seconds. His final score would be 12.2 seconds (a 5-second time fault from the Power section plus 7.2 seconds from the Speed section).

Power and Speed are judged under USDAA Masters rules. Refusals are faulted as are dropped bars and missed contacts.

Course Design

The Power section of the Power and Speed course should be designed to be somewhat inconsequential in terms of handling though challenging in layout. The idea is to allow the handler to direct his dog with a calm touch, making sure to perform the contact obstacles without fault.

The jumping or Speed section of the course should be challenging to an extent. But to a larger measure, this part of the course should be flowing and lend itself to on-the-edge speed.

Strategies

Since completing the "power" portion of the course faultlessly, generally in 40 seconds or less, is enough to qualify for that section,, the handler should not be in a rush to complete that element. When the "Speed" element of the game begins, the handler should push for the best possible speed with a smooth and flowing finish.

When playing Power and Speed at any USDAA event, the exhibitor should pay careful attention to little tricks introduced to the game as a device to dismiss competitors from the ring early (it helps move things along when there is a large entry). For example, when the USDAA played this game at the 1998 Spring Festival of Dog Agility in Lexington, Kentucky, the judge assigned a 30-second Power limit. If the dog had not completed the power section in that time, it was eliminated As a consequence, half the small dogs were dismissed from the ring before getting to the "Speed" element. Another year, the course featured an extended triple-bar hurdle in the middle of the "Power" element, presented at an oppressive angle, and a dummy jump that prevented a square approach. More than 50 percent of the dogs entered in the competition dropped bars on the triple and were dismissed from the ring.

Qualifying and Titles

Power and Speed is an eligible titling game in JFF and TDAA. The course should be nested or reset and numbered appropriately to the level of the classes in competition.

In JFF, no standard course time is observed. In TDAA, the standard course time should be based on the rate established for each class, as set forth in the TDAA rules and regulations.

Variations

- **Style and Sprint variation**—This refinement of the game allows a generous limit on the Style (Power) section so that it doesn't turn into a series of repeatedly downing the dog, interrupted by obstacles. Typically, 50 to 60 seconds are allocated to the overall course. This is long enough to do the Style section carefully but not enough to reposition the before every obstacle (as could happen in the Power section of Power and Speed).

puissance

Puissance is a display of power and strength. The dog agility variation is used mostly as a demonstration event in which the height of the jump bar is raised from round to round until all dogs have failed, save one.

Briefing

In Puissance, the dogs are required to jump one or more hurdles. This is a pass/fail format. If the dog successfully clears the hurdle without dropping the top bar, the dog will advance to the next round. If the dog drops the bar, he is out of the competition.

The jump heights start at 8" or some other height agreeable to the judge and event committee. The hurdle will be raised 2" between each round, making the jump progressively tougher and eliminating dogs from the competition as the height becomes too much for them.

Scoring

The dog that clears the last and highest jump, with all other dogs eliminated, is the winner.

Strategies

In the Trainers' Game variation of a Send Puissance, the most important strategy is to take advantage of the rules of the game that allow incremental steps to reward the dog for performance. Handlers will often want to show off in the early going with their dogs, ignoring the opportunity to reinforce their dogs for going away to the jump. In the later rounds, when other dogs are happily running out to do the jump, the showoff's dog won't understand the game.

Variations

- **Send**—The Send variation of this game is quite different. This is a training competition used by Bud Houston to compel his students to practice sending a dog to perform a jump from a distance. Rather than raising the bar of the jump, the line from which the dog must be sent to jump the hurdle is moved progressively further and further away from the jump until a final winner is determined. The jump remains at the dog's regulation jump height or one step lower throughout the competition.
- **Trainers' Game variation**—Based on the Send variation, this is a game played in seminars and camps taught by Bud Houston. The objective of the game is to teach the handler the value of taking small, incremental steps.

  This is a game of puissance. That means that if a handler succeeds in any round, he will stay in the game with his dog. But if he fails, he'll have to sit down and watch the rest of the contest.

  The game is set over several rounds. In the first round, a line is drawn precisely 10' from a jump. The handlers are briefed to send their dogs over the jump, starting as close as they want to the jump. They may continue sending the dog over the jump so long as they beat their last send and until they actually send from beyond the 10' bar.

  In the second round, each dog will set a new line that represents the longest send. Handlers have three attempts to send their dogs over the jump from beyond the previous high mark. Two attempts may be from in front of the line. The third must be to set a new high mark. An important stipulation is made in this round: once the dog has set a new high mark, the team is done. It doesn't matter whether it's the first, second, or third attempt.

  In the third round, handlers will have two attempts to send their dogs over the jump from beyond the previous high mark. One attempt may be from in front of the line. The second must be to set a new high mark. Again, once the dog has a new high mark, the team is done, whether it's the first or the second attempt.

  In the next and in all subsequent rounds, each handler will have only one attempt to send his dog to the jump and set a new high mark. The game continues until only one dog-and-handler team is still in the game or until there is no more room to move the jump a greater distance.

red rover relay

Red Rover Relay is the invention of Fran Seibert. This is a delightful game of strategy, agility, and teamwork. Because a crossover is a required obstacle, this game is not played widely, as it richly deserves. Red Rover Relay originally appeared in Clean Run *magazine in 1996.*

Briefing

Red Rover Relay is played with teams consisting of two dogs of the same jump height and their handlers. One dog is the red dog and one the blue dog. The red dog runs first.

The objective is to perform all the obstacles on the course but to divide the performance between the red dog and the blue dog. The handlers decide which dog performs which obstacles and the order in which the obstacles are performed. There are, however, certain obstacle performance requirements:

- Each dog must perform at least eight obstacles.
- No obstacle on course can be performed twice by the same dog.
- Each dog must perform two contact obstacles, one of which must be the crossover.

- In performing the crossover, both dogs must make a turn on the obstacle. The blue dog cannot take the same two planks of the crossover taken by the red dog, in either direction.

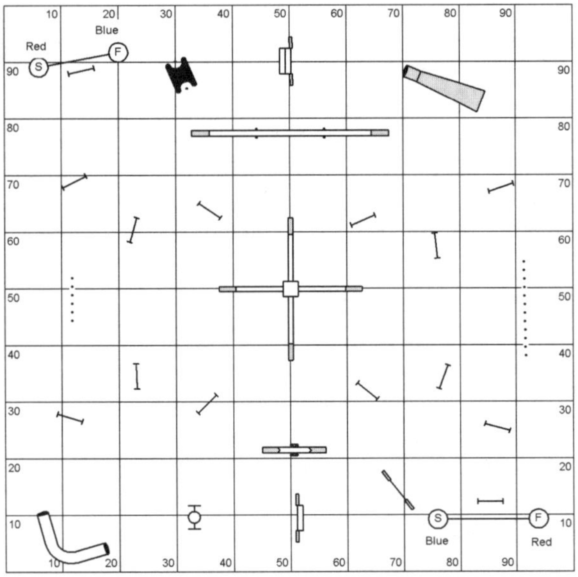

This Red Rover Relay course by Fran Seibert has 25 obstacles plus the crossover, which can be used more than once so long as the planks are taken in different directions. The distribution of obstacles will not make it easy to come up with a perfect strategy to complete everything. But this is exactly the strategy dilemma the teams must solve.

Each dog's start line is the other dog's finish. The start lines are situated on opposite corners of the field. The timer will be positioned at the red dog's start, which is also the blue dog's finish.

There is no baton exchange. The red dog performs whatever sequence the handler has chosen and then crosses his finish line. The blue dog is allowed to go the instant the red dog finishes.

Scoring

Red Rover Relay is scored time plus faults. The lowest score wins.

Faults will be assessed as follows:

- Omission of an obstacle—10 faults
- Obstacle taken twice (four-paws committed to obstacle)—2 faults
- Obstacle not completed correctly (missed weave pole, no turn on crossover, missed contact, fly-off, displaced jump pole)—2 faults

Course Design

The Red Rover Relay course consists of a minimum of 21 obstacles and must include the following:

- Two sets of 6 to 12 weave poles
- Three contact obstacles, one of which must be the crossover
- Two "through" jumps (the tire or wishing well)
- Two tunnels

Strategies

This game demands that the two team members develop a strategy for completing the course together. The paths that the handlers choose to run must have no common obstacles. In addition, each path should favor a specific dog's working strengths, while recognizing that certain obstacles are required to be performed. The team must keep in mind that the fastest course is the key to winning.

relay

In the sport of agility, the relay represents the essence of sportsmanship, teamwork, and humility. Relays are a very special and indispensable form of the game. Just as it sounds, a relay is a competition on an agility course performed by more than one dog and handler. The most common form is Pairs Relay. There are three- and four-dog relays as well.

Briefing

The objective of a relay is for a team to negotiate the course faster than other teams that are competing.

Each team performs a sequence of obstacles as designated by the judge. A relay course can be set up so that one dog will run part of the course and the other dog the remainder, or so that each dog runs the entire course.

The first team starts from a designated area or start line. The handler is required to carry a baton and can choose to lead out or start with the dog. The dog must perform only the obstacles in his designated sequence. After completion of the designated sequence or side, the first handler and dog must move into an exchange area and pass the baton to the second handler, who starts the second part of the course. The second handler cannot lead out.

While performing the exchange, all dogs and handlers must be in the exchange box. Failure to do so results in a faults assessed for passing out of the zone.

The judge may specify whether the inactive dog must be held in the exchange area or whether the dog can be escorted out of the ring after its leg is run.

Relay classes can be conducted with dogs of mixed heights in the same division. For example, a 26" dog can run with a 22" dog.

Scoring

Most frequently, scoring is done on a time-plus-faults basis. The team with the lowest time —after faults are added to running time—is the winner.

Besides standard course faults (see agility), faults are assessed in relays for:

- Dropping the baton—10 points
- Throwing the baton—20 points

After its leg is completed, a dog can earn an off-course by running through the exchange area and taking an additional obstacle.

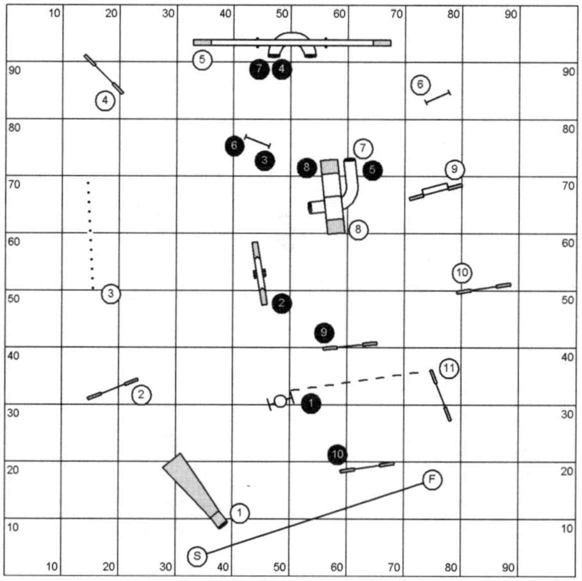

This is an Advanced Pairs course designed by USDAA judge Jean Wilkins for play at Keystone Agility Club on February 20, 1999. The first dog will run the white numbers with a baton exchange after jump #11. The second dog runs the black numbers. To minimize time lost during the baton exchange, it helps to rehearse the switch-off.

Course Design

The layout of a relay course is similar to that of a standard agility course. Typically, however, no teeter or table is used. The course is made up of at least 11 obstacles and often is made up of many more. Each dog on a relay team should be required to perform at least one contact obstacle.

The essential challenge of course design is to balance the difficulty of performance between the dogs in the relay, whether it's a Pairs Relay, a Three-Dog Relay, or a Team Relay (four dogs and handlers). The difficulty should be appropriate to the level of competition.

Course design can have an effect on ring administration. If the exchange area is placed on the opposite side of the ring from the starting line, this means the running of the ring will be slowed as each dog-and-handler team gets into the correct position to begin.

Qualifying and Titles

USDAA

At present, Starters/Novice Pairs Relay is for experience and fun and does not count toward qualifying for titles. As with the other USDAA titling games, however, in Advanced Pairs Relay, a dog-and-handler team can earn the right to move up to the Masters Pairs Relay class by achieving two qualifying scores at the Advanced level. In Masters Pairs Relay, the team can begin earning qualifying scores toward the Relay Master title. As we go to press, the USDAA is revamping its titling process in both the Championship and the Performance Programs, making it possible for dogs to earn games titles at all levels, not just Masters. Please consult *www.usdaa.com* for updates.

To qualify for the Masters Pairs Relay title (RM), a dog must earn five qualifying relay scores, each obtained with a different canine partner. For a relay team to qualify, the time-plus-faults score must be less than the assigned standard course time. Thus, if a team ran a relay course in 60 seconds with a missed contact and a displaced bar, their score would be 70 seconds. If the standard course time were 72 seconds, then the team would qualify. If the standard course time were 65, the team would miss qualifying by 5 seconds. The course rate for a dog to qualify in Advanced Relay is 2.50 YPS, in Masters Relay is 3.00 YPS.

TDAA

Relays, whether as Pairs or three- and four-dog relays, may be played at any level for games titling in TDAA. The design of the course should be appropriate to the level or skill of the dogs engaged in the game. The standard course times should be set at a rate equivalent to the standard course time for the Standard class for each level.

Relays in TDAA will be played time plus faults. If the combined score of the team is under the standard course time, then each dog on the team will earn a qualifying games leg.

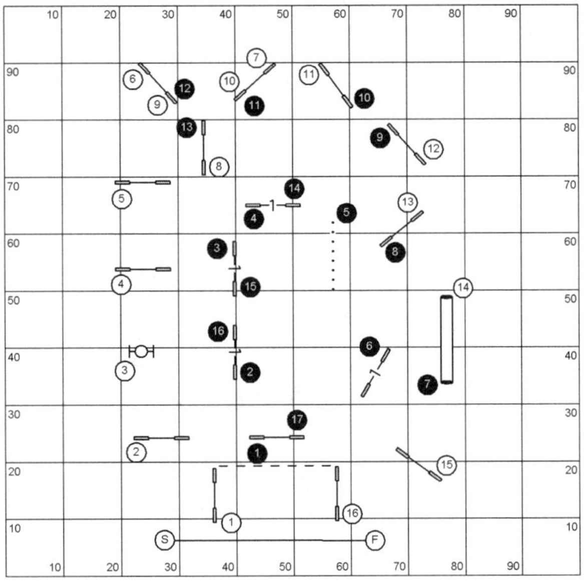

Little is known about the author of this Relay Jumpers course, which was found on the Internet with the notation: "Donyatt 31/5/99, Pairs Jumping, SCT 90 seconds." (The date is evidently a European notation. Donyatt is located in England, or as the Internet says: "a charming little village in the heart of the unspoilt countryside of South Somerset." The trail goes cold there.)

It is certainly a very tight and technical course, containing considerably more obstacles than the traditional Relay course and likely intended for Masters-level dogs and handlers.

Variations

- **Baton exchange**—There are several games based on the baton exchange principle. Some variations become their own unique games and might be discussed elsewhere in this book. In these games, a symbolic representation of the change of lead other than a baton is used (such as giving a high-five, using a picnic basket, putting on an article of clothing, and so on).
- **Reverse baton exchange**—The reverse baton exchange can be used. In a reverse baton exchange, the team member waiting in the exchange area holds the baton. The first handler leaves without the baton; the second handler gives the baton to the first before starting the second leg. This variation is not allowed in the USDAA Relay titling program but is sometimes used in the USDAA Dog Agility Masters Three-Dog Relay.
- **Mini-Maxi Pairs**—Mini-Maxi Pairs is a uniquely British version of the Pairs Relay game. In this variation, a small dog (a Mini) is teamed up with a big dog (a Maxi) for the competition.
- **Three-Dog (Team) Relay**—In this variation, three dog-and-handler teams run the relay. The Three-Dog Relay may be run on a course designed for Pairs Relay. Two dogs run the same side while the third dog runs the opposite side of the course. This is a format used in the USDAA Dog Agility Masters (DAM) tournament. Two dogs must be of one jump height while the third may be any other height or the same height.
- **Four-Dog (Team) Relay**—In this variation, four dog-and-handler teams run the relay. The course might consist of two, three, or four distinct courses.
- **Relay Jumpers variation**—In this variation, the relay is run on a Jumpers course.

reversal of fortune

Marsha Houston with Dogwood Training Center in Ostrander, Ohio, invented Reversal of Fortune as a proofing game for training exercises

Briefing

This game is intended as a relay of four dog-and-handler teams. Every team will have 60 seconds to run a course comprised of three sequences that begin in a central exchange area and finish in that same area.

The three sequences are intended to be run in counterclockwise order, beginning with "A", then "B", and then "C". If a dog faults his sequence, however, the next dog must run the previous sequence in reverse order. Consequently, on a fault, the order of sequences will immediately reverse, as will the order of the obstacles within the sequence.

On any fault, the judge will call "fault" or blow a whistle so that it is clear that a fault has occurred.

On another fault, the order of sequences and obstacles within each sequence will again reverse (returning to the original order and direction of sequences).

The order of the dogs in the relay does not change or reverse. If the second dog faults his sequence, then the third dog in the relay will begin the "previous" sequence in the "opposite" order and direction.

When a dog faults a sequence, the next dog is allowed to begin the next sequence without waiting for the faulting dog to return to the exchange area. However, if a dog runs a sequence without fault, the next dog must wait in the containment area until the active dog has completed the sequence and has gotten back into the containment area. Anticipating the start will be faulted and will cause a reversal of order and direction that could be a bit confusing.

On the 60-second whistle, the dog that is currently active must be directed to the table to stop time. No additional points can be scored on the way to the table.

Scoring

Reversal of Fortune is scored points, then time. Each sequence has a specific point value determined by the judge that represents a total of the point values of individual obstacles in that sequence:

- Hurdles—1 point
- Tunnels and tire—3 points
- Contact obstacles and weave poles—5 points

JFF rules for obstacle performance are used to determine course faults. That means that refusals are not faulted, and only the downside safety zones of contact obstacles are judged.

No points are awarded for any part of a faulted sequence. However, any portion of a sequence under way when the time whistle blows will be earned by the team and added to the score.

Course Design

The essential design for Reversal of Fortune is the construction of three sequences that generate away from a central triangular-shaped exchange area. Each of the sequences must begin at separate boundaries of the exchange area and return to the exchange area on completion.

All obstacles should be bi-directional. Indeed, the sequences themselves should be designed with a sense of symmetry so that they can be run in reverse order.

A table is placed on course to stop time. The table should be placed opposite the third sequence on course.

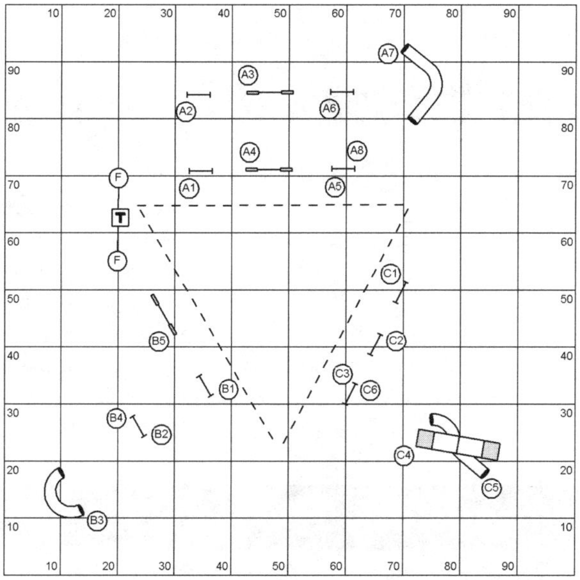

This first-ever design of a Reversal of Fortune course used a medley of training sequences. In this course, the values of the three different loops are dictated by the value of the individual obstacles within each sequence: "A" is worth 10 points; "B" is worth 7 points; and "C" is worth 12 points.

Strategies

The most important skill in Reversal of Fortunes is in knowing what to do on a fault. Each handler must have a mindset that the start he takes with his dog will be one of two sequences, the next in its proper order or the previous in reverse order.

Each member of the team should walk each sequence both in forward and reverse order.

Perhaps a better strategy would be to run each sequence without making any faults whatever.

Variations

- **Natural reversal**—The judge could specify that the team must reverse direction immediately upon the successful completion of all three sequences.
- **Pairs or three-dog teams**—Reversal of Fortune lends itself to be played by multiple dog-and-handler teams of nearly any number.

riddle of two jumps

This is a game played in a seminar format and invented by Bud Houston. The Riddle of Two Jumps tests the handler's ability to adjust for downfield handling requirements. Solving the riddle is sometimes secondary to discovering simple errors in the handler's movement (failing to work through the jumps or not understanding the handling implications on a 180° turn).

Briefing

What difference does it make on which side the handler works his dog? This is a simple enough riddle. What handlers quickly learn is that their dogs turn most naturally in the direction of the handler's position. In other words, if the course turns to the right, the intrepid handler will endeavor to be on the dog's right side. If the course turns to the left, the handler will want to be on the dog's left.

In this game, two jumps are set facing each other with only 12' between them.

The dog must be directed to jump five times. The jumps will be performed alternately, but each time from inside the "box" to outside. It doesn't really matter on which jump the handler starts the dog.

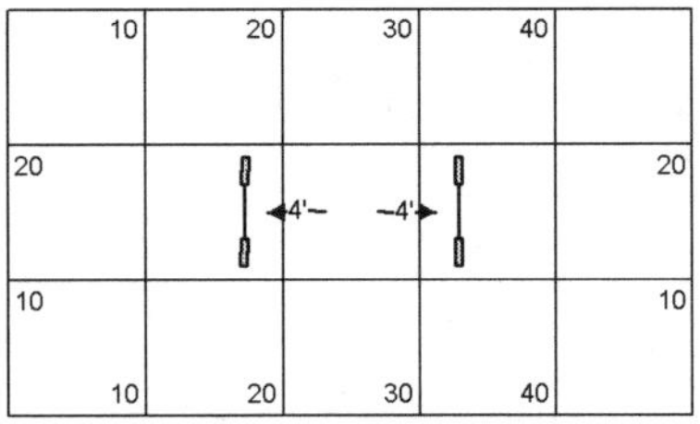

The simplicity of the design for the Riddle of Two Jumps belies its usefulness in assessing the handling skills of agility students. The dog may only take the jumps in the direction indicated by the arrows, from the inside out.

These are the simple rules. The judge will tell the handler which direction the dog must turn on each jump. Additionally, the handler will be prohibited from crossing behind the dog. Rear crosses and tandem turns will not be allowed. This limits the handler to a simple repertoire of a crossing turn or blind cross (when the handler wants to change leads); and a post turn when the handler wants to keep the dog on the same lead.

Course Design

Using this simple course design, the judge can specify several different turning scenarios. Here are some examples:

- LLRLL
- RLRRL
- RRLLR
- RLRLL

Strategies

This game is useful for more than the problem-solving riddle. It is a tool that allows the instructor to see how any agility student will approach a jump with his dog. The jump before an 180º turn is always in danger of being dropped due to errors in the handler's movement.

The game is also used to teach agility handlers that there are always more favorable alternatives to crossing behind the dog. There is no movement in competitive agility that will NQ more handlers than the back cross (crossing behind the dog on the take-off side of a jump). Try running the game in a different way, making the handler solve the entire sequence without allowing any cross "in front" of the dog. This small change in the game will dramatically increase the number of refusals and dropped bars in the simple sequences.

roadside

Roadside is an agility training game invented by Ilze Rukis, who writes, "Yesterday I was so lazy I didn't want to take the time to set out jumps in my freshly mowed backyard, but Zuzu needed 'entertainment,' so I played a game with her that requires no equipment and is something that is actually the result of preparing for my first Dogwood camp with you a couple of years ago. You had sent out 'homework' that one of the things our dogs should know coming into the camp was a 'go around' command. And so I taught Zuzu to go around anything close by: chairs, trees, tables, or car."

Briefing

When you are traveling and your dog needs some exercise, stop at roadside and pick a spot with at least three objects (trees, signs, picnic benches, trash barrel, bench, and so forth) within roughly 30' to 40' of each other, in an area away from other people since this is an off-leash exercise.

Send the dog to go around the first object, for example, a tree. Then send the dog to the table. Send the dog back to the tree or out further to another tree (great *Get Out* practice). Mix up the send patterns, either in big circles or big figure-eight-shaped patterns for a change of direction. Do all of this randomly. It's great mental and physical exercise for the dog.

Five minutes later, a panting dog is happily settled in the car, ready to go on the road again.

Strategies

Training a dog to *Go Around* an object is really quite simple. Start close to the object but do not go around it yourself. Coax the dog into going around and then give the dog a reward, such as food or a toy. As soon as possible, add a bit of distance so that the *Go Around* is the culmination of a *Send*. Dogs are remarkably clever animals and should pick up this game very quickly. This is the foundation of distance training and quite easy to accomplish.

Caution

Be very careful when working your dog in roadside rest areas. You should have an excellent recall on your dog before ever daring to allow your dog off-leash in such a place. Do not treat park benches and stone walls as agility equipment. They may be dangerous to your dog. Dogs have lost their lives in improperly supervised play at a roadside park. Also be careful that your off-leash dog doesn't run off into traffic.

The La-Z-Boy variation is a good place to start your *Go Around* training.

Variations

- **Bud's La-Z-Boy™ variation**—In this variation, the dog's handler can be parked in a nearly horizontal position on the La-Z-Boy™ in the living room (perhaps even while hoisting a beer). Practice sending the dog around furniture, around islands in the house's architecture, or whatever. If the furniture can be layered, this is a great opportunity to work on *Get Out* and *Go Around*. Don't forget that the dog should be rewarded for working. The horizontal position and the bottle of beer will test the handler's dexterity while working with a reward of food treats or a toy.

rock, paper, and scissors

Rock, Paper, and Scissors is a game invented by Becky Dean and Kay Miller, instructors at Dogwood Training Center in Ostrander, Ohio, to teach students to imagine running a course and to hone their dogs' distance-working skills.

Briefing

Rock, Paper, and Scissors is based on the children's game bearing the same name that requires two people. On the count of three, each person chooses either rock, paper, or scissors. Each person must choose a different object; otherwise, the game is repeated until two different objects are chosen. The winner of the selection based on the two choices will be:

- Paper covers rock (paper wins)
- Scissors cuts paper (scissors wins)
- Rock breaks scissors (rock wins)

The agility game Rock, Paper, and Scissors consists of three nested and numbered novice courses. One course is named Rock, the second Paper, and the third Scissors. Each handler will be given course maps of all three courses to review. Each course should be clearly named on the course map. No one is allowed to walk the course at this time. After each handler has reviewed the course map, each handler must play Rock, Paper, and Scissors with the scribe.

If the handler wins the game of Rock, Paper, and Scissors (for example, handler chooses paper and the scribe chooses rock), the handler will run the paper course and have the opportunity to walk the course before running it. However, if the handler loses the game (for example, handler chooses paper and the scribe chooses scissors), the handler will run the paper course but will not be able to walk the course beforehand. The handler can watch others walk the course from behind the start line but cannot ask any questions of others—either before, during, or following walking any of the courses. The handler can only observe others' handling strategies.

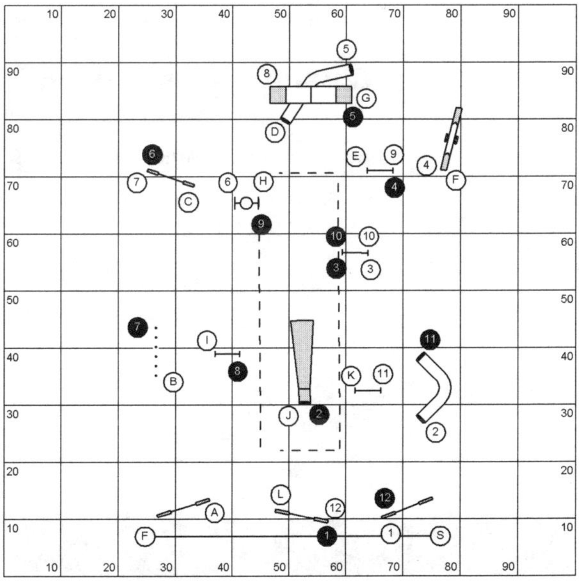

Becky Dean of Columbus, Ohio, designed this example of a Rock, Paper, and Scissors course, which offers both distance (gambler-type) challenges and the potential of having to run a course without walking it beforehand.

Handlers also have the option of handling the entire course from within the containment area. If the handler remains in the containment area throughout the dog's performance, 15 points will be deducted from the dog's score.

If a handler has chosen to use the containment area, the handler must stay within the containment area for the entire run. If the handler crosses the containment area line, no faults are assessed, but the dog will not be eligible to earn the 15-point deduction. Time will stop when the dog has crossed the finish line.

The scribe must note if the handler won or lost the Rock, Paper, and Scissors game for scoring purposes. The scribe may also want to write down which course each handler will be running (not needed for scoring, but to assist the judge).

Scoring

Rock, Paper, and Scissors will be scored time plus faults, minus the bonus. The game is judged using JFF rules.

- Dropped bars, off-course, missed contacts—5 faults
- Failure to perform—20 faults
- Refusals are not faulted
- Missed weave poles are not faulted, but the performance must be corrected or the dog earns a failure to perform.

The bonus (deducted for the total score) is earned if the dog does the sequence while the handler remains within the containment area. The bonus may be earned whether or not the dog earns faults on the sequence, so long as the handler remains within the containment area.

The judge may specify that all teams running the same course (Paper, for example) run before moving to the next course (Scissors, for example). The judge might also determine the running order within a course, for example, specifying that all handlers who walked the course run before those handlers who were not allowed to walk the course.

Course Design

The Rock, Paper, and Scissors course will consist of three unique sequences nested on the field. The complexity of the three sequences should be appropriate to the skill level of the participants.

A containment area must be clearly defined on the course. This area should be centrally located to allow the handler to manage any of the three unique sequences.

Qualifying and Titles

Rock, Paper, and Scissors is an eligible titling game for TDAA and JFF.

- Games I—0 faults on the course the team walked
- Games II—0 faults on the course the team did not walk, or 0 faults on the course walked and handled within the containment area
- Games III—0 faults on the course the team did not walk and handled from within the containment area

seek and ye shall find

Seek and Ye Shall Find is the invention of Mary Jo Lavin. This is a training game that focuses not on how to execute a particular movement, but on the more elusive conceptual skill of "when" to use a particular movement. This game originally appeared in Clean Run *magazine in July 2000.*

Briefing

The following is taken verbatim from Mary Jo Lavin's description of this game: *I have been looking for ways to encourage my students to read sequences to find the best handling strategy for their teams. Although I hope to continue offering insights, I think it is invaluable practice for the handler to plan a strategy of managing a sequence without an instructor's guiding hand. Have you ever had students tell you that they wish you could have been there with them telling them what to do? If so, there is something missing from their training plan! To this end, I designed a course plan where various handling elements might be used and asked students to look for ways to implement them.*

In some cases, I offered a grab bag of skills written on bits of paper. Students could pull from a hat which skill they would try to do. In dealing with larger groups or more novice handlers, it might be best to work as teams. Combine their brainpower and come up with an example. With each opportunity, another member of the team shows the skill. Some examples of these skills were:

- *Front cross*
- *Rear cross*
- *Blind cross*
- *Reverse flow pivot*
- *Lead-out pivot*
- *Counter-hand turn*
- *Get Out*
- *Go On*
- *Distance handling*
- *Serpentine handling*
- *Take a jump, skip a jump*
- *Threadle*

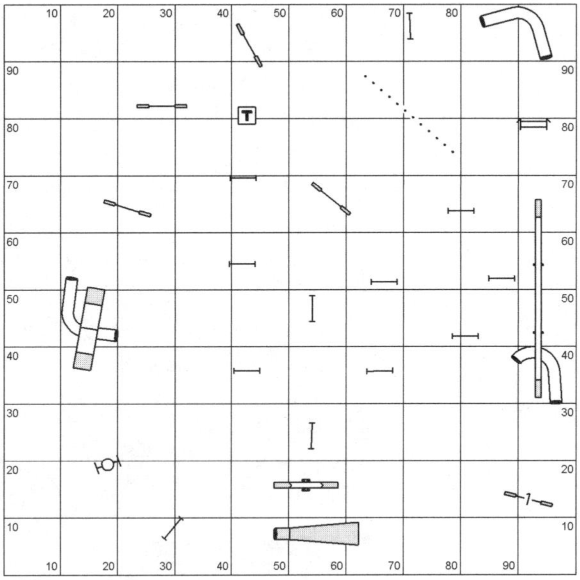

Mary Jo Lavin provided this course as an example of Seek and Ye Shall Find, but just about any course setup would work for this training game.

Can you think of more? Great! Get the class to offer their ideas. Be realistic and don't ask everyone to perform each skill at the same level. One person's sizzling Sheltie and another's Velcro dog won't be looking for the same solutions to challenges on the course.

Course Design

The Seek and Ye Shall Find course should be designed with some thoughtful consideration to creating opportunity for specific movements or handling skills. For example, a serpentine sequence nearly always requires the handler to change sides to his dog. A handling movement is required for the handler to make this change of sides. What movement will be used is left largely to the wit and creativity of the handler.

senility agility

Senility Agility is the invention of the agility staff at Camp Gone to the Dogs in Vermont. It was quite a challenge to come up with a game that could be played by beginner dogs and handlers with only five days of agility experience. The game also had to allow the dogs to work on lead. After giving dogs and handlers a positive and motivational introduction to agility, the last thing the staff wanted was handlers dragging their dogs over obstacles in the heat of competition. Film highlights from this game have appeared on CBS This Morning, Good Morning America, FX Pet Department, *and* Animal Planet.

Briefing

As on a standard agility course, the dog is required to perform each obstacle on the course in the order indicated by the judge.

Here's the catch: if the dog refuses to perform an obstacle, the handler must perform the obstacle. If the dog significantly hesitates or if the handler (in the view of the judge) is being too forceful, the judge will indicate a refusal by blowing a whistle. Either the judge or a ring steward will take the dog (on leash) from the handler. The handler must then perform the correct obstacle.

Often the dog will immediately decide to follow his handler and perform the obstacle. The judge or steward, at his discretion, is allowed to release the dog to follow its handler.

If the handler thinks that the dog will not perform the obstacle, he can direct that the dog be held and immediately do the obstacle himself. This can be an important strategy in achieving the best time.

The handler can also strategically plan for an assisted performance of an obstacle. For each tunnel on the course and at the weave poles, there is a ring steward who at the handler's discretion may hold the dog on leash at one end so that the handler can go to the other end and call the dog through.

The judge will have an assortment of toys and goodies in his pockets in case a dog needs extra motivation.

An instructor or the judge must demo the course and rules with a green dog.

Scoring

Senility Agility is scored time only since no faults are assessed and every obstacle must be performed. Fastest time wins. However, it is suggested that prizes be awarded to all participants.

Course Design

The course should be a simple circle using no more than six obstacles. All obstacles used on course should be training obstacles with which the dogs are very familiar. There should be a start and a finish line.

Because the handler must be able to perform any obstacle on course, the obstacles used must all be examined to ensure they are safe and sturdy. When using the collapsed tunnel, for example, put a piece of carpeting inside the barrel for the handler's comfort. The A-frame should be opened completely and its apex be rested on a low table so that the handler can walk over it safely, if necessary.

Some typical obstacles include:

- A straight or gently curved 15' pipe tunnel
- The agility ladder
- A tire in a stand on the ground or a tire in a frame set at 6"
- A weave pole chute of some type (only 6 poles)
- The A-frame set at about 2' high
- The collapsed tunnel with a 6' chute (held open by helpers if necessary)
- Two 12" wide by 8' or 12' long planks resting on a 6" high table (like half of a crossover)
- A low, non-winged jump

Variations

- **Relay**—This game can be run as a Relay. Set a figure-eight course with a box as an exchange area at the intersection of the circles. In Senility Pairs Relay, the run starts with the first dog leaving the box and stops with the second finishing in the box. No more than six obstacles should be set for each dog.
- **Crowd rule**—In the spirit of fun, it is permissible for the crowd to offer the judge suitable bribes to blow the whistle and require the handler to perform a particular obstacle.

The Simul-Match game represents agility unconstrained by geographic boundaries. It is a game of cooperation and camaraderie that joins disparate regions of the country or of the world. Anne Smith and Bud Houston introduced and popularized the game in the U.S. in the early 1990s. The International Agility Link (IAL), an international agility organization, exists today solely to coordinate Simul-Match competitions around the world.

Briefing

A standard agility course will be run in two or more different locations. The course will be identical in each location, as will the rules for judging.

It is considered a courtesy to videotape the course runs to exchange with the other clubs or organizations that are also running the course.

Scoring

Simul-Match scoring is based on agreement between the groups that are participating in the competition. Any agility game may be used. The participating groups agree to the rules used.

The results will be compiled with the results of other locations running the course. Overall, placements are made for individual dogs. Scores can also be combined to rank how each group did as a whole on the course.

If the competition takes place in virtual time (courses being run at the same time), it is best to be linked by computer for quick results.

In IAL competition, the rules of the International Agility Link (IAL) are typically observed in Simul-Match competitions. These are similar in nature to USDAA Masters:

- Twelve weave poles must be used
- All contact zones are judged
- Refusals are judged on all obstacles
- Almost every fault results in elimination

Course Design

A simul-match competition may use virtually any course or game, or even stipulation of rules, so the design criteria should come from that required for a specific game.

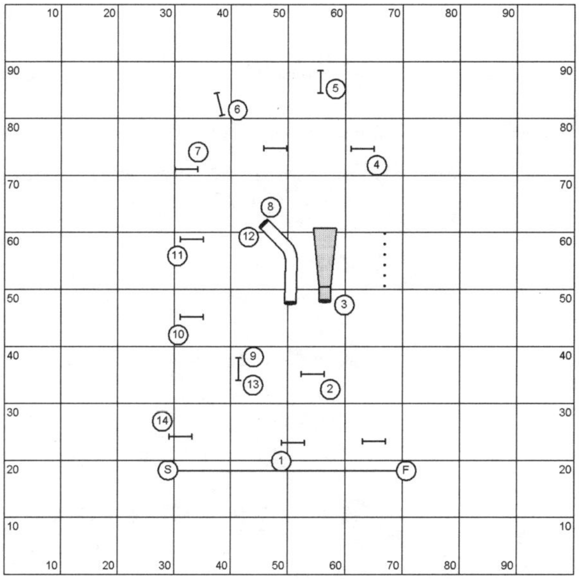

This is the nested Novice course in the simul-match. JFF nearly always nests courses so that novice competitors can run a course or play a game more appropriate to their own level of experience and expertise.

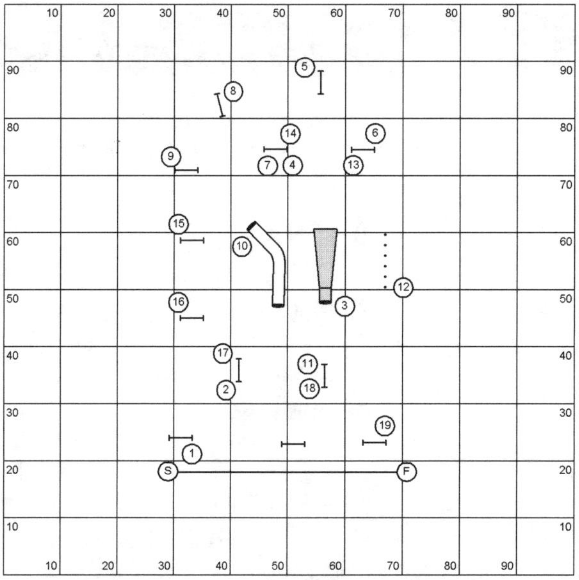

This is the advanced course in a simul-match run by Just For Fun Leagues around the country in December of 2001.

sixty weave-pole challenge

The weave poles represent the most technical obstacle performance in agility. Imagine a line of weave poles 60 long and no other course, just the weave poles. From the dog's point of view and perhaps the handler's, this line of weave poles must seem as though it will go on forever. The 60 weave pole challenge has been played all over the world under various sets of rules. For an example, check out the rules and different competitive divisions in the Clean Run Ultimate Weave Pole Challenge at www.cleanrun.com.

Briefing

This is a simple game. The dog is required to do all the weave poles. There are no faults for missing the entry to the weave poles or for missing a pole. However, any error must be fixed for the dog to receive a score.

The current Guinness world record holder (unofficial) did the Sixty Weave-Pole Challenge in 9.54 seconds. The dog was Quicksilver Ready Aim Fire MX, MXJ, AAD "Mayhem," a Border Collie.

Scoring

The Sixty Weave-Pole Challenge is scored time only.

Course Design

A starting line must be fixed 10' from the first pole and a finish line 10' from the last. A jump may be used at the finish to focus the dog forward. The official spacing of the weave poles is 20". Spring based poles are not allowed. The poles should be flexible only to the extent that 3/4" PVC is a flexible material.

Qualifying and Titles

The 60 Weave-Pole Challenge is an eligible titling game in both JFF and TDAA.

- Beginners—Complete the weave poles within one minute
- Intermediate—Complete the weave poles within 30 seconds
- Superior—Complete the weave poles within 15 seconds

snooker

Snooker is a game of strategy and teamwork. Of all the agility games, Snooker confuses handlers and spectators the most, despite the fact that it uses the fewest obstacles. Indeed, spectators rarely have a clue how Snooker is played, let alone scored. This confusion is due to the fact that the rules appear to be constantly changing, even while the dog is on the field.

Briefing

Snooker is a two-part game. Each part is played and scored on a different basis. The parts are described below.

The judge will establish a time limit for Snooker. This time limit is usually from 45 to 60 seconds. The time is related to the complexity of the Snooker course and the number of obstacles used. Points can only be earned within the allotted time. When the timekeeper blows the whistle, the handler must direct his dog to the designated finish to stop time.

Opening sequence—The game begins with an opportunity for the dog-and-handler team to earn points by successfully performing red obstacles, always jumps, valued at 1 point each. A successfully performed red earns the team the right to attempt one of the colored (non-red) obstacles on the course, valued at 2 to 7 points. The team earns those points if the dog successfully performs the selected colored obstacle.

If the dog faults a red—by knocking down the bar—the dog cannot go on to a colored obstacle. Instead, the dog must perform another red correctly. If a dog faults two of the three reds, he will only be eligible to perform a single colored obstacle. A dog could even fault all three reds. In this case, the dog would not receive any points for the opening sequence. After faulting the third red, the dog would have to go directly to the closing sequence.

The order in which reds are performed is up to the handler. Which colored obstacle is performed after a red is also up to the handler. The handler can choose to take the same colored obstacle after each successful red.

Each red may be taken only once.

The opening sequence ends when the team has performed or attempted all the red jumps specified by the judge and has performed a corresponding colored obstacle after each successfully performed red jump.

Refusals are not faulted in the opening sequence. If the dog commits to an obstacle and then refuses, he is obligated to perform that obstacle, not another. A run-out does not signify commitment.

Performance faults (such as missed contacts) for colored obstacles are not faulted in the opening; the dog just won't receive points for that obstacle. Even if an obstacle is faulted, it must be completed, despite the fact that no points are earned. The dog should then continue the opening sequence by performing another red. If the faulted colored obstacle is the last obstacle in the opening sequence, the dog should start the closing sequence.

At the judge's discretion, two or more obstacles can be combined for a single color. This is called a combination obstacle or an angel. The combination obstacle must be performed in the order and direction specified by the judge. Once a dog has committed to a combination obstacle, all the obstacles in the combination must be performed, regardless of any fault earned on any of the obstacles.

During the opening, scoring will cease if any of the following occurs:

- The dog commits to a colored obstacle without first successfully performing a red.
- The dog performs a red immediately after successfully performing another red.
- The dog performs a red that has already been performed.
- The dog faults a colored obstacle and then attempts to perform the same or another colored obstacle.

Closing sequence—After the opening sequence, the team will perform all colored obstacles in the numerical sequence indicated by their point value (#2, then #3, and so forth, through #7). The dog-and-handler team will earn the value assigned to each of these obstacles as long as the obstacle is not faulted.

If the #2 obstacle was chosen as a colored obstacle for the last red/color combination in the opening sequence, the #2 must be repeated to begin the closing sequence. This is the only instance where an obstacle can be taken twice in succession.

At the close of the scoring period, the dog must be directed to a finish line or point (sometimes the table) designated by the judge to stop the clock.

During the closing, scoring will cease when any of the following occurs:

- An obstacle is faulted
- An obstacle is taken out of numerical sequence
- The #7 obstacle is performed
- The allotted course time expires

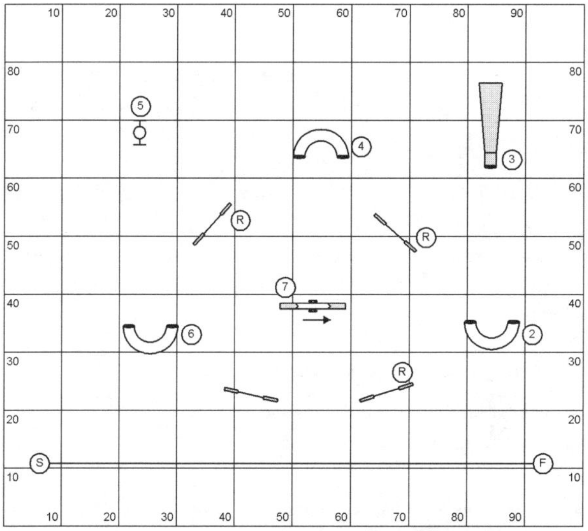

This Masters Snooker course is the design of Mary Jo Sminkey. The high-value #7 teeter in the center will probably result in the winner being the fastest dog to do three 7s (worth the maximum 21 points) in the opening. Note the challenging transitions between obstacles.

Scoring

Snooker is scored points then time. Time is a tie-breaker.

The judge will typically call out the point value of each obstacle performed correctly. The judge will also whistle to end point accumulation if the dog faults during the run.

The timekeeper whistles to signal the end of scoring time. Time does not stop, however, until the dog reaches the designated finish point. Any obstacles performed after the allotted time expires are not counted. The dog keeps all points earned before the whistle was blown. If the dog fails to go to the designated finish, he will retain his points but no time will be recorded.

Course Design

A Snooker course consists of a minimum of nine obstacles or obstacle combinations. Each obstacle or combination is assigned a sequence number and corresponding value. A course will have at least three red jumps and may contain more.

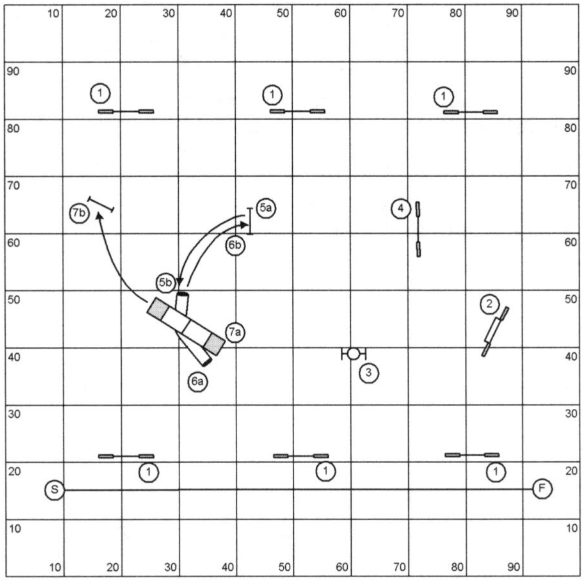

This Masters and PIII Snooker course, designed by USDAA judge Darlene Woz for play on September 1, 2001 at Bay Team in California, illustrates a variation of Snooker that requires teams to perform four or more, rather than the traditional three reds. This course calls for attempts at all six reds.

The judge stipulated that:

- *The dog must use all 6 reds in the opening*
- *#3, #4, and #7 are bi-directional obstacles in the opening*
- *Jump to tunnel is #5*
- *Tunnel to jump is #6*
- *All three combinations must be done with flow across (from one end to the other, and may not be done "inside-out")*

In the closing, the approach/performance of #7 can be jump then A-frame if the dog turns left after jump 6b, or A-frame then jump, if the dog turns right after jump 6b.

Each number on course corresponds to a traditional color (usually indicated on a flag) for that number: 1 is red, 2 is yellow, 3 is green, 4 is brown, 5 is blue, 6 is pink, and 7 is black.

The judge assigns obstacles a color and number based on the difficulty of performance or the distance from a certain point on the course. Any obstacle, except the table, can be used.

All reds must be single jumps.

The table may be used in lieu of start and finish lines.

Strategies

When planning the Snooker run, it is important to know how long it takes your dog to perform equipment and to transition from obstacle to obstacle. With that in mind, the closing sequence should be the first thing that a handler evaluates. Estimating how long it will take you to complete this sequence will indicate how much time is available to accumulate points in the opening.

Pick the smoothest way to go from one obstacle to another.

Evaluate the obstacles on course. If a dog habitually misses contacts, multiple attempts at contact obstacles increase the chance of missing a contact, losing time, and earning no points for the effort. It may be better to try an obstacle that takes longer to perform but one that the dog performs reliably.

Play to win if a win is required in the titling program.

Qualifying and Titles

CPE

Titles can be acquired at each level of competition in CPE by earning two qualifying scores.

JFF and TDAA

Snooker is an eligible titling game in JFF and TDAA. To earn a qualifying score, the dog-and-handler team must earn a minimum of 37 points within the standard course time. The standard course time is typically set at 60 seconds.

The differentiation between Games titles usually should be reflected in the complexity of the Snooker course. For example, a Games I course would use fewer technical obstacles and no combination obstacles. The games might actually be nested so that each level is accommodated on the same course.

USDAA

At present, the USDAA offers a Snooker title at the Masters level. Starters/Novice Snooker is for experience and fun and does not count toward qualifying for titles. In Advanced Snooker, however, a dog-and-handler team can earn the right to move up to the Masters Snooker class by achieving two qualifying scores at the Advanced level. In Masters Snooker, the team can begin earning qualifying scores toward the Snooker Master title. As we go to press, the USDAA is revamping its titling process in both the Championship and the Performance Programs, making it possible for dogs to earn games titles at all levels, not just Masters. Please consult *www.usdaa.com* for updates.

To earn a qualifying score, a dog must earn 37 points. It is not necessary to finish the closing sequence. A dog must earn five qualifying scores in Masters Snooker to obtain the Snooker Master (SM) title. Three of the five qualifying scores must be of the Q-Plus or Super-Q variety, meaning they are in the top 15 percent of the dogs competing at a given height or division. Thus, if five dogs out of twenty receive a qualifying score of 37 points or more, only three will receive a Super-Q. If there are not enough dogs to make up a Super-Q class, the heights are combined. For example, if there is only one dog in the 12" class, that dog will be combined with the 16" class for purposes of determining Super-Qs.

Variations

- **Number of reds**—Several variations exist in which the judge has broad latitude in specifying the number of reds the dog must attempt in the opening sequence. For example:

  Four or more reds must be performed, rather than the traditional three reds.

  Three reds out of four or more available reds must be performed. In this variation, there might be as many as six red hurdles placed throughout the course.

  Three *or* four of four or more reds must be performed.

snooker scramble

Snooker Scramble is the invention of Ken Tatsch. The game debuted at the USDAA Dog Agility Masters tournament in Fair Hill, MD in October of 1998, potentially representing a new approach to the team concept for the USDAA DAM tournaments. This game originally appeared in Clean Run *magazine in January of 1999.*

Briefing

Snooker Scramble is intended for teams of three dogs and three handlers.

Advanced rules are used, except that no refusals are faulted in either the opening or closing sequence. In addition, 10-point penalties will be added for any improper baton exchanges. Time allowed will generally be set between 75 and 90 seconds.

All three dogs and handlers will start and exchange within the designated area. There may be two different jump heights used. If a team has mixed heights, the shortest dog must start. If there are two smaller dogs within the team, these dogs will run first and third. If all three dogs are of the same height, the team may pick their running order.

The game is composed of two opening sequences and one closing sequence. The maximum points available for each team on the course are 102 (three reds each with a color, three reds each with a color, and a closing of #2 through #7 that has a double point value).

The first dog begins with an opening sequence of red-color, red-color, and red-color. He returns to the exchange area and with a reverse baton exchange, the second dog does a second opening sequence using the second set of red jumps, along with the second side's colored obstacles. The second dog may be of a different jump height.

After properly performing the second opening sequence, the second dog returns to the exchange area, and after another reverse baton exchange, the third dog begins. Dog #3 runs a closing sequence of #2 through #7, all worth double-point value for scoring.

The Scramble

If the first dog should break the opening sequence, it will immediately return to the exchange area, and the second dog has the chance of saving some points by picking up where the first dog erred. The second dog will use up any reds unused by the first dog but must perform the colored obstacle at its proper height. A dog need not do the same colored obstacle the first dog was attempting if the break occurred at that point; the handler may choose any available colored obstacle. After completing the first opening sequence, the second dog will then continue to earn points on the second opening course. Examples of a break include any of the following: dog does red-red, red with fault then color, color-color, or repeats a red. A break excludes standard faults on a colored obstacle, such as missed contacts, knocked jump

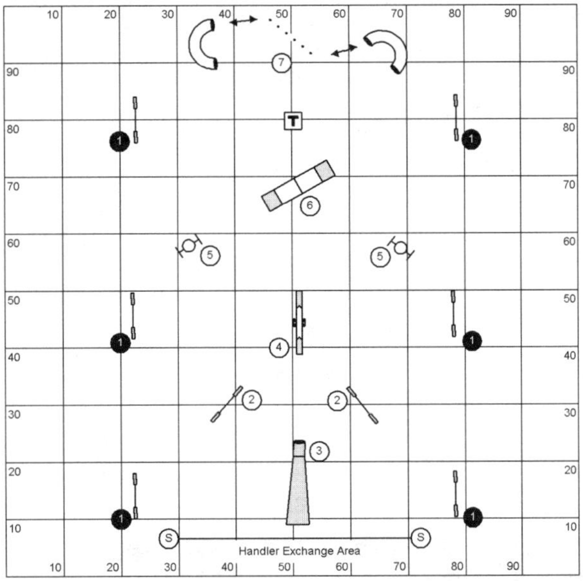

This is a slightly edited representation of the original Snooker Scramble course designed by Ken Tatsch for the USDAA Dam tournament in 1998. In this course, the #3, #4, #6 and #7 colored obstacles are shared by both heights.

The #7 is a combination of tunnel-weaves-tunnel to be done in the direction of flow starting with either tunnel. Besides the correct three reds, only the #2 and #5 obstacles are height specific and offer duplicate obstacles for each height. Each dog must jump its colored obstacles at the proper height.

bars, or missed weave poles. With standard faults, there just will be no points awarded for the obstacle.

If the second dog breaks the sequence, he must be directed back to the exchange area, and the third dog in the scramble must also try to finish up any opening sequence before beginning the closing sequence. Each element of the team is permitted only one error (a sequence-rule violation) and one exchange. If all three breech the rules, the round is over.

This is kind of a "boxed pairs" scenario, with a dog-and-handler team taking over where an error occurs, except that each dog-and-handler team is retired upon occurrence of a single sequence rule error; in other words, there are no repeat substitutions where multiple errors occur.

Scoring

Snooker Scramble is scored points then time. Unlike traditional Snooker, the opening point accumulation will be run twice, and the point values for obstacles in the closing will be doubled. Snooker Scramble has 102 possible points while only 51 are possible in traditional Snooker.

Course Design

The Snooker Scramble course should be designed so that the colored obstacles (those numbered #2 through #7) are balanced on either side by two rows of three red hurdles. Unlike the normal Snooker course, more than one option for a colored obstacle may be included on the course. These are typically duplicated obstacles presented on either side of the centerline of colored obstacles.

The course should include a clearly defined handler exchange area.

steeplechase

In Ken Tatsch's words, "The Dog Agility Steeplechase was actually devised with spectators in mind for USDAA's Spring Festival of Dog Agility. We had been asked two years in a row to put on a mock competition before the stadium jumping finals at the Rolex Kentucky Three-Day Event, and I decided for a third year, why not make it a meaningful competition? To select the dogs to perform in front of the stadium crowd, we ran round one on Saturday, with the finals to be in the stadium on Sunday. The thought for the demos was that the dogwalk, teeter, and table were a nuisance. The A-frame and weave poles were hot items for spectators, along with speed. And of course, they love jumping. So, I set the criteria for the Dog Agility Steeplechase course design and decided it needed to be a time-plus-faults basis to let speed rule. As fate should have it, on that Sunday, they ran behind schedule and cancelled our slot in the stadium time schedule. So, we held the class anyway, and it met with wide acceptance among competitors. We tested it at the Grand Prix and at Fair Hill later that year and announced it would be a tournament the following year."

Briefing

The dog is required to perform each obstacle at the handler's direction in the sequence designated by the judge.

Steeplechase will be run in two rounds with dogs at a given jump height competing against each other. A dog must place in the first round to advance to the second and final round. The final round will stand separately, with all dogs starting with a clean slate.

Scoring

Steeplechase is scored time plus faults. The winners of each round will be the dogs that have the lowest scores.

The number of dogs that advance from the first round to the final round depends largely on the number of dogs in the field. The distribution should reflect the overall distribution of dogs entered in each jump height.

In the final round, dogs run in reverse order of their placement in the first round of competition.

Steeplechase is judged under a special subset of rules. Faults are assessed as follows:

- Off-course (one paw constitutes an off-course), 20 faults
- Missed contact zone, 5 faults
- Knocked jump bar, 5 faults
- Failure to perform, Elimination
- 30 or more faults, Elimination
- Refusals are not faulted, even on contact obstacles.
- Missed weave poles are not faulted as long as they are re-attempted and completed correctly.

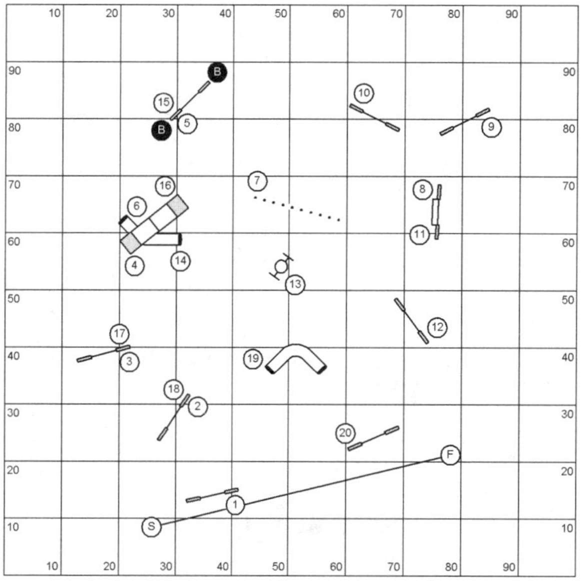

This Steeplechase course was designed by USDAA judge Darlene Woz for Round 1 of the Lexington Spring Festival on April 23, 1999. The Circled Bs on the course map represent large bushes that hedged the #5 and #15 jump.

Course Design

The design of the Steeplechase course seeks speed and flow. The A-frame and weave poles must be used on a Steeplechase course and can be used twice apiece. Other obstacles may include any of the obstacles permissible in a standard USDAA Jumpers class. The teeter, dogwalk, and table are not permitted.

Strategies

On the surface, this class seems easy since it is basically a Jumpers course with one contact obstacle. The difficulty is that the A-frame is often placed in the second half of the course and may be taken twice. After running at full tilt for at least 10 obstacles, many dogs won't slow down for a solid contact performance. Handlers who establish control will have better results.

The handler that places first in round one has the advantage of knowing whether his final run can be conservative or whether he must go for broke. He should pay attention to how other dogs perform before him.

Qualifying and Titles

While the Steeplechase is not a titling game in USDAA, finalists at the regional level are eligible to enter the Dog Agility Steeplechase Championship event, carrying prize money that totaled $10,000 in 2002, which was split among top national finalists in the four separate height classes based upon a pre-approved distribution table.

Steeplechase courses are eligible for qualifying Games scores in JFF and in TDAA. The course should be designed appropriate to the level of competition. TDAA will observe a standard course time comparable to the standard course times used in standard agility classes. In JFF, no standard course time is used.

stop on the contact

Stop on the Contact is a training game played at Bud Houston's Camp Dogwood in Ohio and intended to teach dogs the two-on/two-off method on the dogwalk contact. This game requires the handler to put the dog back on the ramp if he steps off without the handler's release. This game might not be for everyone.

Briefing

This is a game of progression that goes 11 rounds. Whoever makes the most progress in the11 rounds will be the winner. There will likely be a tie for first place.

In the first round, the handler should stop at the bottom of the contact while the dog assumes a two-on/two-off position; then, the handler moves to the dog's opposite side.

In the next round, the handler will leave the dog in position, walk around cone #1, and finish by returning to and releasing the dog.

In the next round, he'll walk around cone #2 and so forth, until the 11 rounds are finished. If the dog is perfect in the 11 rounds, the handler will be walking around the 10th cone in that round.

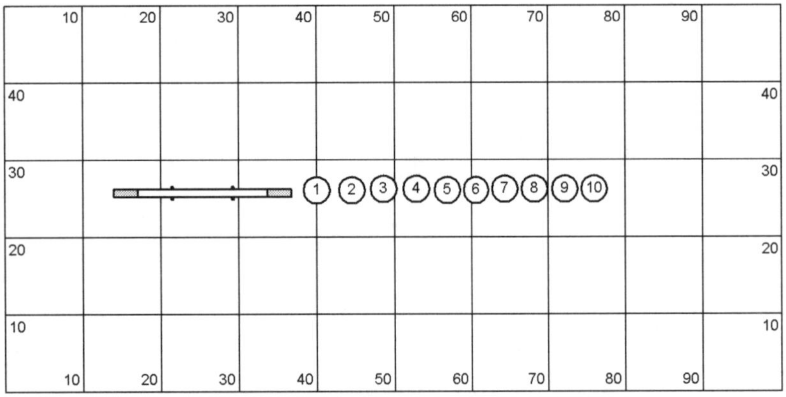

In the Stop on Contact training game, cones mark the extent of the handler's progress as he goes away from and returns to his dog that sticks patiently on the contact until released.

If the dog leaves the two-on/two-off position during any step, the handler will put him back into position and then perform the required step again. In the next round, the dog and handler must repeat that same step.

If the dog actually stays in position during the step, the dog and handler will go on to the next step or cone in the next round.

Scoring

After the 11th round, the handler will earn the number value of that step as the dog's score. The highest score wins the game. If more than one dog has the same high score, the dogs share the win.

Course Design

There's not much to the course design for Stop on Contact. The game needs a contact obstacle (preferably set in a low training position) and 10 cones spaced about 3' apart straightaway from the end of the obstacle.

Strategies

Don't play this game if your dog is "soft" about your physically putting him back in place. It might not even be a good game for a dog with a natural stride through the contacts. If it ain't broke, don't fix it.

Always reward your dog with enthusiastic praise for each step completed.

strategic pairs

Strategic Pairs is the invention of Linda Mecklenburg. This fast-paced and sometimes hectic relay is a game of wit and daring in which both advanced and novice handlers express themselves uniquely. Communication, quick thinking, and cooperation between teammates are essential elements of the game. Strategic Pairs is entertaining for handlers and spectators alike.

Briefing

Strategic Pairs is a pairs relay; two dog-and-handler teams are on the course at the same time. It is run on a single course, numbered #1 through #20 or whatever the judge chooses. The course must be completed in numerical order by either dog.

Dogs must be of the same jump height.

One dog is considered the active dog. The other team is free to move anywhere on course; the inactive dog is not judged. There is no marked exchange area on the course and there is no baton. The teams choose where exchanges will occur and execute each exchange simply by one dog assuming the course from the other. The judge will usually specify a minimum of one or two exchanges, so that both dogs run more than one segment of the course. However, the teams can exchange as many times as is necessary or strategic.

If the active dog faults an obstacle, the judge whistles to signal the fault. The inactive dog becomes active and must successfully perform that obstacle before he can resume the course. If both dogs fault the same obstacle, they must continue, alternately, to attempt that obstacle until it is successfully performed. The course may then be continued.

If one dog drops a bar, one of the dogs must again perform that obstacle even if the performance is simply to send the dog through the jump standards.

There are no off-courses. The judge will only be watching each obstacle in its sequence. For example, the judge will watch #1 until one of the dogs successfully performs it, then #2, then #3, and so on. If a dog performs #1 and #2 successfully but then goes off course, it doesn't matter. The extra obstacle just wastes time. The judge is looking at #3, waiting for a dog, either dog, to perform it.

The inactive dog can do any obstacles it likes without penalty. In some cases, there may even be an advantage to taking a jump on the way to get set up for the next exchange.

Handlers may talk to each other during the run. Outside assistance from the crowd is encouraged.

Scoring

Strategic Pairs is scored time only. The team with the fastest time wins. Faults are penalized by the time it takes to switch dogs. The only number on the scribe sheet should be the total time. There is no standard course time, but it is a good idea to set a maximum course time so that teams aren't on the course for excessive periods.

Strategic Pairs is generally judged under modified USDAA Advanced rules. Refusals are not faulted.

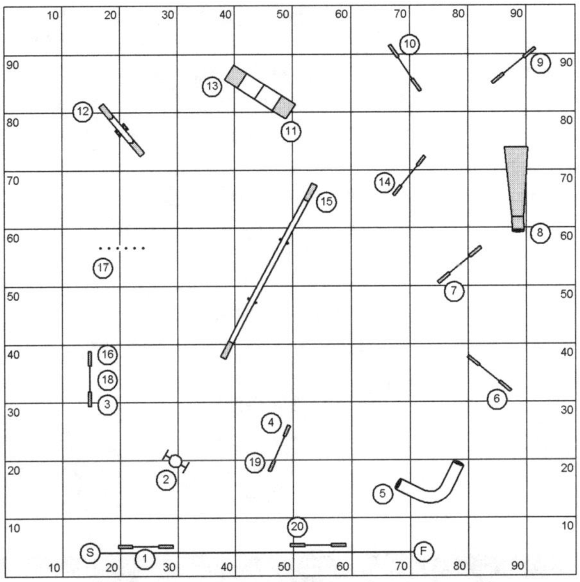

This typical example of a Strategic Pairs course purposefully offers disjointed flow, sharp turns, and seemingly random distances between obstacles—all to encourage handlers to carefully plot their exchanges

Course Design

The course should not be flowing in design and actually should be somewhat disjointed with lots of 180° turns and variable distances—some of them very long—between obstacles.

However, the course should not be so disjointed that it completely dictates the transitions between the dogs. A lot should be left to the imagination and wit of the competitors.

Strategies

The idea is for two handlers to come up with a plan whereby their two dogs can complete the course faster than would be possible for one dog.

How the two handlers communicate with each other is critical. Poor communication results in wasted time. When a dog faults an obstacle, that dog's handler has to quickly convey to his teammate where to resume the course since that handler is intent on positioning his dog for the next segment of the course and is not likely to be prepared to take over.

Each handler must be conversant with the other parts of the course. In case of a fault, an inactive dog's handler has to switch to the active dog. It won't do the team much good if the new active dog doesn't know where to resume the course.

Variations

- **Knocked bars**—A judge may specify that if a dog knocks a bar, the handler must reset the bar before it can be jumped again. This variation should be used only when Strategic Pairs is intended to be an entertaining, silly game.
- **Bi-directional obstacles**—A judge may specify that an obstacle can be taken in either direction so long as it is taken in the designated sequence. Judges must have a firm grasp of the rules before attempting this variation.

strategic teams

Bud Houston uses this variation of Strategic Pairs as a training game at Camp Dogwood. In Strategic Teams, teams of three, four, or five dogs and handlers run the course.

Briefing

A course is laid out that the team must run. Each member of the team must do at least one segment, more if desired or necessary. Where the teams switch dogs does not matter. That's why it's called "Strategic" Teams.

A team will walk a course and determine who will run which parts. Faulting any obstacle complicates the plan. On a fault, a different dog than the one that incurred the fault must resume at the faulted obstacle (on a jump, the jump bar must first be reset). Off-courses are not faulted. However, if the "active" dog takes an obstacle out of sequence after starting any segment of the course, another dog must resume the course at the next correct obstacle.

Scoring

Strategic Teams is scored time only. The team with the fastest time wins. Faults are penalized by the time it takes to switch dogs. There is no standard course time. Strategic Teams is judged under JFF rules.

Course Design

The method for creating the "course" is also unique. Each team will get a number of cones and is instructed to set up a challenging sequence on the field. They are directed to an area or quadrant of the course in which to set up their challenging sequence. The teams actually aren't told that they are going to be playing Strategic Teams or that all the cones will ultimately determine the order and direction of the overall game. This creates a randomness that is as spontaneous as the moment and almost always creates very challenging Strategic Teams courses.

Variations

- **Play It Again Sam**—At Camp Dogwood, the game is always played a second time. Indeed, all the teams get to walk the course again and refine their strategies. This nearly always results in vast improvements in performance and time on course. The score that won the first round will typically be eclipsed in the second round.

strip pairs

The Dallas Agility Working Group (DAWG) dreamed up Strip Pairs, a great mixer that allows dogs and handlers of all levels to compete on a level playing field. It's really not as bawdy as it sounds, but it is a lot of fun.

Briefing

Strip Pairs is run on a standard relay course. Everything about it resembles a standard relay except for one small detail. Instead of exchanging a baton, handlers must exchange an article of clothing. Sometimes this article takes the form of an extra piece of clothing such as a vest or hat. Most of the time, however, the article takes the form of some appropriately strange piece of clothing such as clown pants with suspenders (usually about size 100).

The objective (aside from the relay itself) is to exchange the article of clothing as fast as possible. As most people know, baggy pants and suspenders are very difficult to get into, let alone remove. This means that frequently the first handler must get help (often a lot of help) from the second handler. This can make for some amusing gyrations as well as snide comments. Occasionally, the dogs will even get into the act.

Scoring

Strip Pairs is scored time plus faults. The team with the lowest score wins.

Faults are assessed using modified USDAA Starters/Novice rules. Since there is no baton exchange, there are no baton faults. Shredding the article of clothing, however, is discouraged.

Course Design

The layout of a Strip Pairs course is similar to that of a standard agility course. Typically, however, no teeter or table is used.

swingers relay

Swingers Relay is a game reported by Becky Slanker of the Texas Working Agility Novice Group (TWANG) in which handlers swap dogs in a three-dog relay. This game was first played back in the early 90s at Dallas Agility Working Group (DAWG). Swingers Relay is sometimes known as Spin the Bottle.

Briefing

Dogs and handlers are organized into teams of three dogs and handlers. Each team does part of a standard course while the others are in the start area.

Play is determined as handlers spin a coke bottle. Whoever the two ends point to will switch dogs. The lucky third handler gets to run his own dog.

Scoring

Any rational system of rules can be used to score the teams. This is just an entertaining game, intended for club outings.

However, if a scoring standard is desired, USDAA Novice rules could be used. The game can be scored faults then time.

Course Design

The Swingers Relay course is designed like a simple relay. The course can be divided into three unique sequences or two unique sequences, one of which must be performed by the first and third dog.

The exchange areas should be clearly marked.

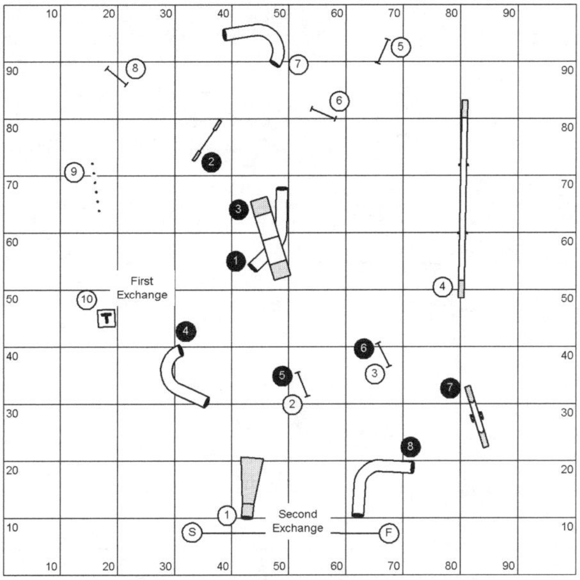

In this example of a Swingers Relay course, the first and third dog will run the same (white-numbered) part of the course. The first handler will hand off the baton to the second handler at the table. The second handler will hand off to the third handler at the original start and finish line.

table in the middle

This is a delightful training game that Carrie Cockerham invented to reward the dog for a fast down on the table and to build a fast and happy down on the first verbal cue. The table is made a very rewarding place for the dog, teaching him that the faster he lies down, the quicker he gets the reward. This game also encourages certain students—with a strong bent for compulsion—to reward their dogs. They are the students that have to be reminded often to give the dog a treat.

Briefing

Each obstacle must be performed in sequential order. However, the table must be performed after each numbered obstacle, except the last obstacle on course.

Time starts when the dog crosses the start line and ends when the dog crosses the finish line.

The required table performance will be a down. Only one verbal cue and signal (treat in closed hand down on table) is allowed. There will be no table count. When the dog is in a down position, the judge will say *go* to cue the handler to open his hand and reward the dog. The team may then proceed to the next obstacle.

As soon as the dog dismounts the final obstacle, the handler is encouraged to toss the dog's favorite toy or a food tube across the finish line and race the dog to get it, with a game of tug or food from the tube as a jackpot.

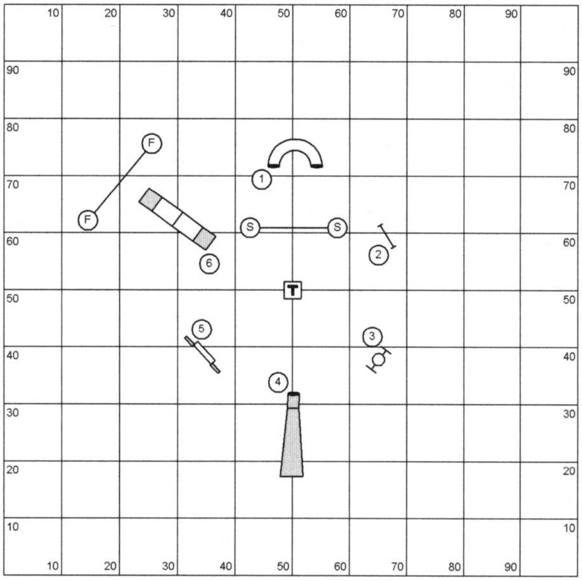

This is the original Table in the Middle Game designed by Carrie Cockerham to encourage students to reward their dogs for fast downs on the table.

Scoring

Table in the Middle is scored time plus faults.

Faults are assessed for any of the following:

- 10 faults for each additional verbal *Down* cue given. It would be beneficial for the handler to wait the dog out rather than reissue the down cue since the dog will likely lie down before 10 seconds have passed. If dog has not assumed position after 10 seconds, the instructor will ask the handler to take the dog off the table and reattempt with the same rules applied. There will be no faults incurred for the reattempt.
- 10 faults for failure to reward the dog while on the table or failure to reward the dog at all.
- 5 faults for failure to toss reward across the finish line as the dog dismounts the final obstacle.
- 5 faults for each off-course obstacle taken.

It is advisable that the judge has a stopwatch to monitor 10 seconds accurately.

Course Design

Six obstacles are set in a circle with the table in the middle. When beginner teams are playing this game, obstacles should be limited to jumps, tunnels, and very low-set contact obstacles. No weave poles should be used. Enough space should be allowed between obstacles to make off-courses unlikely and to set the beginner teams up for success. More advanced teams may choose other obstacles with variable spacing.

Strategies

The handler should be prepared with a handful of small, soft treats to reward on the table as fast as possible. The handler should also have the dog's favorite toy or a food tube tucked away for fast access at the finish line.

Clearly, the handler should be careful to give only one down cue and wait the dog out. The training goal is for the dog to figure out what will get the reward. The handler should take care to reward the dog while in a down position on the table rather than after the dog jumps off the table.

table tag

Table Tag is the invention of Laura Manchester who trains with Valley Agility Sports Team (VAST) Agility in Turlock, California. This is a training game used to work on quick and happy table positioning, Snooker skills, quick thinking, and quick side changes while on the table. The class really gets into it, and it's a crowd-pleaser as well,

Briefing

The dog starts and ends on the table. Time starts as soon as the dog leaves the table. Time ends when the dog gets on the table and assumes an obedience position after completing the last obstacle. The judge will specify the required obedience position.

Each obstacle must be completed correctly from #1 to #5, in order. After each obstacle, the dog must get back on the table and assume a position (sit or down) at which time the judge will immediately release by saying "Go!" No other obstacle may be taken while coming or going from the table. The judge will not award points until the dog completes the obstacle and then correctly assumes the required position on the table.

The maximum course time is generally 60 seconds. If a dog goes off course or misses a contact, he must run back to the table and assume the position. The team may then continue to the next obstacle in order. The dog just does not get the points for the previous faulted obstacle. Refusals are not faulted.

Scoring

Table tag is scored points then time, with 5 maximum points possible. Time is a tiebreaker only.

Course Design

In Table Tag, the table is placed on the field with five to six obstacles around it. The obstacles may be made up of combinations. Traps may be placed depending on the level of competition.

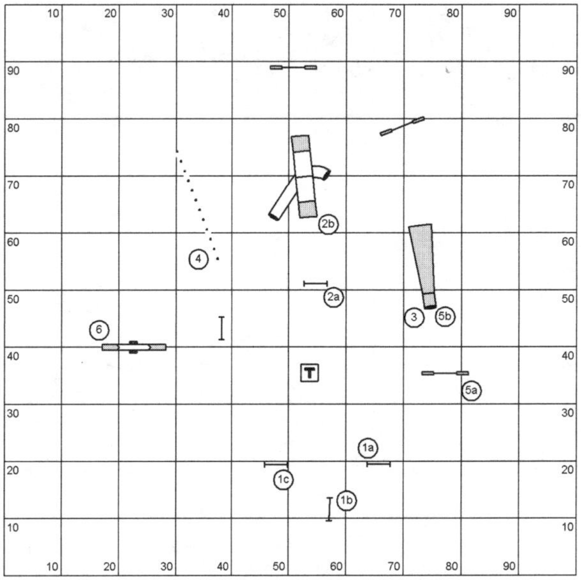

This is an example of a Table Tag course that rewards fast table performance and quick maneuvering among obstacles.

tag 10

Tag 10 is the invention of Martin Gadsby and Lisa Brownschilde as a game of strategy for pairs. The game described here is an adaptation of the original set of rules to make it playable for individuals in the JFF format. This game was played for the first time with Dogwood's agility league on April 16, 2001. Tag 10 was submitted to satisfy a homework requirement for Dogwood's Instructors' Certification Camp.

Briefing

The purpose of Tag 10 is to accumulate points in 10-point blocks and to accumulate as many of those 10-point sets as possible. Sixty seconds are allotted for play.

The team starts with the first "tag," the performance of one of the two tires on course, and then proceeds to gather a 10-point set. Upon successfully securing the 10-point set, the team must again tag and seek to accumulate another 10-point set. The team continues in this fashion until time expires.

The team may not repeat a scoring sequence at any time, either forward or in reverse. Each scoring sequence must be unique. Dogs *cannot* take the same obstacle back-to-back. However, they can take the same obstacle twice (and only twice) in a sequence as long as a different obstacle is taken in between. An obstacle can *only* be used twice in a single 10-point set.

Upon the 60-second whistle, the handler is to direct his dog to tag the nearest tire. When the dog hits the ground on the landing side of the tire, time will stop.

Scoring

Tag 10 is scored points then time. Time is a tiebreaker only. Each set earns the team a score of 1. Each point earned for performing obstacles is worth $1/10^{th}$ of a set.

The schedule of points is:

- Jumps—2 points;
- Tunnels—3 points
- Contacts and weave poles—5 points

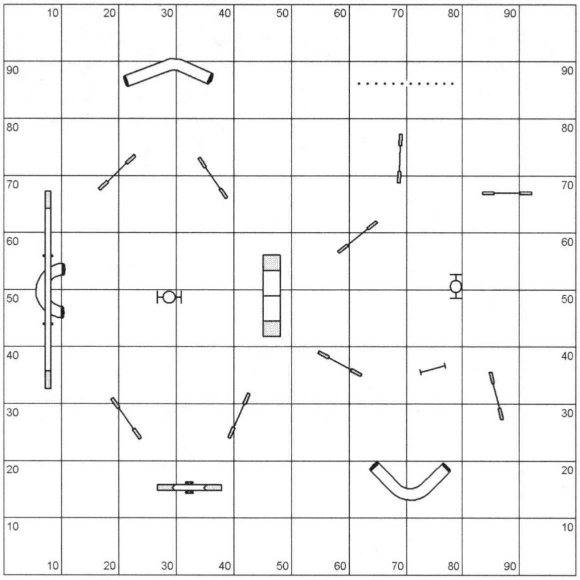

This Tag 10 course designed by Bud Houston was played July of 2001 in agility leagues at Dogwood Training Center in Ostrander, Ohio. The game encourages on-the-spur thinking and creative approaches to combining obstacles for performance.

If a dog faults an obstacle, no points are awarded for that obstacle. The handler must go on to another obstacle before repeating the faulted obstacle. If a bar is dropped on a jump, that jump is out of play for the remainder of the course run.

If the dog tags with more than or less than 10 points, he will receive no score for the set. If the dog is in the middle of accumulating a set when time is called, the points earned in that set will be converted to a decimal score, for example, 4.6 points are earned for the fourth attempted set in which the dog accumulated 6 obstacle points .

Course Design

The Tag 10 course should be designed somewhat symmetrically. The obstacles are distributed around the position of the tagging obstacle (usually the tire). Obstacles of different values should be somewhat evenly distributed.

If two tires are used, both will be ringed with obstacles, and a transitional path should be provided between the tires.

Strategies

The handler must understand very well how to put together the blocks of 10 points. The stipulation against repeating a sequence or running a sequence already used in reverse does not adversely limit the handler's ability to score points. It just keeps things from being repetitive and boring. For example, the handler may do the A-frame, a tunnel, and a jump, and may repeat this point collection strategy so long as a different jump or tunnel is used in each repetition.

Also, the prohibition against running the same sequence in either direction does not limit the handler from doing the same three obstacles in different sequences. For example, the handler could do A, B and C. He's not allowed to repeat with C, B, and A, but he could do B, A and C, and then he could do B, C, and A.

It is strategic to conclude 10-point sets as close as possible to the "tagging" tire to minimize wasting time.

Qualifying and Titles

Tag 10 is an eligible titling game for qualifying in TDAA and JFF.

- Games I—Two sets, or at least 20points
- Games II—Three sets, or at least 30 points
- Games III—Four sets, or at least 40 points

tag team

Tag Team is the invention of Mary Mersereau from Mystic, Connecticut, where the game was first played in June 2002 at My Dog's Place training center. An English couple, Simon and Deb Dominey, that both run their Boxer, Laurel, inspired this game. Deb was running Laurel and was having a little trouble so she called dad and he took over running the dog. Because both handlers can play, this is a particularly enjoyable game for people who share the handling responsibilities of their dog.

Briefing

One handler starts with the dog and the second handler must sit (not down) on the table. The first handler runs the course until the table. The second handler gets up and the dog jumps on the table and lies down. Then the second handler finishes the second half of the course with the dog.

The first handler must immediately sit on the table when the second handler is under way with the dog and must remain on the table for the finish of the course.

Scoring

Tag Team is scored time plus faults. There is no standard course time. The schedule of faults is:

- Knocked bars—5 faults
- Missed contacts—10 faults
- Off-courses—10 faults
- Missed weave poles—0 faults, but any error must be corrected
- Failure to perform—20 faults
- Dog jumping on and kissing second handler—0 faults
- Either handler failing to sit on table—20 faults

Course Design

The course can be designed either like a relay course or like a standard course that uses a table in the middle of the course. The table will be the designated "exchange" area where one handler adopts the task of handling the dog from the other.

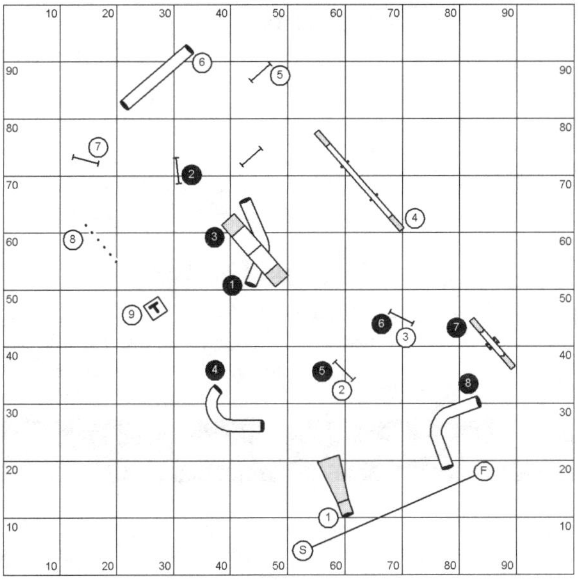

This is an example of a Tag Team course in which two handlers trade off running one dog.

team relay–mixed levels

This variation of the traditional relay game is the inspiration of Anna Carr, who trains with Winston-Salem Dog Training Club and Leaps and Bounds. Anna wanted to develop a relay consistent with the USDAA's Dog Agility Masters relay, but one that can be played by dogs and handlers of mixed levels, allowing them to be more successful and have a lot of fun. By all accounts, Anna's game is a great success.

Briefing

In Team Relay—Mixed levels, the relay is divided into four loops, each with 4-10 obstacles that are designed to take into account players of different skill levels. The teams each consist of four dog-and-handler teams with one pre-Novice dog, one Novice dog, one Advanced dog, and one Masters dog per team. Each dog-and-handler team runs a different loop depending on its level. Faults are assigned for different errors.

If the teams don't work out perfectly evenly, a more advanced dog might run a simpler element of the relay. However, that handler will be handicapped in some manner. For example, the handler might be required to run without arms (hands in pockets or behind his back) or he could be required to run without using his voice.

A dog must finish all obstacles correctly. If a dog misses the dogwalk contact, the handler must redirect the dog to the dogwalk until the dog correctly performs the contact. If handicapped handlers use their voice or their arms, they must redo all obstacles performed with the illegal aid.

There is no set order in which loops must be run. Teams can decide the most efficient transfers and organize accordingly. The clock starts to run when the first dog leaves the line and stops when the last dog hits the table.

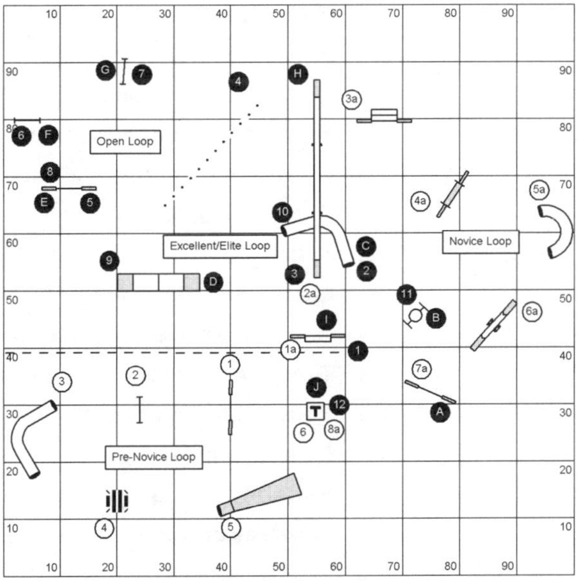

This course shows a design for the Team Relay–Mixed Levels, developed by Anna Carr. Although on the surface, the course seems a bit confusing and complex, since each dog is running a discrete loop, it shouldn't be too difficult for the individual handler to figure out his

Scoring

Team Relay—Mixed levels is scored as time plus faults.

Any rational system of scoring faults can be used for Team Relay—Mixed Levels (if there really is such a thing as a rational system of scoring). It might make the game more interesting to recognize the differences in faults in a USDAA scoring system, so that the different levels of play required in the "loops" are judged using slightly adjusted scoring systems. An off-course at the Novice level would be 5 faults while an off-course at the Advanced level would be 20 faults. The judge must be well versed in the rules used and aware at what skill level a dog is performing.

Course Design

The design of the Team Relay—Mixed Levels course is not the typical relay, which usually strives to present sequences of roughly equal complexity. In the Team Relay—Mixed Levels course, the different sequences are intentionally designed for "mixed levels," and so are of varied complexity.

three-day eventing

Three-Day Eventing that combines Dressage, Show Jumping, and Cross Country comes to us from the U.K. Eleanor M. Thomas of Guildford in the U.K related these rules to us.

Section A: Dressage

Dressage is a preset test that handlers must perform from memory. The judge will allocate points for each movement. These points are added up and then subtracted from the overall mark allocated to the test. This leaves penalty points, which is the score given to the dog.

The dog with the lowest score (the lowest number of penalty points) at the end of the class wins.

The test is judged on accuracy (carrying out movements at the markers), harmony of dog and handler, and the overall impression given.

The arena is 20 meters long and 10 meters wide and is marked out using letters as for horses.

A **Enter at walk**—10 points
X **Halt, sit, salute**—10 points
Proceed at trot—10 points
C **Track right**—10 points
B **Turn right and, at E, turn left**—10 points
A **Circle left 10 meters and, on returning to A, walk**—10 points
B **Turn left and at E, turn right**—10 points
H **Trot**—10 points
C **Circle right 10 meters and, on returning to C, walk**—10 points
B **Halt, sit, remove lead, and proceed around the arena to A**—10 points
A **Turn down centerline**—10 points
G **Halt, salute, leave arena at A**—10 points
Overall impression—10 points
Harmony of dog and handler—10 points
Accuracy of test—10 points

Section B: Show Jumping

A dog is required to run, at the handler's directive, a course of approximately 15 agility obstacles, including the long jump and the collapsed tunnel. No contact obstacles may be used.

Faults will be assessed for the following:

- Knocked jumpbar—4 faults
- Refusal—3 faults
- Wrong course—10 faults

Section C: Cross Country

The dog is required to run, at the handler's directive, a course of approximately 15 rustic obstacles. An optimum time or standard course time is allocated to the course. However, the competitors are not informed of the time until after the competition is finished. The dog with the time nearest the optimum time wins (as in Time Gamble), not the fastest dog.

The height of the fences is 24" maximum, except for dogs less than 15" when the maximum height of fences is 15".

Dogs will not be penalized for jumping on the fences.

three strikes

Three Strikes is a game invented by Fran Seibert. The JAZZ Agility Club meets once a month and has playtime after each meeting. They are always in the market for a good game, especially one that moves quickly (they only have about an hour) and that lends itself to a mixed group with different skill levels. JAZZ has played Three Strikes at several meetings, and members declare it a lot of fun.

Briefing

A fairly large group, members of which are at about the same skill level, usually plays the traditional Three Strikes game.

Numbers (1 or 2) are drawn from a hat to form two teams. All those drawing #1 are on Team #1; those drawing #2 are on Team #2.

Team #1 is at bat first and continues at bat until it has earned three outs or until every one on the team has run. Then Team #2 takes over, and so on. Play continues until everyone on both teams has run. The game may be played for a fixed number of innings.

The same dog will make the "pitch" and then run the "batter's" course. Each play begins with a "pitch." The handler directs the dog through a pitching sequence, and then, as the batter/base runner, must perform each obstacle between bases. The dog must put all four feet on each base to continue.

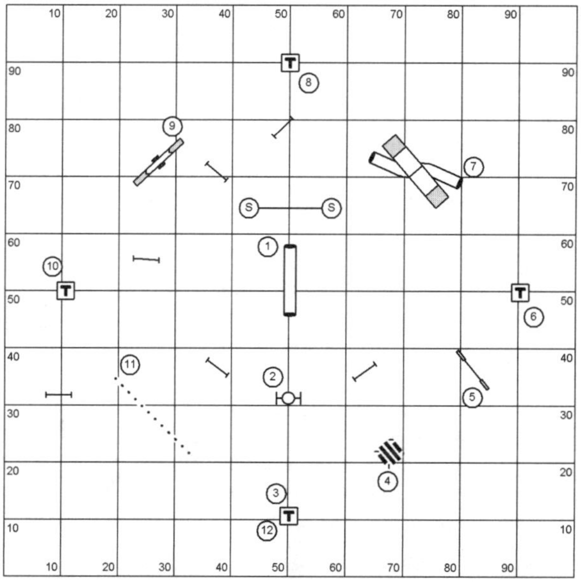

This is an example of an advanced Three Strikes course, designed by Fran Seibert. The "pitcher"" runs obstacles #1 through the table at #3; the "batter" runs obstacles #4 through #12.

Scoring

Three Strikes is scored runs, then time. Time is kept cumulatively for the team. The team with the most runs wins. Time is used as tiebreaker.

The umpire (judge) calls strikes and outs. The timekeeper records time from start line to the "home base" table at completion of a run. The scorekeeper records runs scored and times.

The pitcher gets a strike for any wrong course or a refusal, and three strikes puts the pitcher out. On a strike, the pitcher must start over. Any strikes earned by the pitcher are carried over to the batter.

The batter gets strikes for a wrong course or a refusal, and three strikes puts the batter out. The batter is out for any missed contact, dropped bar, or a refusal at a table. On a strike, the batter must return to last base and continue from there.

Course Design

The Three Strikes course should be set up baseball-diamond-style with tables for home plate and the bases. Alternatively, pause boxes may be used. The pitcher pitches through the tunnel, through the tire, or over a jump to the "home base" table. Other obstacles may be placed nearby to cause the pitcher to incur a strike. The base runner portion of the course begins with the dog and handler in the pause box. Two or more obstacles should be placed on a straight line between the bases. Dummy obstacles should also be present.

The difficulty of the obstacles should be appropriate for the skill level of the players. If weave poles are part of the course and a dog cannot perform them, the handler must perform them.

Strategies

Think of the batter's run as a slow-motion swing of the bat. If the batter misjudges during the swing, he'll probably get a strike and then another pitch. If he executes his swing perfectly, he'll probably hit a home run. The batter's base run is three chances to score a run.

The only strategy, except handling to avoid off-courses or refusals, is to try to stay cool under the pressure of trying to make the best possible time. The more often a handler has to return to the last successfully attained base, the more frantic he is likely to get.

In the traditional team variation of the game, time becomes a tiebreaker. Indeed, time may win the game. The team should be thinking about working briskly and not making a big production of each dog and handler moving into position to begin the next pitch and base run.

Taking a modest lead-out might enhance the batter's chances for success whether starting a run or resuming the course from any of the bases.

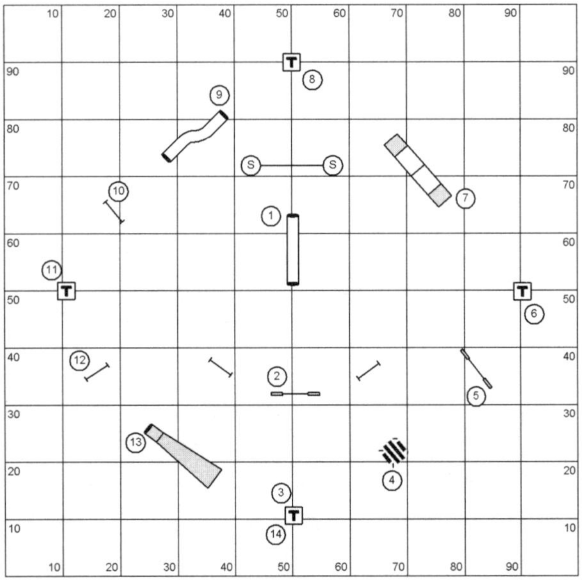

In this novice Three Strikes course, designed by Fran Seibert, aside from the two jumps alongside jump #2, the dog and handler aren't faced with a lot of discrimination problems.

Variations

- **Mixed levels**—This variation is for a fairly large group, members of which are at different skill levels. Beginning dogs and handlers are paired with dogs and handlers that are more advanced. Teams are formed as in Method #1 with one member of each pair drawing a number to determine the pair's team placement. The beginner in each pair has a baton and runs the first three obstacles (the pitch), and then passes off the baton to the base runner in the pause box. The beginner and dog must all have all feet in the pause box while passing the baton to the runner who will be standing to the right of, but not in front of, the box. Play continues as above.
- **Sandlot**—The Sandlot variation is for smaller groups. Each dog-and-handler team runs as an individual, achieving an individual score. For those that score a run, the winner is determined by time. The game can be set to go for one, two, or three innings at the discretion of the group. When everyone has had one chance to score, the inning will be over.
- **Alternate timekeeping method**—Time is kept individually for each dog in one-inning games. The fastest time for a completed run wins; in multiple-inning games, highest number of runs wins. Time is used as tiebreaker.
- **Different pitcher**—The game can be played with a separate pitcher. The pitcher is finished as soon as he hands off the baton to the runner. At Jazz Agility, the split team is used to accommodate beginning dogs and family members who want to play. This variation might also be used as a round-robin rotation so that the pitcher becomes the base-runner/dog-on-deck.

three-tunnel barrel racing

Three-Tunnel Barrel Racing is a game invented by Nancy Creel for the annual Gallatin County Summer Fair Competition in Bozeman, Montana where there are plenty of horse people around. This game is modeled after rodeo-style barrel racing. In the barrel race, the horse and rider run a cloverleaf pattern around three barrels.

Briefing

The dog is required to run the cloverleaf pattern of tunnels.

In the equine barrel race, the horse and rider run a cloverleaf pattern around three barrels. In Three-Tunnel Barrel Racing, the dog must do the same. There are no specific performance faults, but the dog must complete the pattern.

A 10 percent reduction in time will be given to small dogs (less than 13"), junior and veteran handlers, small veteran dogs, and dogs that meet the NADAC 3:1 ratio.

Scoring

Three-Tunnel Barrel Racing is scored time only. Off-courses and refusals usually add so much extra time that it is not worth the effort to score them, and in effect, represent elimination. With only three obstacles, an off-course adds enough time that even the fastest dog will place out of the awards but ahead of plodding inattentive dogs that are looking for resident gophers. Dogs do need to finish all three tunnels in the correct direction to get a time. Usually, this game is won in 10-12 seconds when just three tunnels are used.

Teams will be handicapped using the following system:

- Small dogs = time multiplied by .90
- Veteran dogs = time multiplied by .95
- Heavy-bodied dogs = time multiplied by .95
- Veteran handlers = time multiplied by .90
- Junior handlers = time multiplied by .95

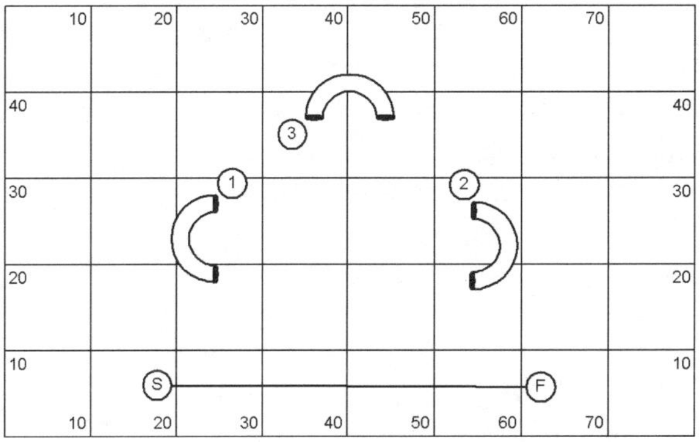

The Three-Tunnel Barrel Racing course echoes the pattern used in barrel racing for horses.

Course Design

In the Three-Tunnel Barrel Racing course, the pattern around the three tunnels is the same pattern used in barrel racing for horses. In a traditional Barrel Race, the horse can start on the left or right. It is easier to number the course than to explain this rule. No faults apply.

time and score

Time and Score was one of three games introduced in the U.S. by Kenneth Tatsch and Jean MacKenzie in the early 1990s after they returned from an agility trip to the U.K. Time and Score likely inspired the Steeplechase game played today because of its frantic pace and reliance only on the A-frame to slow and test a dog on contact obstacles. Time and Score is played rarely in the U.S. today.

Briefing

Time and Score is run like a standard agility course. The dog is required to perform each obstacle on the course at the handler's direction in the sequence designated by the judge. However, the dog may start the course over again if there is time remaining on the clock after his first time through. The dog will accumulate points for each obstacle successfully completed.

The judge will assign a fixed course time. This is usually 60 seconds. At the end of course time, the timekeeper will blow a whistle. From wherever they are on course, the handler and dog must go directly to the finish line to stop the clock. No points are awarded for performance of any obstacle after the whistle.

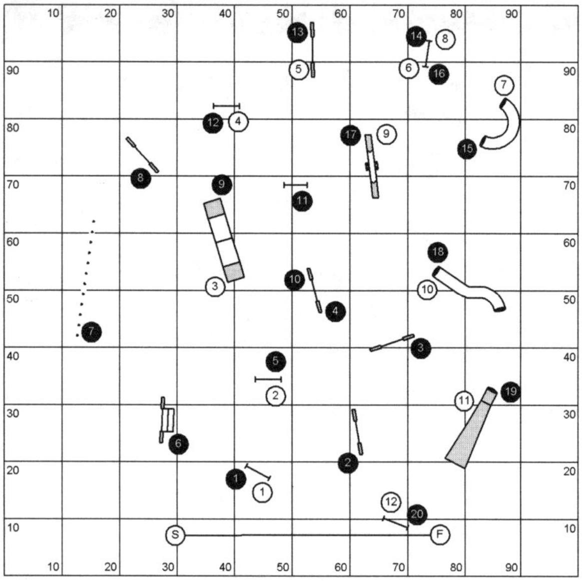

This is a "nested" Time and Score course with the white numbers representing the course for Novice competitors and the black numbers representing the course for Advanced or Masters competitors.

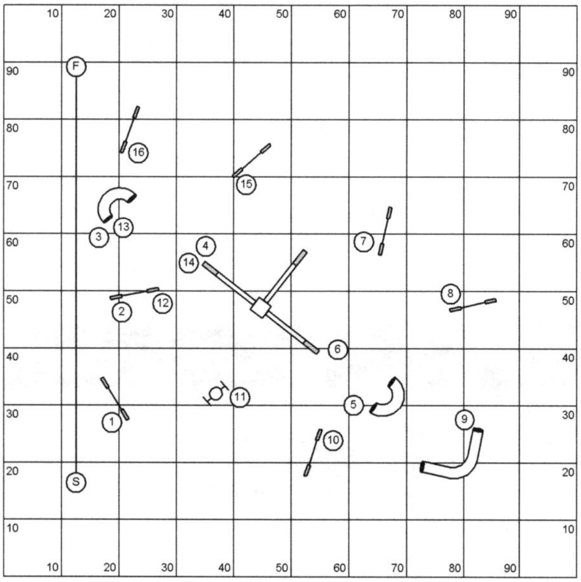

This is the original Triple Cross variation of Time and Score designed by USDAA judge Brian McGunigle for play at Contact Agility on June 8, 1997.

Scoring

Time and Score is scored points, then time. The dog-and-handler team with the most points wins. Time is used as a tiebreaker only.

Points are awarded for obstacles on the following schedule:

- Jumps—1 point
- Tire and tunnels—3 points
- Contact obstacles, full set of weaves—5 points

USDAA Starters/Novice rules are used for judging, except that the four-paw rule will not apply on the contacts. If a dog begins ascending a contact obstacle and jumps off, the handler must attempt the obstacle again.

Course Design

In the beginning, Time and Score courses were usually just circular and fast. However, as dogs and handlers have become more skillful competitors in this country, Time and Score courses should be designed with elements that challenge the dog and handler for control as well as speed.

Qualifying and Titles

Time and Score and the variation Triple-Cross are eligible titling games for qualifying in TDAA and JFF. In both of these organizations, the qualifying score for this game is left fairly to the judge's discretion.

Qualifying should reflect the standard of performance set forth for the appropriate level of the class. In the given 60 seconds, the dog should be able to do the number of obstacles, without fault, for the level at which the dog is competing. If the dog does more, it may be eligible for placement. For example, in 60 seconds

- Games I—zero faults; 12-14 obstacles
- Games II—zero faults; 14-17 obstacles
- Games III—zero faults; 17-20 obstacles

Variations

- **Time, Fault, and Out**—This is a variation of the game from the U.K. In Time, Fault, and Out, the dog continues to run until the time expires or the dog faults an obstacle. A faulted obstacle results in the immediate end of point accumulation. The handler must direct his dog to the finish line for a time.
- **Triple Cross**—This variation uses the crossover at the center of the course. Triple Cross is the invention of Brian McGunigle, who was asked to create a "silly" game for the Long Island Agility club. This is what he came up with. Brian writes of the game, "Apologies if this is not silly enough. I am a new judge, and I will undoubtedly become sillier as I gain more experience." Amen to that.

Despite having gamble in the title, Time Gamble has nothing to do with distance work. The gamble is that the handler must guess the time it will take his dog to run the course. This game has been played regularly at the USDAA Nationals since 1993. Although it started as a familiarization exercise, it has evolved into a regular class that handlers take some delight in playing, and if everything goes right, in winning.

Briefing

Time Gamble is played on any standard agility course. The dog is required to perform each obstacle on the course at the handler's direction in the sequence designated by the judge.

What makes Time Gamble different from standard agility is that the course distance and standard course time are not given. The purpose of this game is for the handler to guess how much time it will take to do the course with his dog. The class is scored time plus faults so that the handler's guess must also include any faults he thinks the dog might pick up on course.

After the course walk-through, and before the class is started, all handlers are required to give the scribe (or another specified ring official) the guess of their final score.

Scoring

Time Gamble is scored time plus faults, minus the handler's guess. The difference between the dog's actual score and the handler's guess is the dog's final score. The winner is the handler with the lowest difference.

If two handlers guess 40 seconds as a course time, and the first team runs the course in 35 seconds while the second team runs 39 seconds, the second team would win despite the first team being faster through the course.

If one handler guesses 60 seconds and runs the course in 59 seconds while a second handler guesses 45 seconds and runs in 40 seconds, the first team would win since they are closer to their estimated time.

Faults are added to the dog's time. The fault schedule is unique:

- Missed contact—3 faults
- Knocked bar—3 faults
- Refusals—not faulted

If one handler guesses 50 seconds and runs the course in 47 seconds with 3 faults while a second handler guesses 45 seconds and runs in 40 seconds, the first team would win since they are closer to their estimated time (the 3 faults are added to the running time of 47 seconds) although the second dog was faster and had no faults.

Course Design

A Time Gamble course will typically consist of at least 11 obstacles and no more than 14 obstacles. Only two contact obstacles are used. No table is used.

Strategies

- Before playing this game, figure out how fast your dog works by keeping track of your dog's yards per second in standard classes. To determine this, divide the course distance by the dog's actual time on course, less 5 to 7 seconds for the table performance. This will give you the yards per seconds that your dog works. Knowing how fast your dog works means all you have to do is estimate the length of the Time Gamble course.
- In addition to knowing how fast a dog runs, the handler might anticipate incurring any faults and add those into the estimate for the guess. Good teams often come within 1/10th second of their estimated times.

Qualifying and Titles

Time Gamble is an eligible game for titling in both JFF and TDAA.

- Games I = Guess within 12 seconds

- Games II = Guess within 7 seconds
- Games III = Guess within 3 seconds

Variations

- **Pre-Novice**—Elizabeth Evans designed this variation as a simple circular course with a table, wingless jumps, a very low A-frame (4' or so) and a tunnel. Handlers have to guess how long it will take for their dogs to do the course. Dogs will start and end on the table. Whoever is closest (over or under) to his actual time will win. Folks with puppies can run the circle without doing all the obstacles, or they can do the ones the puppy knows how to do, like the tunnel, low table, or run between the wings of the jump. They can run the dog on leash if necessary.
- **Elimination for overestimating**—At the 1997 USDAA Nationals, the judge specified that if a handler's guess was over the dog's time, then the team was eliminated. The insinuation of this variation is that a low guess is somehow superior to a high guess.

time warp

Time Warp is the invention of Ilze Rukis. She writes, "Thirty seconds are taken off the final time if weaves are successfully completed with the handler behind the line. Therefore, there is a possibility for negative course times, hence my name for the game. My Border Collie, Zuzu, has proven this time warp theory. She did this game in minus 4 seconds!"

Briefing

The objective of Time Warp is to run all the obstacles in sequence as fast as possible without faults. All obstacles must be completed.

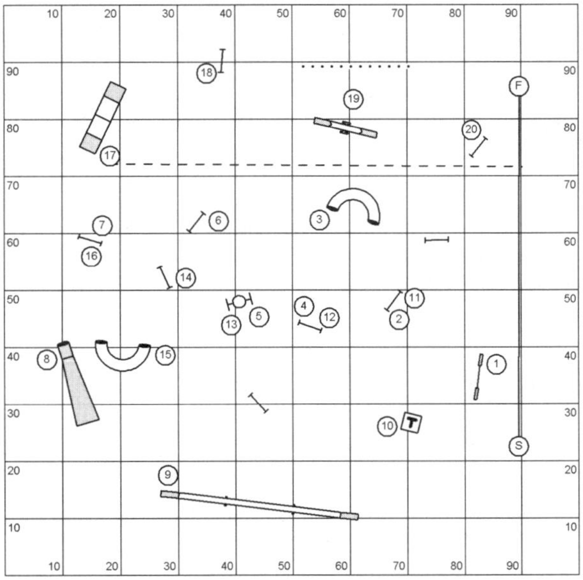

This Time Warp course for Advanced competitors was designed by Bud Houston for agility league play at Dogwood Training Center in Ostrander, Ohio.

In performing the table, the dog will demonstrate both a sit and a down, in either order. The handler simply continues when the dog has done these two performances.

At the end of the course, the handler has a choice, either the teeter or the weave poles. Thirty seconds are taken off the final time if the weaves are completed with the handler behind the line. The handler must be behind the containment line by the time the dog gets into the weaves. Therefore, there is a possibility for negative course times, hence the name of the game.

If the dog comes out of the poles, it is permitted for the handler to switch performance to the teeter.

If the dog puts a single paw on the teeter, the handler must finish the course via the teeter. This is to keep handlers from pulling their dogs off the contact obstacle. If the teeter is chosen, no time bonus is granted and there is no handler restriction.

Scoring

Scoring is time plus faults. Knocked bars and missed contacts earn a 5-point fault.

A 30-second reduction in the dog's time is awarded if the dog performs the weave poles while the handler remains on the opposite side of the containment line.

Refusals and wrong-courses are not faulted (since the dog is already being penalized for wasting time).

Strategies

The handler should be very aware of the capacities and limitation of the competition. A dog that does not attempt the distance challenge might win the game, but it is unlikely unless there is no dog in the field of competitors that will do the weave poles without the attendance of the handler alongside. Moreover, the handler should trust the dog's understanding the performance of the weave poles, even if this performance has not been intentionally tested in the dog's training program.

The handler should be aware that a dog would work nicely in a parallel path to the handler's path. The handler should seek a path of movement complimentary to the dog. The biggest mistake a handler can make in lateral distance work is to come to a stop and rely on the flapping of arms and jaw to direct the dog.

Since refusals are not faulted, the handler should not get mental if the dog should happen to refuse an obstacle. It is possible to recover from such an error and still place highly in this game.

If the handler knows that his dog will not do the weave poles from a distance, it makes more sense for the handler to draw the dog to the alternate obstacle and never mind making the attempt for the Time Warp bonus obstacle.

Course Design

The Time Warp course is usually designed as a standard course except that the weave poles are the last obstacle. The Time Warp course can also be designed as a Jumpers course.

In the traditional Time Warp course, the designer will seek a closing challenge offering a performance of the weave poles to the dog at a lateral distance from the handler.

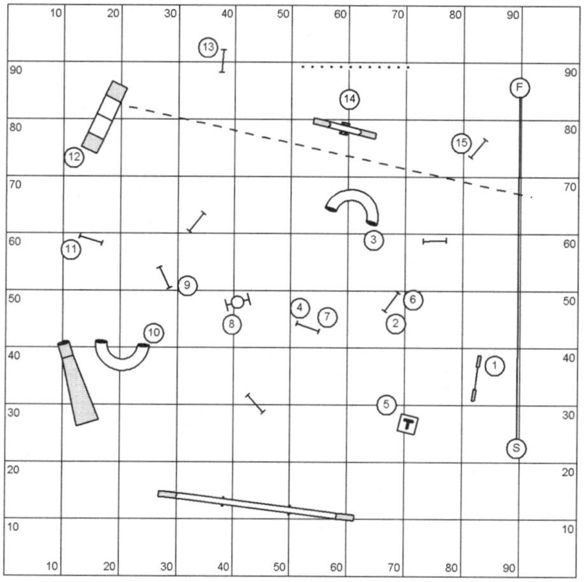

This Novice Time Warp course is nested with the Advanced course.

Qualifying and Titles

Time Warp is an eligible titling game for qualifying in TDAA and JFF. In both of these organizations, qualifying criteria for this game are left fairly to the judge's discretion.

Qualifying should reflect the "Time Warp" quality of the game, such that when the bonus is subtracted from the time-plus-faults score, the team might arrive at an improbable course-time score. For example:

- Games I—40 seconds or less (novice course)
- Games II—25 seconds or less (novice course); 50 seconds or less (competition course)
- Games III—30 seconds or less (competition course)

touch n go

The goal of the Touch N Go class is to demonstrate the dog's ability to perform contact obstacles at speed on a course comprised of tunnels and contact obstacles.

Briefing

This course consists of contact obstacles and tunnels only. The handler must direct the dog to perform the obstacles in the order specified by the judge. Under NADAC rules, refusals are not faulted, and there are no jump bars to drop. All the handler has to worry about is the dog touching the contacts and staying on course.

Scoring

Touch N Go is scored faults, then time. The dog with the fewest faults will win. Time is a tiebreaker only.

The schedule of faults will be:

- Failure to complete—20 faults
- Running the wrong course—10 faults

Touch N Go YPS Table

	Small Dogs	Medium Dogs	Large Dogs
Novice	3.50	3.75	4.0
Open	4.0	4.25	4.5
Elite	4.50	4.75	5.0

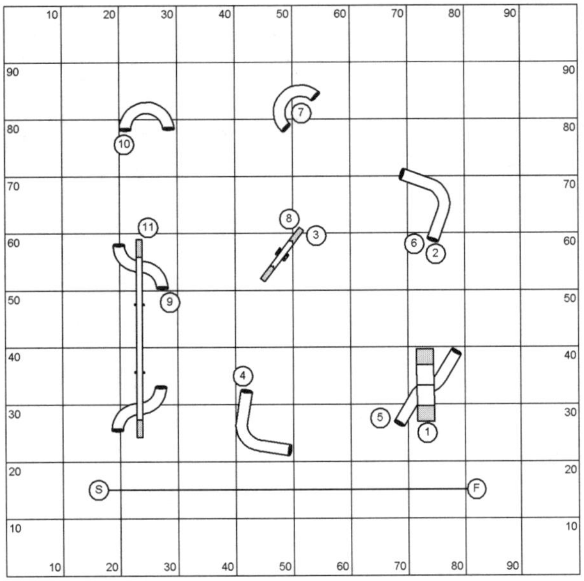

This Touch N Go course was designed by judge Lora Del Page for Ace Agility on April 8, 2002.

- Missed safety zone (descent only)—10 faults
- Body blocking—10 faults
- Time faults—The dog will be assessed time faults for each second or fraction of a second that it exceeds the standard course time

Course Design

The Touch N Go course is made up exclusively of contact obstacles and tunnels. No weave poles or hurdles are allowed. The course should present challenges appropriate to the level of competition.

Qualifying and Titles

Touch N Go is a titling game under NADAC rules. A clean run under the standard course time earns the dog 10 points. Certification in Touch N Go requires 30 points. NADAC offers these Touch N Go titles:

- Novice—TG-N
- Open—TG-O
- Elite—TG-E

All dogs at each of the levels run an identical course. Only the qualifying time changes from one level to the next based on the yards-per-second table.

For each performance of a teeter or A-frame, one second will be added to the standard course time. For each performance of the dogwalk, two seconds will be added. Other adjustments to time may be made at the discretion of the judge.

Touch N Go is an eligible titling game under JFF and TDAA rules. A qualifying score is earned for a clean run under the standard course time.

triathlon

This is an advanced game concocted by Bud Houston and intended as a team game that emphasizes the various skills and games of USDAA agility: Snooker, Jumpers, and Gamblers. Only the most intrepid and advanced handlers and dogs should undertake to play this game. To our knowledge, this game has been played only at Camp Dogwood in Ostrander, Ohio.

Briefing

This is a three-handler and three-dog team game. Each handler in his turn will send his dog over the release jump and play the game indicated by which tunnel the dog elects. These games and tunnels have no set order and can be taken in whichever order the handler (or the dog, as the case might be) prefers.

One tunnel is designated as the start of a snooker course. As the dog emerges from the tunnel, the dog will have 60 seconds to play. On the timekeeper's whistle, the handler must direct the dog to the table to stop time.

Another tunnel is designated the start of a gamblers course. As the dog emerges from the tunnel, the dog will have 40 seconds to accumulate points then 20 seconds to perform the gamble. On the second whistle, the handler must direct his dog to the table to stop time.

The final tunnel is designated the start of a jumpers course. Weave poles may be used in this course. The dog's time stops on the table.

When the first dog gets to the table, the second dog may be released. When the second dog gets to the table, the third dog is released. The team's time will stop when the last dog gets to the table.

Each team may report only one score for each of the three games. However, a dog electing a tunnel and a game that has already been played may finish by playing the game elected by the tunnel. The team will keep whichever is the better of the two scores but will lose the scoring opportunity for the game not played.

Scoring

Triathlon is scored points then time.

The jumpers course is scored on a 100-point deduction system. The dog begins with 100 points. Both time and faults are deducted from these 100 points. No standard course time will be specified.

The gamblers course is scored points only and judged under USDAA Advanced rules. This is significant, since refusals are faulted on contact obstacles. The team is given 25 bonus points for successfully performing the gamble in time.

The snooker course is scored points only and judged under USDAA Advanced rules. Taking an obstacle that is not a part of the Snooker course results in immediate end of scoring (and the judge's whistle).

The three scores are combined and the overall time of performance noted for tie-breaking purposes. This course requires three timekeepers: one to keep overall time, one to keep snooker time, and one to keep gamblers time.

Course Design

Nesting courses for any game can be quite a complicated matter. Nesting courses for three different games is incredibly complex. In the Snooker and Jumpers courses, the first indicated obstacle should be placed in such a position that the handler has some hope of getting into position to direct his dog after sending the dog away to the respective tunnel.

Each course should be designed with challenges appropriate to the level of competition.

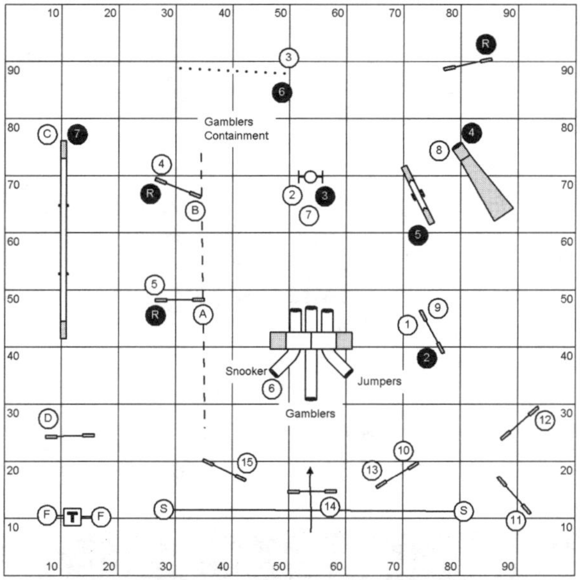

This example of a Triathlon course was designed by Bud Houston. The release jump is the center jump, labeled #14, with a directional arrow drawn through it. Black numbers refer to the closing sequence of the snooker course; white numbers show the jumpers course; and the letters A through D mark the gamble.

Strategies

The team should divide the course on the basis of the relative strengths and weaknesses of the dogs and their handlers. The dog that works best at a distance should do the gamblers course. The most savvy and strategic handler should do the snooker course. The dog most likely to fault contact obstacles should do the jumpers course.

Each handler should be completely familiar with all three of the games and courses on the field. It's not just a matter that a handler might send his dog to the wrong tunnel. Either of the first two handlers to run might send the dog into the wrong tunnel. The handler on deck should be prepared to run the course that the prior handler had intended. With this in mind, the dog designated to be the Gamblers dog probably should go last, because he's more likely to have the directional control to get into the tunnel not taken (even though it might not be the Gamblers course).

Variations

- **U.K. Triathlon**—In the U.K., an agility Triathlon is run with a single dog in three events: standard, jumpers, and gamblers. The three are separate classes. After all classes have been run, and three winners decided, an overall winner is computed from the three classes.

trim the tree

Is your agility club looking for some new games to play at your annual Christmas party? Here's the perfect seasonal game. Trim the Tree is the invention of John Ostrowski.

Briefing

As in Gamblers, the object of the game is for the dog-and-handler team to accumulate as many points as possible in a specified time. However, in Trim the Tree, the handler must hang a Christmas ornament on the tree after each obstacle is successfully completed for points. The proper sequence would be obstacle–ornament–obstacle–ornament–obstacle and so on. The handler will also receive points for each ornament that is hanging on the tree at the end of the run.

Each obstacle on the course may be performed only once for points.

The judge will assign a fixed course time, usually around 45 seconds. At the end of course time, the timekeeper will blow a whistle, and the handler will go to the finishing point designated by the judge.

Scoring

Trim the Tree is scored points plus ornaments, then time. The dog with the highest score wins. Time is used only as a tiebreaker.

The point system used for assigning values to obstacles is at the sole discretion of the judge. Obstacle performance faults will result in the team not earning the points for that obstacle.

Scoring will cease when any of the following occur:

- The handler fails to hang an ornament between the performance of two obstacles
- The handler hangs two ornaments in a row without successfully performing an obstacle in between
- Course time expires

When any of the above occurs, the dog cannot receive any additional points but will keep all points accumulated to that point.

Traditionally, special awards are given for odd circumstances such as most broken ornaments or most ornaments falling from the tree. Awards for watering the tree are optional.

Course Design

This is a great game to play as a pick-up game. You can take whatever course was on the field for the last class, tweak the angles of a couple of obstacles, and then add a Christmas tree and a box of ornaments.

Obstacles should be arranged on the field in a random fashion without any discernible flow. High-point obstacles should be placed some distance from the Christmas tree.

Safety note: It's better not to use breakable ornaments!

triple-true team baton relay

Triple-True Team Baton Relay is the invention of Linda Northrop. The game was originally submitted for the Clean Run *magazine Games Contest in 1995. This is a fun twist on the standard relay, perfect for novice and advanced dogs alike.*

Briefing

Triple-True Team Baton Relay is an up-and-back team relay with multiple legs for teams of three dogs and three handlers.

The course layout consists of four straight lines of obstacles, each of which contains an equal number of obstacles. The flow of each line of obstacles goes in the opposite direction as the line before it.

Handler A directs his dog over the first line of obstacles and passes the baton to Handler B. This handler and his dog run the next line of obstacles before passing the baton to Handler C. Once Handler C and his dog complete the third line of obstacles, all members of the team must perform the final line of obstacles. Any running order for the final sequence can be used. No baton exchange is required between team members for the final leg.

Time stops when the last dog and handler of the team complete the final line of obstacles and cross the passing line.

All baton exchanges must occur behind the appropriate passing line.

Scoring

Triple-True Team Baton Relay is scored time plus faults. The team with the lowest score wins.

USDAA Starters/Novice rules should be used for judging faults with the following exception: bars that are displaced must be replaced by a team member and performed correctly.

According to traditional relay rules, faults should be assessed for dropping, throwing, kicking, or beating someone with the baton.

Course Design

For a novice Triple-True Team Baton Relay, no more than 12 obstacles should be used. These 12 obstacles must be arranged in four lines of three obstacles. Each set of three goes in the opposite direction. No contact obstacles should be used. Obstacles should be restricted to weave poles and other obstacles that are permissible in Jumpers. Set the height of all jumps to 12".

For more advanced handlers, more obstacles, including contacts, may be added to each line. In addition, jumps in each of the first three lines of obstacles could be set at the regulation jump height of the dog running that leg and jumps in the final line could be set at the height of the smallest dog on the team.

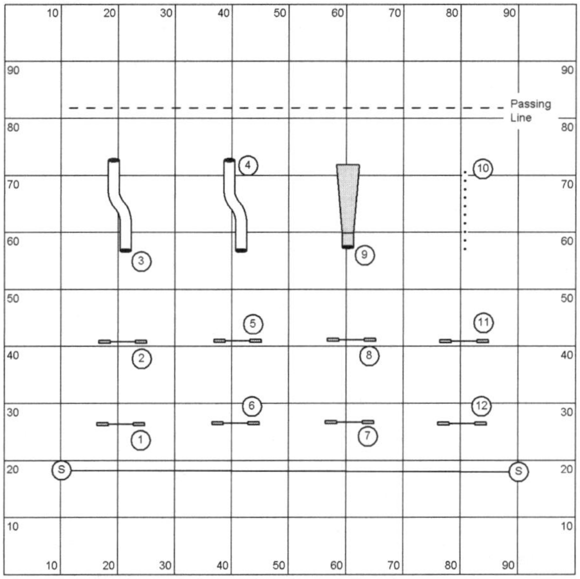

This is a representative example of a Triple-True Team Baton Relay for novice handlers.

tunnel-crossover game

Darlene Woz created the Tunnel-Crossover Game or Tunnel Game for a USDAA event held in Detroit, Michigan in 1994. This game is great fun and often hilarious as handlers find their dogs sucked straight through the crossover of tunnels when they are supposed to turn. Dogs and handlers with a minimum amount of experience can play the game, but it takes a dog and handler team of some experience to do well. When the Tunnel Pretzel obstacle was added, the game was renamed The Ultimate Tunnel Game.

Briefing

The Tunnel-Crossover Game is run on a course consisting only of tunnels and weave poles. The main "obstacle" is a crossover area consisting of a 10' square marked on the ground with a straight pipe tunnel placed on each edge of the square.

The dog must perform obstacles in the numerical order specified by the judge, and the dog must perform each obstacle correctly before going to the next. There is no penalty for an off-course (the handler is just wasting time) as long as the order is eventually completed correctly.

The 10' center zone of the tunnel crossover will be treated like any other obstacle on the course in that handlers cannot touch the obstacle without penalty. If at any time the handler steps into the center zone, intentionally or by accident, the handler must do three jumping jacks before he is allowed to leave and continue on course. It is recommended that the judge have all handlers practice jumping jacks during the briefing so that proper form can be demonstrated.

There's one special bonus in this game. If the handler starts and stays in the center zone of the crossover, directing his dog through the entire course from there (start line to finish line), a 25-second bonus is subtracted from the dog's course time.

The judge will set a standard course time. This is generally in the range of 60 seconds. At the end of course time, the timekeeper will blow a whistle. This is an all-or-nothing game so that dogs must complete the course before the whistle blows to receive a score.

Despite all the silliness of the game, the Tunnel-Crossover Game actually has the profound effect of teaching the importance of handler body position and movement on course.

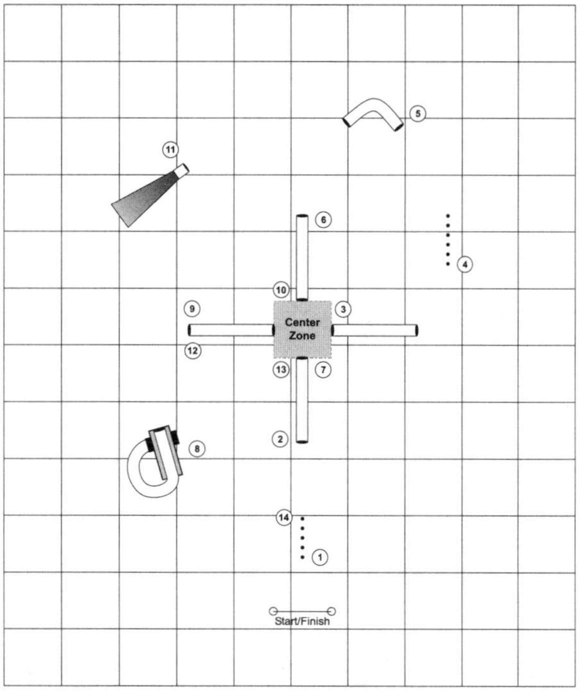

This is the original Tunnel Crossover Game designed by Darlene Woz.

Scoring

The Tunnel-Crossover Game is scored solely on time. The winner is the dog with the fastest time.

There are no faults because each obstacle must be completed correctly before proceeding. The only adjustments to a dog's actual running time will be the application of the 25-second bonus, if earned.

Course Design

The course layout must consist only of tunnels, both open and closed, and weave poles. Contact obstacles and jumps may not be used. Generally, the course should contain no more than 14 obstacles.

An elevated ramp forming a tunnel pretzel may also be used.

Note: Plans for building the base for the tunnel pretzel are available, see page 179 for plans

Strategies

- The goal of this game is to get through the course as smoothly as possible. This is very difficult. Since the only objects are tunnels and, possibly, weave poles, the handler must rely more on body language and posturing rather than verbal commands to direct his dog.
- To handle a dog from the center zone of the crossover and earn the 25-second bonus deduction, a dog-and-handler team must have exceptional distance control and communication.

Variations

- **Scoring option**—The game can also be scored points then time. The number of the final obstacle performed before the whistle blows represents the points earned. For example, if the dog completes the course up through #12 when the whistle blows, the dog's score would be 12 points. Time is used as a tiebreaker, if more than one dog has the same number of points.

tunnelers

The goal of the Tunnelers class is to demonstrate the dog's ability to respond quickly to directional commands from the handler while rapidly negotiating a course consisting only of tunnels.

Briefing

This course consists of tunnels only. The handler must direct the dog to perform the obstacles in the order specified by the judge. Under NADAC rules, refusals are not faulted, and there are no jump bars to drop. All the handler has to worry about is staying on course.

Tunnelers Qualifying YPS

	Small Dogs	Medium Dogs	Large Dogs
Novice	3.50	3.75	4.0
Open	4.0	4.25	4.5
Elite	4.50	4.75	5.0

Scoring

Tunnelers is scored faults then time. The schedule of faults is:

- Failure to complete—20 faults
- Running the wrong course—10 faults
- Body blocking—10 faults
- Time faults—The dog will be assessed time faults for each second or fraction of a second that it exceeds the standard course time.

Course Design

The course is composed solely of tunnels. Tunnels can be reused to make the most of only a few tunnels. The complexity of the handling challenges and number of tunnels should be appropriate to the level of competition.

Qualifying and Titles

Tunnelers is a titling game under NADAC rules. A clean run under the standard course time earns the dog 10 points. Certification in Tunnelers requires 30 points. NADAC offers these Tunnelers titles:

- Novice—TN-N
- Open—TN-O
- Elite—TN-E

All dogs at each level run the identical course. Only the qualifying time changes from one level to the next based on the yards-per-second table on the page opposite.

Adjustments to the standard course time may be made at the discretion of the judge.

Tunnelers is an eligible titling game under JFF and TDAA rules. A qualifying score is earned for a clean run under the standard course time.

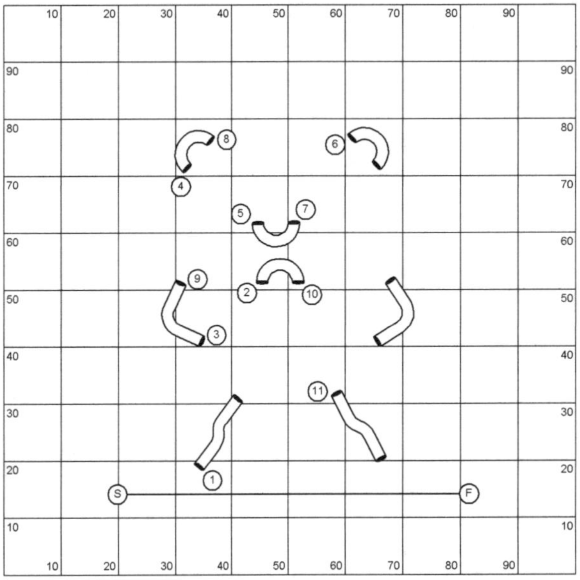

This Tunnelers course was designed by NADAC judge Lora Del Page for Agility Junkies on April 13, 2002.

tunnel vision

Tunnel Vision is the invention of Darlene Woz, one of the foremost innovators in agility games development. This is the perfect game for clubs that are rich in pipe tunnels and want something really fun and really different to play.

Briefing

Tunnel Vision is played on a course consisting of only pipe tunnels, jumps, and weave poles. The obstacles must be taken in the numerical order specified by the judge with these caveats:

- All obstacles can be taken in either direction.
- Each clump of tunnels may be performed in any order and in any direction, so long as each tunnel is ultimately performed. This could mean that the handler has to adapt his running strategy on the fly if the dog chooses a tunnel other than the one intended by the handler.
- The handler must remain behind the indicated containment line for each group of tunnels.

The judge will specify a separate standard course time for each different skill level competing, for example:

- Masters—30 seconds
- Advanced—35 seconds
- Starters/Novice—40 seconds

If the closing whistle hasn't blown by the time the dog reaches the jackpot jump (#15 on the sample course), 100 points will be awarded. The dog may then attempt to complete the inner circle of obstacles (sans tunnel groups) for an additional 100 bonus points.

As long as the whistle hasn't blown by the start of the dog's inner circle run, the turn may be completed although the dog may finish with some time faults.

Scoring

Tunnel Vision is scored points, minus faults, then time. The winner is the dog with the highest score.

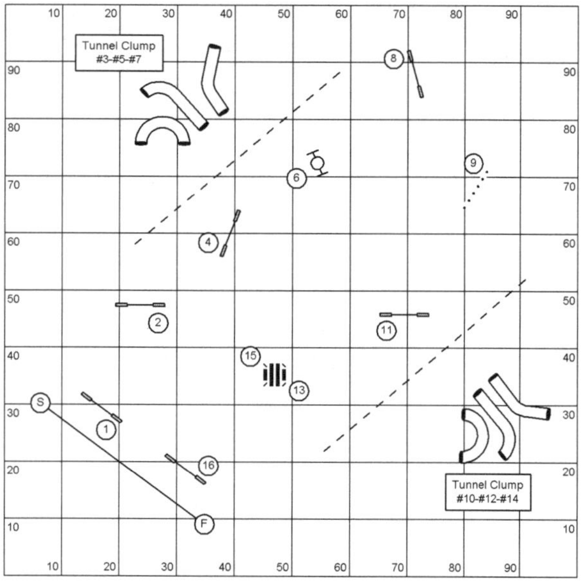

This is an example of a Tunnel Vision course, a crowd-pleaser that presents dogs with entertaining choices at the tunnel clusters.

USDAA Advanced rules will be used for assigning faults:

- Dropped bars or missed weave pole—5 faults
- Wrong-course or failure to perform—20 faults
- Stepping on or over a containment line with one foot—10 faults
- Stepping over a containment line with both feet—20 faults
- Refusals—not faulted (no contact obstacles on course)

Any time faults (whole numbers) will be subtracted from the dog's total score. Any time remaining on the clock (whole numbers) will be added to the dog's total score.

Course Design

Tunnel Vision uses only tunnels, hurdles, and weave poles.

The course is based on an inner, roughly circular, sequence of obstacles. The tunnel clumps are positioned on opposing sides of the inner circle.

twelve-tone row

Twelve-Tone Row is the invention of Becky Dean, an instructor at Dogwood Training Center. The game is modeled after an obscure musical analogy. You'll have to ask her if you're really curious. Otherwise, just read the rules below and have a good time with this game.

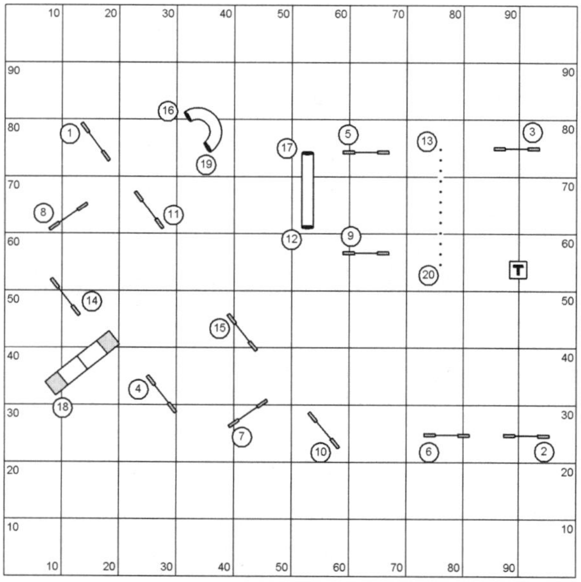

This Twelve-Tone Row course was designed by Becky Dean for play in an agility league at Dogwood Training Center in Ostrander, Ohio.

Briefing

The purpose of Twelve-Tone Row is to accumulate as many points as possible. Each obstacle's number on course represents its point value. The same obstacle may have different values, depending on the direction in which it is performed.

The handler may direct his dog to perform the obstacles in any order he chooses. If the dog chooses the obstacle to perform, the handler will have to live with it. Only 12 obstacles may be performed. The 12th must be the weave poles, in either direction. The dog-and-handler team will earn the assigned point values of the obstacles taken. No obstacle may be repeated, whether performed correctly or faulted.

The game starts and stops on the table. Time starts when the dog leaves the table. Time ends *only* when the dog gets into a *down* position on the table.

If the dog faults an obstacle, he will not earn the points for that obstacle. Further, the obstacle may not be repeated. It will not be counted as one of the dog's 12 required obstacles.

For each obstacle more or less than 12 total obstacles, the dog will be penalized 20 points. Any obstacle taken after the 12th obstacle, on the way to the table, will earn the extra obstacles penalty.

Scoring

Twelve-Tone Row is scored points, minus faults, then time.

The judge will call out the value of each obstacle as the dog performs that obstacle. It will be up to the scorekeeper to determine if the dog has performed the correct number of obstacles and that the value for the weave poles is earned in the 12th obstacle position.

Faults will be assigned as follows:

- Each obstacle performed over or under the 12 allowed—20 faults
- Refusals—not faulted
- Missed weave poles—not faulted but the performance must be corrected, or the dog earns 20 faults for failure to perform.

Faults are deducted from the points earned by the dog. No standard course time is used.

Course Design

In Twelve-Tone Row, the numbers are randomly assigned to the obstacles on the field. Obstacles may have different values if performed by the dog in different directions, at the discretion of the course designer. Numbering obstacles for performance in either direction should be reserved for the A-frame, weave poles, and tunnels.

The weaves (the last obstacle to be performed) should be placed close to the table or other designated time-stopper.

Strategies

The greedy man's strategy will be to seek the most possible points. It's a simple matter to figure this out. If only 12 obstacles can be performed, the handler should seek the performance of the 12 with the highest value. In a 20-obstacle course, that would be #9 through #20. Once this is known, the approach to these high-point obstacles becomes a bit of a "What's My Line?" problem to determine the best approach to pick each of them up in some kind of logical flow.

The handler should remember that taking an off-course obstacle is not a tragedy. It just means that the handler will have to balance the accumulation of points by omitting an obstacle that was in the plan to make up for taking the one that wasn't.

Qualifying and Titles

Twelve-Tone Row is an eligible qualifying game for both TDAA and JFF.

- Games I—78 points or better
- Games II—126 points or better
- Games III—170 points or better

Note that this system is based on a course of 20 numbered obstacles. It is impossible to get such high values with a course numbered with only 15 obstacles. Indeed, the most points that could be scored in a 15-obstacle course would be 114. And so, for a 15 obstacle course, the qualifying criteria might have to be redefined as:

- Games I—78 points or better
- Games II—95 points or better
- Games III—112 points or better

The qualifying number for Games I is the same in a 20-obstacle course as it is in a 15-obstacle course. The reason for this is quite simple: it is impossible to earn points for 12 obstacles and earn a lower number. But, doing 12 obstacles without fault, without repeating any obstacle, making up your own course, and finishing with a performance of the weave poles, is about all you could ask of a Novice or Beginners student. And so, the same Games I qualifying score is justified whether it is a 15-obstacle course or a 20-obstacle course.

Variations

- **Start and stop method**—The method for starting and stopping the game can be adapted by the judge. For example, the judge may allow the exhibitor to begin on any obstacle he likes. Time would begin when the dog commits to that obstacle. This allows handlers to develop many diverse strategies for solving the course.

  The method of stopping time could be changed from the table to a finish line. The judge may also stipulate that the dog's time stops as the dog makes his exit from the weave poles.

weakest link

The Weakest Link is a game invented by TDAA judge Tara Choate for a Teacup Dogs judging assignment. Tara is a member of Columbia Agility Team in Portland, Oregon.

Briefing

The objective of The Weakest Link is to score as many points as possible in the allotted time. Only "banked" points will count toward the final score.

The dog-and-handler team have 60 seconds to accumulate the best score possible.

The handler starts the round by directing the dog to any obstacle to earn points. Each obstacle taken by the dog must be worth *as much as or more than* the previous obstacle taken, with the gamble, whose obstacles are scored at twice their normal value, worth the most. The dog's potential score will increase as each obstacle value is added to the overall total. Points earned for the performance of obstacles will be credited to "potential" points. But the dog can't keep or count on these points until they are "banked."

Points are banked when the dog gets on the table (or other obstacle specified by the judge as the "banking" obstacle). When the dog banks his points, they are kept secure toward the final score and cannot be lost. On the table, no obedience position or counting is required; all the dog has to do is get onto the table to bank points. When points are banked, the potential points score is set to zero.

After banking points, the dog-and-handler team start over so long as time remains.

Each sequence banked must be unique. That means there must be at least one difference from any sequence previously banked. This stipulation is optional and up to the discretion of the judge.

If a dog faults, all potential points are lost (banked points can never be taken away from the dog). Faults include:

- Dropped bars
- Missed contacts
- Taking an obstacle of a lesser value than previously taken
- Taking an obstacle out of sequence in the gamble
- Failing to bank points before the final whistle

When a dog faults the judge will call "fault." The handler is obligated to direct the dog to the first obstacle in a new sequence to earn potential points.

If a bar is dropped on a jump, that jump is out of play for the remainder of the game, except when that jump is in the gamble sequence. Every attempt will be made to reset the bar on a gamble sequence; if it has not been reset, the dog must be directed between the standards of the jump.

Scoring

Weakest link is scored points, then time. Time is a tiebreaker. The point values are:

- Jumps—2 points
- Tire or tunnels—4 points
- Contact obstacles—6 points

- Weave poles—8 points
- Gamble—double the usual value of the obstacles in the gamble

In the dog's score, each number earned is added to the potential points until the dog "banks" those points. Points that are not banked are lost on a fault or when time expires.

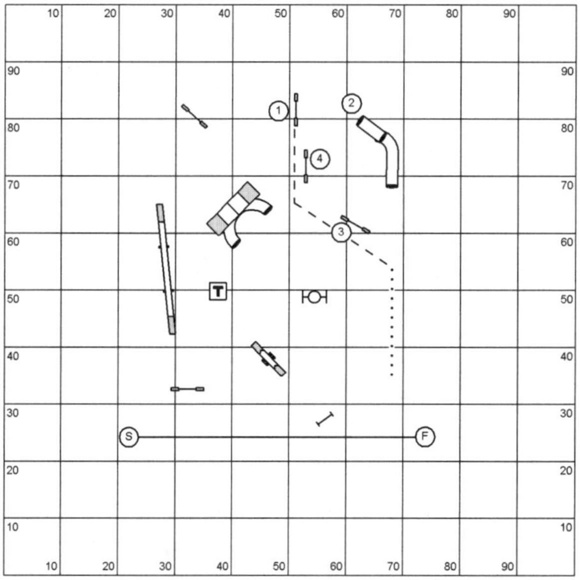

This is the original Weakest Link course that Tara Choate designed for the TDAA, so the transitional distances between obstacles are considerably shorter than for the big-dog venues.

Course Design

The design of a Weakest Link course is much like the design of a gamblers course in that the obstacles are arranged with no discernable flow. All standard obstacles should be used; a gamble should be marked with the containment area clearly defined.

Strategies

The boldest strategy with the highest scoring potential requires the handler to work for continuous performance while being sure to score on each obstacle value in succession: 2-point obstacles, 4-point obstacles, 6-point obstacles, 8-point obstacles, and the gamble, then to bank the points earned and begin the process again.

It is better to do the longer sequences first, and then finish with shorter sequences in anticipation of time expiring. It is better to be caught short of finishing a three-obstacle than a fifteen-obstacle sequence.

If the dog tends to drop bars, the handler might want to minimize the number of 2-point obstacles. If the dog doesn't work reliably at a distance, it would be better to bank points after the last 8-point obstacle.

Qualifying and Titles

Weakest Link is an eligible titling game under JFF and TDAA rules. A qualifying score is earned for:

- Games I—30 or more points
- Games II—40 or more points
- Games III—50 or more points

weavers

The goal of the Weavers class is to demonstrate the dog's ability to correctly enter weave poles at a variety of angles and weave accurately at speed on a course comprised solely of tunnels and weave poles.

Briefing

This course consists of weave poles and tunnels only. The handler must direct the dog to perform the obstacles in the order specified by the judge. Under NADAC rules, refusals are not faulted, and there are no jump bars to drop. All the handler has to worry about is staying steady in the weave poles and staying on course.

Scoring

Weavers is scored faults then time.

- Failure to complete—20 faults
- Running the wrong course—10 faults
- Missed weave pole (one or more)—20 faults
- Body blocking—10 faults

Weavers Qualifying YPS

	Small Dogs	Medium Dogs	Large Dogs
Novice	3.0	3.75	4.0
Open	4.0	4.25	4.5
Elite	4.50	4.75	5.0

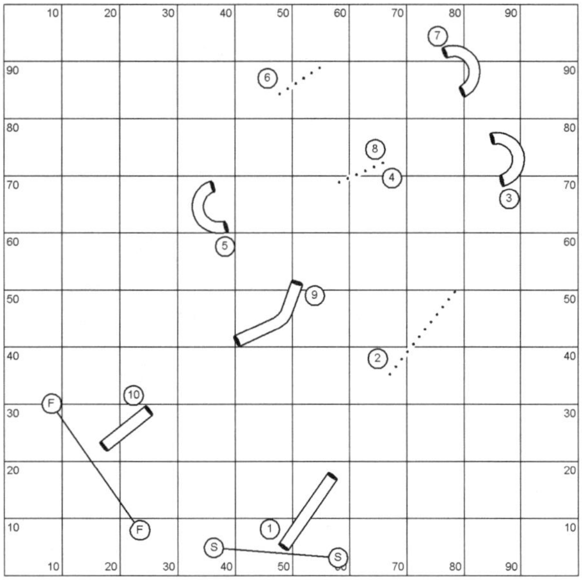

NADAC judge Ilze Rukis designed this Weavers course for play at A-1 Training Club, Brooklyn Park, Minnesota on March 30, 2002. This Weavers course is a good example of the flowing and logical lines that are so characteristic of NADAC courses.

- Time faults—Time faults are assessed for each second or fraction of a second that the dog exceeds the standard course time.

Course Design

A Weavers course is made exclusively of pipe tunnels and weave poles. No contact obstacles or hurdles are allowed.

Qualifying and Titles

Weavers is a titling game under NADAC rules. A clean run under the standard course time earns the dog 10 points. Certification in Weavers requires 30 points. NADAC offers these Weavers titles:

- Novice—WV-N
- Open—WV-O
- Elite—WV-E

All dogs at each of the levels run the identical course. Only the qualifying time changes from one level according to the yards-per-second table at on the previous page.

For each performance of a long set of weave poles, two seconds will be added to the standard course time. For each performance of a short set of weave poles, one second will be added to the standard course time. Other adjustments to standard course time may be made at the discretion of the judge.

Weavers is an eligible titling game under JFF and TDAA rules. A qualifying score is earned for a clean run under the standard course time.

what's my line?

Named after the old television game of the '50s and '60s, What's My Line? presents the obstacle course in the form of a puzzle. The game provides all handlers the opportunity to come up with a strategy for running the most efficient course possible. In the U.K., this game is known as Take Your Own Line.

Briefing

What's My Line? uses obstacles laid out in a random pattern on the field with no discernible course flow. Obstacles may be numbered at the judge's discretion. These numbers are for the judge's reference only and in no way suggest a sequence for running the course.

The objective is to perform all the obstacles on the field as quickly as possible without repeating or omitting any.

The handler earns one point for each obstacle his dog performs successfully. Each obstacle has the same value, regardless of the difficulty of performance and regardless of the number assigned to the obstacle.

If an obstacle is performed twice, scoring will stop immediately. The team keeps points earned and must be directed to the time-stopper to end the game.

If an obstacle is faulted, the team will receive no point for that obstacle. The handler may choose to retry the obstacle until it is performed correctly. At the judge's discretion, a four-paw safety rule may be observed on contact obstacles. Under this rule, if a dog commits to a contact obstacle with all four paws, then bails off, the handler may not redirect his dog onto that obstacle and will be eliminated if he does so.

Time will be started and stopped at points designated by the judge. A maximum course time can be applied at the discretion of the judge.

Scoring

What's My Line? is scored points, then time. Time is a tiebreaker only. The team with the most points will win.

Performance faults can be based on any rational system. Typically, USDAA Starters/Novice rules are used.

Course Design

What's My Line? can be played on virtually any configuration of obstacles. It is an ideal game to nest with another game or standard course so that only a minimal amount of tweaking of the obstacles is required.

Strategies

The handler's job is to find the most economical path for the dog to perform all the obstacles. The handler should be ingenious in looking for lines through the course, which should not be limited by vertical and horizontal lines. Diagonal lines in the course should also be considered.

Qualifying and Titles

What's My Line? is an eligible qualifying game in both TDAA and JFF. The qualification should be set on the basis of the number of obstacles on the course, using a number consistent with those required in the standard classes. To earn a qualifying score, no course faults will be allowed and no standard course time will be imposed.

When a limited number of obstacles are used for more advanced classes, the judge can stipulate a standard course time that will challenge the field to solve the course in a specific timeframe.

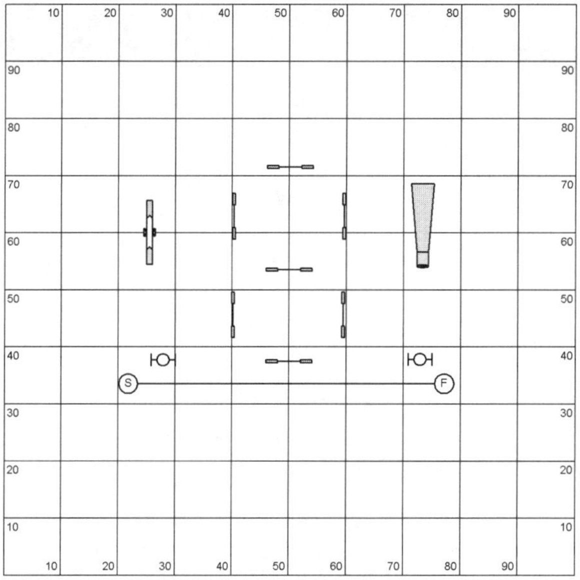

This What's My Line course, designed by Bud Houston and first played in Dogwood's agility league, challenges participants to see the lines that might be less obvious.

Variations

- **Never Cross the Line variation**—In this variation, invented by Helix Fairweather, in addition to the stipulation that the dog cannot repeat any obstacle, he is not allowed to cross his own line (meaning, no crossing patterns).
- **Zero value obstacle**—The judge mentions the zero value of the obstacle in the general briefing. Whether the handler directs his dog to perform that obstacle depends on whether he was paying attention in the briefing, or whether he wants to give the dog time on the obstacle as a warm-up for a later class. There is no penalty for the dog performing the zero-valued obstacle. Frequently, the valueless obstacle is the dogwalk.
- **Scoring variation**—Another scoring variation is to award the obstacle point values as in Gamblers, instead of just one point. Higher numbers are assigned to the more difficult obstacles. The more obstacles on course, the higher the maximum possible score. This assignment of numbers might affect the handler's strategy, since the handler might attempt the higher-point values earlier in the solution to the course.

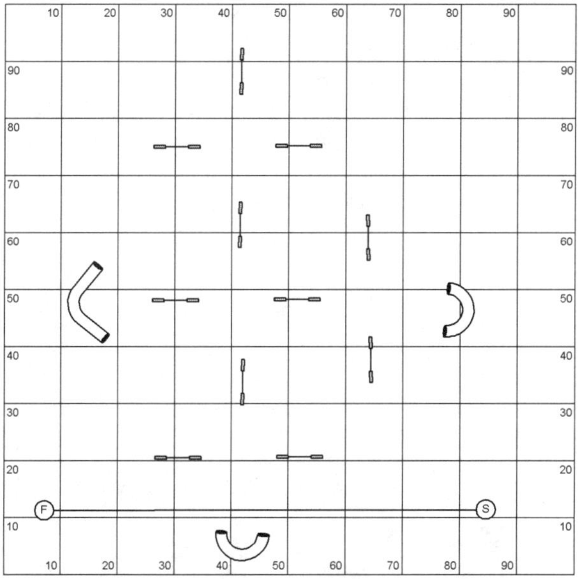

This example of Helix Fairweather's "Never Cross the Line" variation requires the dog to do all of the obstacles without repeating any—and without crossing his own path.

This game was invented by Francis Harvey to satisfy a judging examination for the Australian Dog Agility Association (ADAA). This is a game of daring in which the handler must understand the capabilities of his dog.

Briefing

The object of Who Dares Wins is to accurately estimate how many points your dog can score in the standard course time (50 seconds).

After walking the course, all handlers must estimate, using a 3-2-1 scoring system, how many points they can score in the standard course time. The handler and dog can complete more than one circuit of the course and may start anywhere on the course providing they run the course in the correct order.

- 3 points for contact obstacles and the long set of weave poles
- 2 points for tunnel, tire, and short set of weave poles
- 1 point for jumps

Handlers must report their estimate to the scorekeeper before any dog runs the course. Handlers are not to use their wristwatches or stopwatches to gauge their time. Neither spectators nor timekeeper are to indicate time to any handler while running the course.

The handler and dog proceed to their chosen starting point on the course.

Dogs are started with the timekeeper's whistle and will not accumulate points before the whistle. Dogs are not faulted. They just do not accumulate points for an obstacle faulted or out of turn. A dog must attempt every obstacle in turn. There are no refusal faults. Jump bars are not replaced. However, a dog must run between the uprights if attempting a hurdle with a dropped bar a second or subsequent time.

Weave poles have no refusal, and a dog must complete 50% of the poles before continuing. There are no specific faults associated with the weave poles. However, the handler must correct an improper entry or a missed pole to earn points for that obstacle. No points are awarded for any partial performance of the weave poles.

The timekeeper will signal the end of scoring at 50 seconds. The dog may not earn additional points after the whistle, and the handler must direct his dog to the table to stop time.

Scoring

Who Dares Wins is scored points only. The dog with the most Points Earned (see below) wins. In a tie, the dog with the most points scored wins. If an additional tiebreaker is required, the dog with the highest estimate wins.

Errors—At the end of each run, errors are calculated.

- Points error—the difference between the estimated points and the points scored for the run.
- Time Error—The difference between the dog's time and the standard course time is calculated. The dog's time is rounded down to the nearest second.

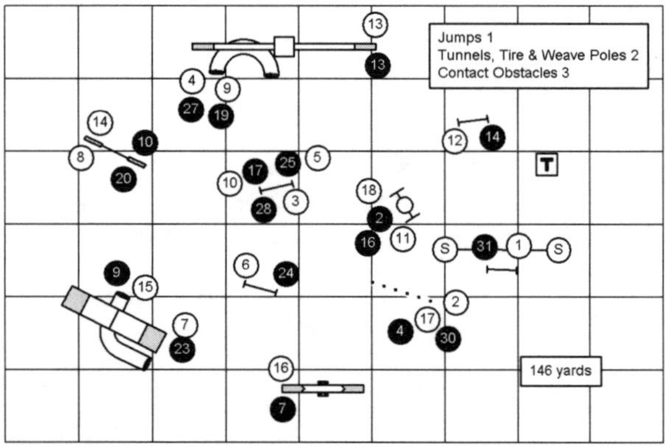

Total errors—Time errors are added to the point errors.

Points scored—Points the dog earned for successful performance of obstacles on course.

Points earned—Total errors are deducted from the points scored. This total score determines placement.

Scoring Example

In Who Dares Wins, the handler must make a reasonable estimate of how much course he can complete in 50 seconds. The course at left measures 146 yards. If the handler figures his dog will cover 3.5 yards per second, that means they'll have 8 seconds to play with. Going directly to the table would create an unacceptable time error. So the handler might be bold and begin his run at the teeter (#16) with the expectation that his dog might do #16 through #18, and then run the entire course without fault and before the whistle blows (can't earn points after the time whistle).

Using the key (for this very bold exhibitor), you would take the value of obstacles #16 through #18 (6 points) and add it to the value of the entire course (31 points) for the value of the dogs run (a total of 37 points). The dog would have deducted from his score the difference between 50 seconds and the actual time to the table.

That sounds simple enough, but it's not that simple at all. Using the same plan, let's say that the dog faults the A-frame at #7. The judge will call out "Fault!" So, after running his entire plan, the handler turns and does jump #1 after the tire at #18 to make up points. His dog enters the weave poles, but the whistle blows and he has to take his dog to the table. For this scenario, the estimate would be the same 37 as in the previous example, minus 5 for the A-frame that was faulted (giving 32), plus 1 for the jump that was not a part of the plan... making a total of 33 points. Since the handler's guess was 37, he'll get 4 points errors, and whatever time error.

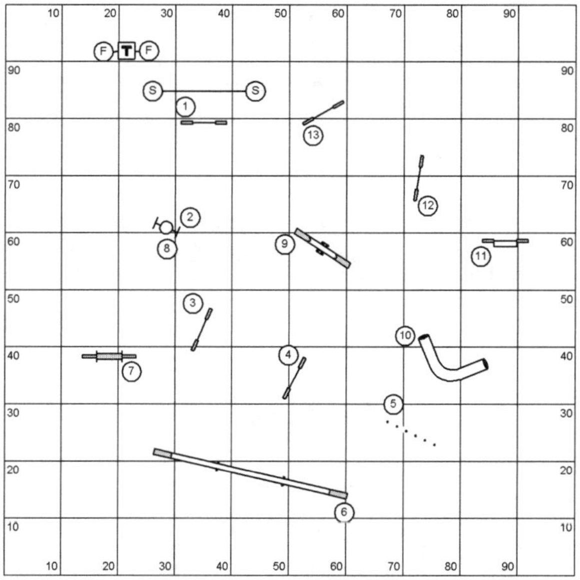

This sample of a Who Dares Wins course was designed by Bud Houston for play at Dogwood's agility league in June, 2002.

Course Design

The course should be fast and flowing and should form a continuous simple or complex loop, with a table placed in a safe spot to stop time.

Strategies

In the course at left, the handler's estimate should calculate for the course to end at jump #13 in order to proceed to the table. If the handler believes he can do four more obstacles than in the course, for example, the handler would bid 26. That's 21 for the course and five for the last four obstacles. The handler would start his dog on obstacle #10.

If the dog faults an obstacle during the performance of the sequence of obstacles that was bid, the handler may direct the dog on to the first obstacle or two (or more) at the beginning of the course to try to make up the points not earned, providing the time whistle has not blown.

Alternatively, the handler might also anticipate faults and omit points from the bid.

Qualifying and Titles

Who Dares Wins is an eligible titling game for both TDAA and JFF.

Qualification should be based upon the number of obstacles a dog might be required to do in a standard titling class and given a leeway of about 5 seconds for the dog's time to the table. Using the sample course as a baseline, the qualifying criteria would be:

- Games I—16 points or higher
- Games II—19 points or higher
- Games III—26 or higher

Variations

- **Least errors wins**—At the end of each run, the difference between the estimated points and the points scored for the run is called the points-error. The difference between the time the dog took and the standard course time is called the time error. The time errors are added to the point errors to determine total errors. The dog with the least total errors wins. In the event of a tie, the dog with the highest points scored wins. In a further tie, the dog with the highest estimate wins.
- **Penance**—Arranged around the table are four jumps allowing the dog and handler to make up points for point errors earned. Points earned in excess of the points estimated are also point errors. That is, if a handler estimated 40 points and accrued 41 points, the dog has one point error.

- **Suicide variation**—Going over time or under points knocks the handler out. This variation is suitable only for the very bold.
- **Team play**—When running in a team format, each dog earns individual time errors. Before the final dog in each team runs, the total points that the dog and handler must earn are posted. The final dog in the team can attempt to reach the total estimate for the team or can run for minimum time faults. The winning team has the least total of time-error plus points-error. In a tie, the team with the highest estimate wins.

wildcard

The invention of Linda Eickholdt, Wildcard is a titling game in CPE, TDAA, and JFF. Wildcard includes an element of strategy and daring.

Briefing

A Wildcard course is run like any standard agility course in that the dog is required to perform a sequence designated by the judge. However, Wildcard is different from standard agility in that, at three designated points on the course, the handler, or possibly the dog, will have a choice of taking one of two obstacles for that number in the sequence. This is called a Wildcard. The two obstacles for the Wildcard are placed approximately parallel to each other. One of each pair of Wildcard obstacles is valued at 1 point; the other is worth 2 points. Depending on the dog's level, the handler must develop a strategy to collect the appropriate combination of 1- and 2-pointers to qualify.

A standard course time will be established by measuring the course using the path for the obstacle in each Wildcard that is easiest to perform. Time faults will be assessed on a 1:1 basis; that is, one second equals one fault. Fractions are dropped for scoring. The timekeeper will report time in 1/100th of a second for placement.

Scoring

Wildcard is scored faults, then time. The lowest score wins. Time is a tiebreaker only.

For scribing purposes, the judge will call 1 or 2 (points) when the dog successfully performs the respective Wildcard obstacle.

A faulted Wildcard obstacle can only be corrected if it is an open or collapsed tunnel, tire, window jump, or weave poles. A 5-point fault for off-course or other faults may be assessed. Any other Wildcard obstacles that are faulted cannot be corrected and will be scored as 15 faults (failure to perform) and will result in an NQ due to not having completed all three wildcards. A handler cannot change the wildcard obstacle once a dog has touched or started an obstacle (such as the tunnel, collapsed tunnel, weave-pole entry, contact obstacles) whether the handler instructed the dog to that obstacle or not. If the handler does so, the wildcard will be scored as 15 faults (failure to perform).

Points for type of wildcard obstacle will be awarded as follows:

- 1 point—bar jump, tire, broad jump, pipe tunnel, collapsed tunnel, ascending double jump, and two-obstacle combinations composed of a tire to a tunnel if the dogwalk is a 2-point option
- 2 points—teeter, A-frame, dogwalk, double or triple spread, pipe tunnel, collapsed tunnel, weave poles and two-obstacle combinations composed of single bar jumps, tire, tunnel (open or closed)

Wildcard Required Obstacles

	Minimum	Maximum with Wildcards
Contacts	0	3
Tire or window jump	1	3
Collapsed tunnel	1	1
Pipe tunnel	1	4
Weave poles, level 1 and 2	0	6
Weave poles, level 3, may be 2-3 sets	5	18, maximum 12 outside wildcards
Weave poles, level 4, 5, and "C" , may be 2-3 sets	10	18
Bar jumps	4	12
Broad Jump, double jump, triple spread	1	2

Course Design

Wildcard will be designed like a standard agility course. The course will contain 10 to 12 obstacles and 6 Wildcard obstacles. There will be three Wildcards on the course. One of the obstacles in each wildcard is included as the regular course obstacle. The Wildcards are two obstacles placed approximately parallel to each other and 5' apart.

Strategies

The handler's choice of path must be based upon his dog's performance strengths and weaknesses, balanced by the risks and advantages imposed by the selection of a given path.

Qualifying and Titles

Wildcard is a qualifying game for CPE. A dog must have the correct number and type of wildcards respective to its level to qualify. It is possible to NQ within the fault limits if the correct wildcards are not collected.

For example, the dog NQs if:

- Level 1 and 2: dog takes three 1-point wildcards *or* more than one 2-point wildcard
- Level 3/4/5/C: dog takes more than one 1-point wildcard *or* three 2-point wildcards

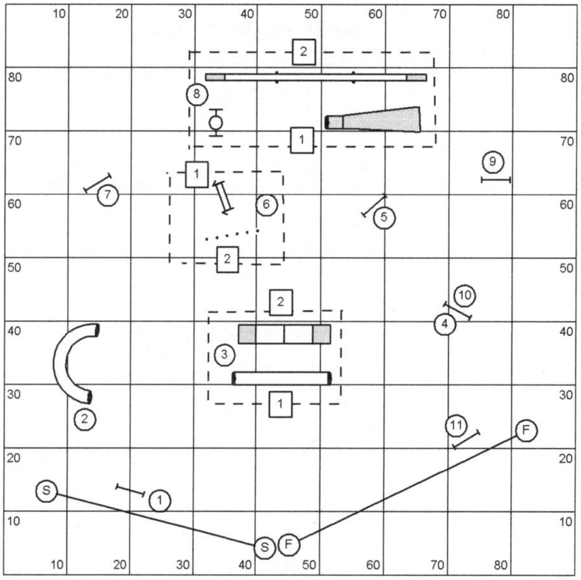

Ray Wheeler designed this CPE Wildcard course for Levels 1 and 2 for play at the All Dogs Gym in Manchester, New Hampshire in March 2003. The Wildcards occur at #3, #6, and #8. Note that #8 presents the option of a combination obstacle (tire to collapsed tunnel).

wild west pinball

Wild West Pinball is the invention of Ilze Rukis, one of the preeminent agility games inventors in the world. The game was designed as a qualifying game in TDAA for play at Decatur Dog Training Club in Warrensburg, IL on April 12, 2002.

Briefing

The purpose of Wild West Pinball is to accumulate as many points as possible in the time allotted: 50 seconds. All dogs start at Gold Bone Tunnel. Open tunnels have no point value. Obstacle point values are:

- Jumps and the tire are worth 10 points and may be taken any number of times, but not back-to-back. If the dog drops a bar, then 10 faults are assessed. The bar is not reset and the jump is out of play.
- "Gold Nuggets" are worth 50 points and may be taken no more than two times (not back-to-back). The Gold Nugget weaves must be completed in their entirety (no pop-out fixes). Multiple attempts to correctly complete the weaves are allowed.
- The "Cowdog Cliff Hanger" (the teeter) is worth 100 points. The Cowdog Cliff Hanger may be taken no more than two times (not back-to-back) and is only approachable by passing through the Dead Dog Round Up. If the dog enters either one of the Dead Dog Round Up tunnels, it must repeat the tunnel before moving on to attempt the Cowdog Cliff Hanger.

At the whistle, point accumulation stops and team must cross the finish line to stop time.

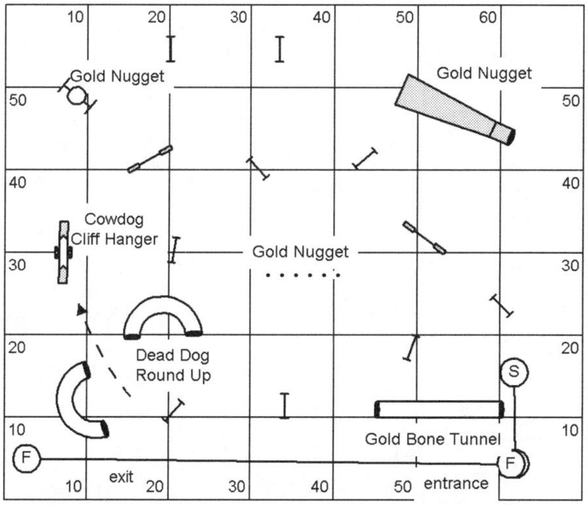

TDAA judge, Ilze Rukis designed this sample course for play at the Decatur Dog Training Club TDAA trial on April 12, 2002.

Scoring

Wild West Pinball is scored points minus faults, then time. Time is a tiebreaker only.

Course Design

The course should be flowing enough to encourage rapid point accumulation, with lots of jumps and tunnels to build up speed and provide access to high-point obstacles. The Cowdog Cliff Hanger should provide appropriate off-course enticements on its approach.

Qualifying and Titles

TDAA

Wild West Pinball is eligible as a qualifying game under TDAA rules.

- Games I—300 points
- Games II—450 points
- Games III—600 points

JFF

Wild West Pinball is eligible as a qualifying game under JFF rules using the same qualifying criteria as TDAA.

The Challenge

Inventing an agility game is no simple matter. If you have a vision for a game, you should go through the following checklist to help you nail down the game so that is it ready to play.

What Makes Your Game Different?

Obviously, there are many agility games out there right now. But that doesn't mean there aren't more and interesting turns we can put on agility contests.

You should be familiar with the games that are defined in this book (*The Clean Run Book of Agility Games*, Second Ed.) and their variations. If you have a game that looks similar to an existing game, but is not quite the same, you might have invented a variation of an existing game.

There are different kinds of games. You should know what type game you have invented:

- **Training Games**—These games have specific training objectives and might not be the kind of game you'd play in open competition.
- **Silly Games**—These are games you might play on a holiday or an outing with your agility club. They might involve dressing up in funny clothes, the handler doing the agility obstacles, or using water cannons as part of the play.
- **Team Games**—Team games involve play by two or more dogs and their handlers, possibly being on the course at the same time.
- **Strategy Games**—These are games like Snooker, Pairs Pursuit, Pole Jacks, and Twelve-Tone Row that require the handler to develop a careful strategy to qualify or to win the game.
- **Qualifying and Titling Games**—These are games that might be appropriate as a titling game for organizations like JFF and TDAA. A qualifying or titling game must have the same level or equal basis for all dogs. For example, you couldn't play "Pass the Secret" as a titling game because the sequence might change from run to run. Qualifying criteria must be fairly well-established.

What Are the Rules?

When you define the rules of the game, you should take the role of the judge who will brief the field of exhibitors. Explain how the game is played and what the players need to understand. Anticipate any question that might be asked.

How is the Game Scored?

There are several methods of scoring games. Here are some to think about:

- Faults then time. This is the usual basis for the standard agility run. The dog with the fewest faults wins. In case of a tie, the fastest dog wins.
- Time plus faults. In this game, time and faults are added together. This might favor the faster dog that, even with faults, will have a better score than a dog that ran slower without faults.
- Points then time. This is the basis for games like Gamblers. The dog with the most points wins. In case of a tie, the fastest dog wins.

How Are Ties Broken?

It's almost always a good idea to add a time element to a game so that winners can be clearly differentiated. Imagine a game like Pole Jacks, in which there are only eight possible scores. There are bound to be many ties for points. The time the dog takes to complete the game becomes an important tiebreaker.

Have You Thought of Everything?

How does the game begin? How does the game end? Are all performance faults accommodated by the rules?

It might be a good idea to play the game with a group of interested agility competitors. It's amazing how many things pop up that you might not have anticipated in the rules you defined for the game.

Report Your Game!

If you've invented a new game, I'll want to know about it for future volumes of *The Clean Run Book of Agility Games*. Write:

Bud Houston

8738 Slocum Road

Ostrander, OH 43061

info@dogwoodagility.com

tunnel pretzel plans

The Tunnel Pretzel obstacle is the invention of Darlene Woz of Michigan. It consists of three pipe tunnels attached together and fixed on two raised ramps and a center base. These are the instructions for building the ramp base.

Here's what you will need:

- 2x4s for legs and cross supports
- 2x8 for sides of ramps
- 2x12 for bottom of ramps
- 4 hinges for attaching ramps to center base
- 10 eye hooks
- 5 bungee cords

All joints are glued for extra strength. No screws or nails used, except to mount the hinges.

Eye hooks and bungee cords across

FRONT VIEW OF BASE

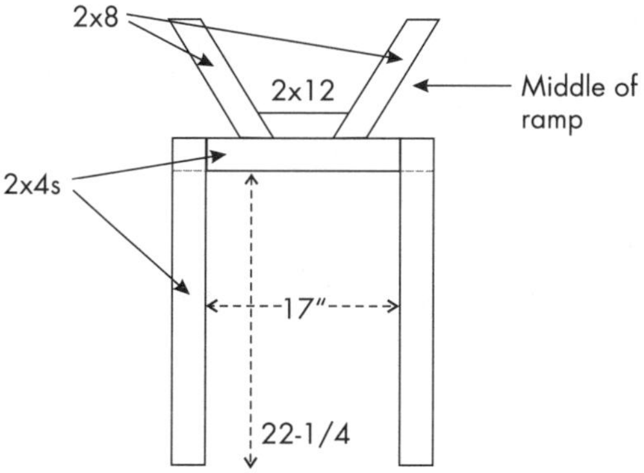

SIDE VIEW OF BASE

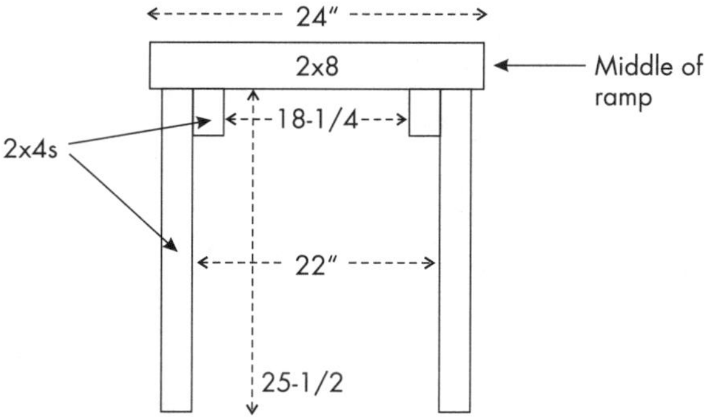

SIDE VIEW OF RAMP

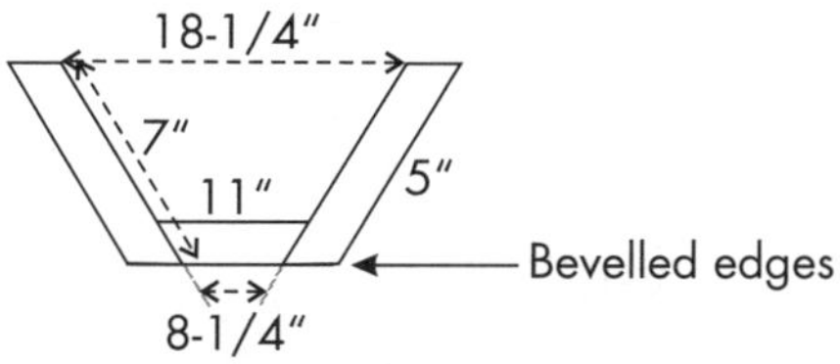

BOTTOM VIEW OF RAMP

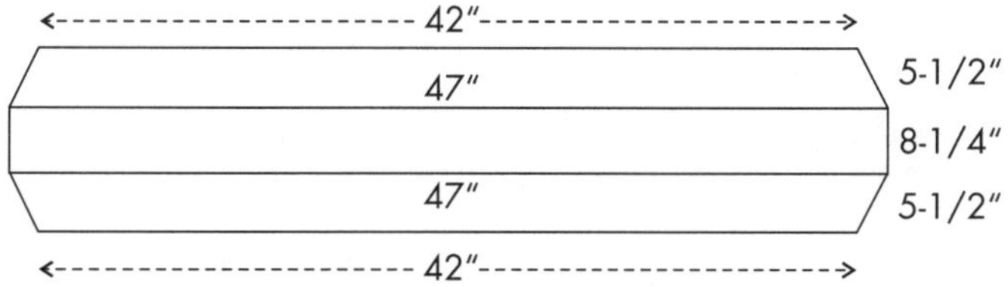

games type index

Distance games

Silly games, games for a holiday outing

Games formats

Games of strategy

Games using non-standard agility obstacles or props

Sequencing games

Team games

Training games

games description index

Clean Run
Class Ideas for Agility Instructors
Exercises for Backyard Trainers
Course Analyses – What Worked, What Didn't
America's #1 Source of Dog Agility Information Since 1995!
Training Problems: Cures and Prevention

Oh, my dog!
It's not just an agility magazine. You wouldn't believe all the great stuff...
Everything for the Performance Dog
www.cleanrun.com